THE MODERN LIBRARY

of the World's Best Books

⪼⪼⪼

A NEW ANTHOLOGY OF

MODERN POETRY

The publishers will be pleased to send, upon request, an illustrated folder setting forth the purpose and scope of THE MODERN LIBRARY, *and listing each volume in the series. Every reader will find titles he has been looking for, handsomely printed, in unabridged editions, and at an unusually low price.*

A NEW
ANTHOLOGY OF
MODERN
POETRY

>>

EDITED, WITH AN INTRODUCTION BY

SELDEN RODMAN

>>

THE MODERN LIBRARY

NEW YORK

THE MODERN LIBRARY
is published by RANDOM HOUSE, INC.

Manufactured in the United States of America by H. Wolff

ACKNOWLEDGMENTS

For permission to use the copyrighted poems included in this volume, acknowledgment is made to the following publishers and poets:

GEORGE ALLEN & UNWIN LTD.

for "Indian Day," "In Hospital: Poona" and "The Jungle" from *Ha! Ha! Among the Trumpets* by Alun Lewis

R. P. BLACKMUR

for "All Things Are A Flowing" and "October Frost" from *For Jordan's Delight*, published by Arrow Editions

BRANDT & BRANDT

for "Moriturus" by Edna St. Vincent Millay from *The Buck in the Snow*, published by Harper & Brothers. Copyright, 1928, by Edna St. Vincent Millay

for "Litany for Dictatorships," by Stephen Vincent Benét from *Burning City*, published by Farrar & Rinehart, Inc. Copyright, 1933, 1935, 1936, by Stephen Vincent Benét

for "my father moved through dooms of love" from *50 Poems* by E. E. Cummings, published by Duell, Sloan & Pearce, copyright 1939, 1940 by E. E. Cummings

ALBERT & CHARLES BONI, INC.

for two selections from *Blues: An Anthology*

JONATHAN CAPE LTD.

for the selections from *Quiver's Choice* by 'Sagittarius'

EUNICE CLARK

for "The People Has No Obituary"

SARAH N. CLEGHORN

for selections from *Threescore*

HUBERT CREEKMORE

for "It's Me, Oh Lord, Standing With A Gun"

COMMON SENSE

for "Millions Are Learning How" by James Agee
for "Spiritual Exercises" by Stephen Spender
for "In Panelled Rooms" by Ruth Herschberger

COVICI-FRIEDE, INC.

for "Boy With His Hair Cut Short" from *U. S. 1* by Muriel Rukeyser

MALCOLM COWLEY

for "The Hill Above the Mine" and "For St. Bartholomew's Eve"

COWARD-MCCANN, INC.

for "These Are the Live" from *Angel Arms* by Kenneth Fearing

CURTIS BROWN, LTD.

for "Lines in Dispraise of Dispraise," "Song of the Open Road" and "Autres Bêtes, Autres Moeurs" by Ogden Nash

JOHN DAY CO.

for "Fife Tune" from *Selected Verse* by John Manifold

THE DIAL PRESS, INC.

for "The Serf" by Roy Campbell
for "The Soldier Walks under the Trees of the University" from *Little Friend, Little Friend* by Randall Jarrell

DODD, MEAD & CO.

for "The Ballad of Jesse James" by William Rose Benét

DOUBLEDAY, DORAN & CO.

for the selection from *American Song* by Paul Engle

FABER & FABER

for "In Arcadia" from *A Private Country* by Lawrence Durrell
for "Ignorance of Death" from *The Gathering Storm* by William Empson

ACKNOWLEDGMENTS

FARRAR & RINEHART, INC.

for "Pole Star For This Year" by Archibald MacLeish

for "Litany for Dictatorships" by Stephen Vincent Benét and Four Rhymes from *A Book of Americans* by Stephen Vincent and Rosemary Benét

for Canto XVII by Ezra Pound

KENNETH FEARING

for "Dirge" from *Poems*

ROBERT FITZGERALD

for "Horae" and "Mementoes" from *A Wreath for the Sea* published by Arrow Editions

THE FORUM

for "Rapid Transit" by James Agee

JEAN GARRIGUE

and to New Directions for "From Venice was that Afternoon"

W. C. HANDY

for the fragment from "Sundown Blues," copyright, 1923, and "St. Louis Blues," copyright 1914, both published by Handy, Bros. Music Co., Inc., New York

HARCOURT, BRACE & CO.

for selections from *The People, Yes* by Carl Sandburg

for selections from *Collected Poems* by E. E. Cummings

for "I Paint What I See" by E. B. White from *The New Yorker Book of Verse*

for selections from *The Rock* and *Collected Poems* by T. S. Eliot

for "Tombstone with Cherubim" and "Salvos for Randolph Bourne" from *No Retreat* by Horace Gregory

for "Pondy Woods" from *Selected Poems 1923–1943* by Robert Penn Warren

HARPER & BROS.

for "The Conspirators" by Frederic Prokosch

for "Moriturus" from *The Buck in the Snow* by Edna St. Vincent Millay

[*vii*]

ACKNOWLEDGMENTS

RUTH HERSCHBERGER

for "Hymn to Texture." "In Panelled Rooms" and "The Lumberyard"

HENRY HOLT & CO.

for "The Listeners" by Walter de la Mare

for "Two Tramps in Mud Time" by Robert Frost

for "Others, I am not the first," "1887," and "Terence, this is stupid stuff" from *The Shropshire Lad* by A. E. Housman

for "Carapace" from *Take Them Stranger* by Babette Deutsch

for "Rapid Transit," "Millions Are Learning How" and "Sunday: Outskirts of Knoxville, Tennessee" by James Agee

THE HOGARTH PRESS

for "January 1940" from *The Middle of a War* and for "A Wry Smile" and "The Statue" from *A Lost Season* by Roy Fuller

for "River" from *The Sun, My Monument* by Laurie Lee

HOUGHTON MIFFLIN CO.

for selections from *Collected Poems* by Archibald MacLeish

for "Little Ivory Figures Pulled With String" by Amy Lowell

ALFRED A. KNOPF, INC.

for selections from *Harmonium* by Wallace Stevens

for "Here Lies A Lady" from *Chills and Fever* by John Crowe Ransom

for "The Elephant Is Slow To Mate" from *Pansies* by D. H. Lawrence

for "Wild Peaches" and "Castilian" from *The Collected Poems of Elinor Wylie*

JOHN LEHMANN

and to *New Writing and Daylight* (London) for "Abel" and "Lazarus" by Demetrios Capetanakis

LIVERIGHT PUBLISHING CORPORATION

for selections from *Collected Poems* by Hart Crane

ROBERT LOWELL

for "Dea Roma," "Children of Light" and "On the Feast of the

[*viii*]

Immaculate Conception" from *Land of Unlikeness*, published by the Cummington Press, and for the hitherto unpublished poems "Where the Rainbow Ends" and "Caron, Non Ti Crucciare"

HUGH MACDIARMID

for "Reflections in an Ironworks" and "At the Cenotaph"

FLEMING MACLIESH

for selections, both published for the first time in this anthology, from *The Destroyers* (John Day Co.) and *In Time of Foreign War*

for "Spirit: A Spiral: A Spire" published for the first time in this anthology

THE MACMILLAN CO.

for selections from *Selected Poems* by Marianne Moore

for lines from *Reynard the Fox* by John Masefield

for "Afterwards" and "Channel Firing" by Thomas Hardy

for selections from *Collected Poems* and *Last Poems* by W. B. Yeats

for selections from *Collected Poems* by Vachel Lindsay

for "The Military Harpist" from *The Spirit Watches* by Ruth Pitter.

for the three poems by Alun Lewis from *Ha! Ha! Among the Trumpets*

for "Sonnet" and "Munich Elegy Number 7" from *Selected Poems* by George Barker

EDWIN MARKHAM

for "The Man with the Hoe"

EDGAR LEE MASTERS

for "Mrs. Williams," "Chandler Nicholas" and "Howard Lamson" from *Spoon River Anthology* and *New Spoon River*

JOHN MURRAY

for "In Westminster Abbey" from *Old Lights for New Chancels* by John Betjeman

NEW DIRECTIONS

and to James Laughlin for the poems by Delmore Schwartz

from *In Dreams Begin Responsibilities;* for the poems by Dylan Thomas from *The World I Breathe* and *New Poems;* for "Father" from *Selected Poems* by John Wheelwright; for "Spiritual for Nine Voices" from *A Glad Day* by Kay Boyle; for "The Trappist Abbey: Matins" and "For My Brother Reported Missing in Action, 1943" from *Thirty Poems* by Thomas Merton; for "Now on this day of the first hundred flowers," "Here I sit, reading the stoic," "Remember that breakfast one November" and "Adonis in Summer" from *The Phoenix and the Tortoise* by Kenneth Rexroth; for the two poems by Mark Van Doren; for Malcolm Cowley's "The Long Voyage"; for the poems of Ezra Pound and Mark Van Doren not acknowledged elsewhere; for "From Venice was that Afternoon" by Jean Garrigue; and for the poems by Robert Fitzgerald and Kenneth Patchen acknowledged elsewhere.

THE NEW MASSES

for "Death of a Craneman" by Alfred Hayes

THE NEW REPUBLIC

for "The Yachts" by William Carlos Williams from *An Early Martyr*

OXFORD UNIVERSITY PRESS

for "Johannes Milton, Senex" by Robert Bridges

for "Pied Beauty," "Duns Scotus's Oxford," "Fragment" and "Felix Randal" by Gerard Manley Hopkins

for "Now is the air filled with chiming balls," "I walked out to the graveyard to see the dead," "I wish I could live at the pitch that is near madness" and "The Humanist" from *Song and Idea* by Richard Eberhart

PANTHEON BOOKS, INC.

for the two sonnets by Ralph Gustafson from *Flight Into Darkness*

KENNETH PATCHEN

for "He Thought of Mad Ellen's Ravings . . .," "The Character of Love . . ." from *First Will & Testament;* for "The Grand Palace of Versailles" from *Teeth of the Lion;* and for "What Is the Beautiful?" from *Cloth of the Tempest*

RANDOM HOUSE, INC.

for "Shine, Perishing Republic," "Night," "Practical People" and "The Beaks of Eagles" by Robinson Jeffers

for "The Express," "I think continually of those who were truly great," "The Funeral," and "Oh young men oh young comrades" by Stephen Spender

for "The Eremites" and "The Laureate" from *Selected Poems* by Robert Graves

for selections from *The Airmen* by Selden Rodman

for "It is time for the destruction of error," "Look, Stranger," "Prologue," "Musée des Beaux Arts" and selections from *For the Time Being* by W. H. Auden

for "Museums," "Their Last Will and Testament" and "Prayer Before Birth" by Louis MacNeice

for "Tempt Me No More; for I" by C. Day Lewis

REYNAL & HITCHCOCK

for "Auto Wreck" and "The Fly" from *Person Place and Thing*

for "Nigger" and "The Leg" from *V-Letter and Other Poems* and for selections from *Essay on Rime,* all by Karl Shapiro

GEORGE ROUTLEDGE & SONS, LTD.

for the three poems from Sidney Keyes' *Collected Poems*

CHARLES SCRIBNER'S SONS

for "Miniver Cheevy" and "George Crabbe" by Edwin Arlington Robinson

for "Prelude LVI" by Conrad Aiken

for "Idiot" from *Selected Poems* by Allen Tate

for "The Burning Wheel" and "This Dim and Ptolemaic Man" from *Selected Poems* by John Peale Bishop

for "Old Countryside" and "Baroque Comment" from *Poems, New and Selected* by Louise Bogan

and to Maxwell E. Perkins for the selections from Thomas

Wolfe as arranged by Sgt. John S. Barnes in *A Stone, A Leaf, A Door*

SEDGWICK & JACKSON, LTD.

for "In Time Like Glass" by Walter James Turner

SIMON & SCHUSTER, INC.

for "Final Autumn" from *Year's End* by Josephine W. Johnson
for "Memorare" from *Poems* by Dunstan Thompson

EDITH SITWELL

for "Said Sir Pompey," "Still Falls the Rain" and "An Old Woman"

STACKPOLE SONS

for a selection from *The River* by Pare Lorentz

VIKING PRESS

for "I hear an army charging upon the land" by James Joyce
for "The Sea" and a selection from "The Ship of Death" by D. H. Lawrence
for "The Snake" from *Collected Poems* by D. H. Lawrence. Copyright 1929 by Jonathan Cape & Harrison Smith, Inc. Reprinted by permission of the Viking Press, Inc.
for selections from *The Book of American Negro Spirituals*
for "John Henry tol' his Cap'n" from *Rolling Along in Song* by J. Rosamond Johnson
for "The Legion of Iron" by Lola Ridge
for "Be beautiful, noble, like the antique ant" from *Have Come, Am Here* by José Garcia Villa
for "War Experience" from *Vigils* by Siegfried Sassoon, and for the same author's "At the Grave of Henry Vaughan"
for "Song of Songs," "The Show," "Strange Meeting," "Arms and the Boy" and "Greater Love" by Wilfred Owen
for "Fighting Words" and "Bohemia" by Dorothy Parker
for "Last Speech to the Court" by Bartolomeo Vanzetti from *The Letters of Sacco and Vanzetti*

ACKNOWLEDGMENTS

ANN WATKINS, INC.

for "Spiritual for Nine Voices" by Kay Boyle

for the three poems by Edith Sitwell

for "Museums," by William Abrahams

for "The Return" and "The River-Merchant's Wife" by Ezra Pound

OSCAR WILLIAMS

for "Subway" from *That's All That Matters,* published by Creative Age Press

EDMUND WILSON

for "The Omelet of A. MacLeish" from *Notebooks of Night,* published by The Colt Press, San Francisco

YALE UNIVERSITY PRESS

for "City of Monuments" and "Citation for Horace Gregory" by Muriel Rukeyser from *Theory of Flight*

for "McSorley's Bar" and "The Laboratory Midnight" from *The Connecticut River* by Reuel Denney

for "Notes for an Elegy" and "A Kodiak Poem" from *Letter from an Impossible Land* by William Meredith

CONTENTS

CONTENTS

PART TWO

CONTENTS

CONTENTS

PART THREE

CONTENTS

[xx]

CONTENTS

PART FOUR

CONTENTS

PART FIVE

CONTENTS

[*xxiv*]

CONTENTS

[xxv]

CONTENTS

INTRODUCTION

By Selden Rodman

MODERN poetry, like all other poetry, is a language devised to communicate those experiences or ideas which defy the deliberate order and pace of prose. The most intense prose, whatever advantage it may have in explicit presentation, is less highly charged with suggestive ambiguity and direct tonal quality than the special language we attempt to describe by the word poetry.

What is modern poetry, and where does it begin? Did it begin in America with Edgar Allan Poe? It certainly began in France toward the middle of the nineteenth century when the younger poets rejected the romanticism of Victor Hugo as inadequate protest against what they considered the anti-poetic materialism of "bourgeois" civilization. But these first poets of the ivory tower—Baudelaire, Rimbaud, Verlaine, Laforgue, Mallarmé—didn't start to influence English poetry until the time of Yeats, and not with any widespread effect until after World War I. Symbolism, then,— the highly personal, associative approach which these poets invented, and which will be discussed later on—is an important (perhaps the most important) element in modern poetry, but it is only one. It doesn't cover the quite different revolt against tradition in America that began with Whitman and survives in Sandburg. Nor do such modern poets as Hopkins and Housman, Elinor Wylie and Edna St. Vincent Millay, Masefield and Hardy and Frost have anything to do with it. Walt Whitman and Emily Dickinson, with whom the older contemporary anthologists start off, are modern to be sure—but so are Blake and Marvell and Donne. A simpler criterion will have to be found.

W. B. Yeats (who was still alive in both senses when this anthology first appeared) not only knew Gerard Manley Hopkins
before the latter's death in 1888; he also attended the famous
Tuesday receptions at the apartment of Stephen Mallarmé in Paris
fin de siécle. There also came the young Paul Valéry. And there
symbolist innovation became symbolist doctrine. Ten years later
John Masefield, establishing another link with the past, tells us
that he was stimulated by the Monday evenings at the London
home of W. B. Yeats. Later he would go to the reading room of the
British Museum, where he would see that incorrigible old Vic-
torian, Swinburne, deaf and roaring to himself over some obscene
impropriety.

Chronologically I have begun with Hopkins, whose poems
(though written outside of any tradition whatsoever in the
seventies and eighties) appeared in my generation and have had
their first influence, already a considerable one, on the younger
living poets. Otherwise my rule of thumb has been simply whether
the poet lived and wrote in the twentieth century—with Carroll's
"Jabberwocky" as the single irrepressible exception.

I say "rule of thumb" because obviously a more important test
has been whether the poet, or the poem, seemed "modern" to me.
Kipling, for all the recent efforts to trim his imperial feathers, belongs with the great Victorians. A simple definition, broad enough
to be comprehensive, would be too broad to be sensible. I shall
therefore list a few of what seem to me the characteristics of
"modernity," though it may be difficult to dissociate some of them
from the hallmarks of true poetry at any time—

Imagery patterned increasingly on everyday speech
absence of inversions, stilted apostrophes, conventional end-
rhymes, "poetic" language generally, except where used deliberately
for incantatory effect
freedom from the ordinary logic of sequence, jumping from one

image to the next by "association" rather than by the usual cause-effect route

> *emphasis on the ordinary, in reaction against the traditional poetic emphasis on the cosmic*

> *concern with the newly identified "unconscious" or with the symbolic "father" as against "the soul"*

> *concern with the common man, almost to the exclusion of the "hero" or extraordinary man*

> *concern in secular verse with the social order as against "heaven" and "nature," and in non-secular verse with religion as a new field of discovery and imagery like psychoanalysis*

A few of the poets, such as Housman, answer only to the most general of these criteria. But these few have contributed nothing to technical innovation or fresh outlook, and for that reason have had no significant influence.

II. THE ARRANGEMENT

To avoid rigidity, I have given no titles to the five sections into which this anthology is divided. Their contents should speak for them. The introductory poems set the tone.

In the first part are the immediate forerunners of contemporary poetry as well as certain poets and poems that belong to no classifiable revolt against tradition.

Clearly the second embraces the poets who derive their inspiration from the people and the soil, in rebellion for the rights of both, but rebelling within an accepted historical tradition, and in a less experimental style than the poets included in Part IV.

While Yeats himself was influenced not a little by the French symbolist movement, it was not until Pound and Eliot that the whole course of modern verse was transformed by it. Here then is Part III. Pound had been something of a scholar in the Latin,

Provençal, Italian and Chinese, as well as in the symbolist language. He had lived in self-imposed exile for twenty-five years. Eliot, whose use of symbolism has been more deliberate and intellectual, has had the largest influence of any living poet. I have concluded the section with Gregory and MacLeish whose styles are clearly evolved from this movement, but whose concern with social and political issues marked a distinct finish to the exile and aristocratic phases of symbolism.

Part IV, in a sense, brings together the matter of II and the manner of III, but in addition many new things of its own. Here, for the first time, the influence of Hopkins' "sprung rhythm" [1] was felt. Satire assumed new strength and importance, especially in the work of W. H. Auden. Revolt against society drove revolt against form into the background. And the new synthesis (social-symbolism, it might be called) inevitably seemed less sharply original, if more outspoken and robust. The transition poet at the end of this section is Auden.

In their original shape Parts I–IV were assembled in 1937. A number of poems have been added since and a like number dropped. But Part V is entirely new and represents only work produced between that date and the beginning of 1946. Advisedly it is introduced and signed off with passages from an elaborate critique of modern poetry—a critique in my opinion refuted by everything printed between these quotations, and most convincingly perhaps by the poetry of Karl Shapiro himself. The dominant theme of these new poets, naturally enough, is war, and the prevailing tendency—religious. The soldier-poets this time (almost all of them) turned away from a materialistic resolution of the paradox that increase of knowledge was engendering increase

---

[1] This form, occasionally used in old ballads, by Langland in *Piers Ploughman*, and by Milton in the choruses of *Samson Agonistes*, has the advantage of opening up verse to include easily scientific words and conversational rhythms; its principal limitation is the indeterminacy of the stress, since the stresses rather than the syllables are counted. One foot may have one or many syllables.

of suffering, while the religious poets (all of them) seized upon the catastrophe as a flaming symbol of their quest for God.

The number of poems by which a poet is represented should not necessarily be taken as a judgment of his relative importance. Graves and Frost, Stevens and Sassoon, for example, are fairly represented by one or two poems, while Yeats, whose style has undergone a great many changes and whose influence persists, is inadequately represented by five. The important younger poets, with whose work the public cannot be acquainted, are given space accordingly. A few poems have been chosen not as representative of an author, but for their intrinsic excellence alone. Poems that appeal particularly to the editor—"Channel Firing," "Two Tramps in Mud Time," "Emblems of Conduct," "I think continually of those who were truly great," "Nigger"—are to be found in all sections. His inability to include more of the work of Hardy and Moore is the editor's only regret.

III. TAKING POETRY OFF THE SHELF

The two outstanding American anthologists of recent years have been Louis Untermeyer and Conrad Aiken. Untermeyer has been notable for his catholic taste (a recent edition of *Modern American and British Poetry* contains no fewer than 1,604 poems). Aiken has been distinguished by his discriminating partiality to the "metaphysical" poets. Very broadly their choices have reflected two viewpoints: that of the New Poetry (heralded by the Chicago "renaissance" of 1912), and that of the Lost Generation whose roots extended back even beyond symbolism to the so-called metaphysicals like Donne.

Neither of these anthologists showed much favor in the thirties to the significant new poetry of social protest, or in the forties to the religious counter-current stimulated by the war. Neither has included any folk-verse. Both have favored the lyric almost to the exclusion of the characteristic narrative and satirical poetry of our time. Both anthologists have suffered, in my opinion, from an excess of high seriousness; there is hardly a humorous poem or even representation of light verse in the collections of either. Yet:

> *"According to his powers each may give;*
> *Only on varied diet can we live . . .*
> *The pious fable and the dirty story*
> *Share in the total literary glory."*

And one of the major blocks to the popular appreciation of poetry, especially modern poetry, is the conviction that it must be Highly Serious—and consequently Highly Dull. People who dislike the very idea of poetry, says Auden, dislike it as they dislike over-earnest people, "they imagine it is always worrying about the eternal verities. . . . Poetry is no better and no worse than human nature; it is profound and shallow, sophisticated and naïve, dull and witty, bawdy and chaste in turn."

So, I think, the haunting songs of the Negro people, the Benéts' verse for children, the bitter *vers de société* of Dorothy Parker, the raucous rhymes of Ogden Nash, the political needling of 'Sagittarius,' the parodies and ballads, when phrased with a master's precision, help to make up what is poetry in our time.

IV. THE EXCITEMENT OF POETRY

To read poetry, however, and get the best out of it, does require effort. Poetry may be read on several levels—for its sound, for its content, for its pith, for excitement or for relaxation. But those who read it for merely sentimental reasons, the associations and the pleasing cadences, can hardly expect a visitation of the famous trouble Housman professed to have with his razor when a line of poetry strayed into his mind. "The sentimentalists," says Yeats, "are practical people who believe in money, in position, in a marriage bell, and whose understanding of happiness is to be so busy.

whether at work or at play, that all is forgotten but the momentary aim." The aim of poetry is not momentary, though its enjoyment may be. Its full enjoyment is lasting, precisely because it is not written by sentimentalists.

I will mention a few of the many things that are exciting to me in the poems of this collection, not because my reactions are important to anyone but myself, but because they may help some readers to look for other specific things themselves.

I would call attention to the *speed* of Masefield's lines, to the dropping sensation induced by the step-like arrangement of vowel sounds in the line

> "*Then down on the mile-long green decline.*"

I find exciting transitions like that of the first line of the fourth sonnet in Elinor Wylie's "Wild Peaches," where the lush, dreamy South suddenly becomes the austere, bitten North. Or the frightening shift from contemporary politics to legendary symbolism in Yeats' "The Second Coming."

I would mention the broken last line of the seventh Negro spiritual, where the effect of a sob and of defiance poignantly mingle. Or the intricate weaving of place and time into "Purgatorio," Crane's cry of despair before suicide. Or the effect of the rhyme, like a blow, in the last word of Fleming MacLiesh's "Speech of the Sentry."

Assonance [2] is not new in Wilfred Owen, but it is employed by him to extraordinary effect:

> "*They will be swift with swiftness with the tigress,*
> *None will break ranks, though nations trek from progress.*
> *Courage was mine, and I had mystery,*
> *Wisdom was mine and I had mastery . . .*"

Observe the "lift" in the sprung rhythm of Spender's limpid

[2] The use of imperfect rhyme, where the consonants but not the vowels of the end-words are similar.

early verse, the combination of delicacy, nobility and tensile strength:

> "*It is too late to stay in great houses where the ghosts*
> *are prisoned . . .*
> *Oh comrades, step beautifully from the solid wall*
> *advance to rebuild and sleep with friend on hill*"

Or the effect of clean distinction when life is breathed into old words under the impact of new ideas—by Muriel Rukeyser's

> "*Before they die the brave have set their hand*
> *On rich particular beauty for their heirs . . .*"

Do these examples seem trivial? Is it a poor definition that a poet's stature may be measured by the number of memorable lines he has written? Of such small things is the stuff of poetry fashioned. . . . But the "grand manner" is no more absent from modern poetry than from any other poetry. You will find it in the conclusion to "Felix Randal" when Hopkins abruptly passes from the pathetic details of his friend's illness to the triumph of his homely deeds. You will find it in the opening lines of Robert Lowell's "Where the Rainbow Ends," and in fact throughout the work of this powerful writer. Or in the magnificent peroration of Auden's vision of a future England:

> "*As when Merlin, tamer of horses, and his lords to whom*
> *Stonehenge was still a thought, the Pillars passed*
> *And into the undared ocean swung north their prow,*
> *Drives through the night and star-concealing dawn*
> *For the virgin roadsteads of our hearts an unwavering keel.*"

V. IS MODERN POETRY DIFFICULT?

If it is the business of poetry not merely to convey information, but to provide for the reader precisely those "vibrations" experienced by the writer, is it small wonder that the demand upon the reader's sensitivity and concentration is great? Shall we be shocked to find that much poetry in every age has been "difficult"? And is it surprising that for the full enjoyment of important poetry as much attention and understanding are required as an intelligent music-lover will devote to the intricate structure of a fugue? Yet superficially the music, like the poem, may be enjoyable to everyone who hears it. For like music "poetry often communicates when one does not understand it, and even when written in a language which one knows very imperfectly."

There has been difficult poetry in every age, then. But in periods of transition and social upheaval, when ideas, attitudes and even language are uprooted or in process of reconstruction, poetry has been correspondingly complex. That it has proved, at such times, to be correspondingly rewarding, is a fact that has sometimes been left to later generations to discover. Such epochs, and our own is no exception, have produced plenty of poetry that may be enjoyed with a minimum of effort. And the most subtle craftsmen in such a period, as witness James Joyce in our own, have occasionally written with piercing directness. But the fact of complexity remains.

"If a poet writes entirely in metaphor, using rare words only," said Aristotle at a time when poetry was going through another of its periodic crises, "the result is jargon." "But," he wisely added, "he who uses merely commonplace words sacrifices all to clarity." There is a new directness perceptible in the work of the poets included in the final part of this anthology. The intimately personal communication of Rexroth, the brutally frank sentiment of Patchen, the almost-flat honesty of Fuller and Lewis, the colloquial wit of Shapiro, bear witness to it in their fashions. But simplicity of utterance is not to be confused with simplicity of thought, or with naïveté. These are sensitive writers at grips with an ever more complex environment. They are not satisfied with appearances. "If you seek the kernel," Meister Eckhart wrote, "then you must break the shell. And likewise if you would know the reality of Nature, you must destroy the appearance, and the farther you go beyond the appearance, the nearer you will be to the essence."

VI. WHAT MAKES IT OBSCURE?

Let us admit, however, that two characteristics of contemporary verse have stood between the poets and a healthy audience: a philosophy of isolation and a private language.

The first of these began in France in the mid-nineteenth century when artists, as we observed, were expressing their revolt by retiring into some form of dream-world of their own making. Great poets, intense but too isolated to contribute to the development of a tradition in accord with the new social and scientific facts, rose on the crest of this first symbolist tide. One of them, Rimbaud, carried his escape so far as to anticipate such a recent phenomenon as surrealism. The following passage from his most mature work is self-explanatory—and prophetic:

"One must be modern completely . . . I loved meaningless door-tops, backgrounds, acrobats' back-cloths, signboards, popular prints, old-fashioned literature, church Latin, misspelled erotica, . . . I invented the color of the vowels!—A black, E white, I red, O blue, U green . . . I accustomed myself to simple hallucination: I saw quite freely a mosque in place of a factory, a school of drums made by the angels, a drawing-room at the bottom of a lake . . . I finished by finding the disorder of my senses sacred."

Poets who followed him, if they did not carry their burden to the same extremity, were content to develop some particular facet of the hard symbolist jewel. The late Paul Valéry, for example, battened upon the precious myth of the poet's unproductivity. Self-consciously he would work upon a single poem, for years and years, treating it as a piece of sculpture to be admired for its form only.

Ruling out verse that is full of passion or deliberately intelligible, he likened poetry to a heavy load which the poet carts to the roof bit by bit and then drops all at once on the poor unsuspecting reader who passes below. "Enthusiasm," he stated, "is not an artist's state of mind." And small wonder that the puritanism of this doctrine (which found American spokesmen in Yvor Winters and Allen Tate) was capable of awakening small enthusiasm in the reading public.

But symbolism, as I have endeavored to show in explaining the arrangement of the present collection, is not a piece of eccentric baggage to be tossed overboard lightly. For better or worse, it is part of the structure of the ship. And modern poetry, unless we would scuttle it entirely, must be an intricate, nicely balanced vessel if it is to ride the troubled cross-currents of our world.

If the philosophy of much modern poetry contributed to isolating it from all but a priesthood, the language which that philosophy called into being acted as a still more serious deterrent. For the style was bound to persist long after the attitudes themselves became unfashionable. Thus, for example, much of what has been loosely called "proletarian" poetry was written (ironically) in the same private, filigree manner with which the poet was wont to embellish the interior of his ivory tower.

C. Day Lewis [3] once pointed to the association-of-ideas technique, employed by T. S. Eliot and his followers, as a major cause of obscurity in post-World War I poetry. The poet takes over a sequence of images from psychology's exploration of the "unconscious"—and then presents them *as in psychic life* without the logical connections.

Another source of obscurity has been the modern poet's attempt

[3] A short list of the best studies of modern poetry, for which this introduction may serve as a summary, might include Mr. Lewis's *A Hope for Poetry, Axel's Castle* by Edmund Wilson, *Hart Crane* by Philip Horton, *The Name and Nature of Poetry* by A. E. Housman, *This Modern Poetry* by Babette Deutsch and Stephen Spender's *The Destructive Element.*

to compete with the clanging rhythms and inchoate life of the city. This often leads, when the material is poorly digested, to more confusion than one finds even in the poet who deliberately escapes from the city into a private, pastoral world of his own. Furthermore the city poet, often finding himself isolated from any genuine contact with his fellows, fails to derive that benefit from the group which has enriched art in all periods of great achievement. At such a time, he finds himself necessarily talking to those fellow-intellectuals who can readily share his frustration.

VII. DOES SCIENCE CONFLICT WITH IT?

Every five years or so, somebody announces in a solemn voice that poetry is dead. Coleridge, great romantic that he was, started the critics off a hundred years ago when he announced that poetry, in opposition to science, was after pleasure, rather than truth. Even so astute a critic as Edmund Wilson fell victim to this delusion. In the twenties he shook his head when T. S. Eliot ventured the belief that poetry would be reinstated on the stage. In the thirties, with that miracle on the way to modest accomplishment (by Eliot himself, among others), Mr. Wilson sadly noted the decline of Edna St. Vincent Millay and informed us that prose, and prose alone, was the medium of the future.

Both of these arguments arise from a fundamental misconception of the role of poetry. Poetry, as Hart Crane said, is an architectural art "based not on Evolution or the idea of progress, but on the articulation of the contemporary human consciousness *sub specie aeternitatis*, and inclusive of all readjustments incident to science and other shifting factors related to that consciousness." The function of poetry in this age is similar to its function in any age; and it is notable that the machine is being assimilated by the younger poets today with far less self-consciousness than by Crane himself—and for the very reasons which he himself described with such insight:

"The emotional stimulus of machinery is on an entirely different psychic plane from that of poetry. Its only menace lies in its capacities for facile entertainment, so easily accessible as to arrest the development of any but the most negligible aesthetic responses . . . Unless poetry can absorb the machine, i.e. *acclimatize* it as naturally and casually as trees, cattle, galleons, castles and all the other human associations of the past, then poetry has failed of its full contemporary function. This process does not infer any program nor does it essentially involve even the specific mention of a single mechanical contrivance. It demands, however, along with the traditional qualifications of the poet, an extraordinary capacity for surrender, at least temporarily, to the sensations of urban life. . . ."

Max Eastman, one of the leading literary worshippers of science, maintains that science has withdrawn intellect from literature. He goes so far as to say that nothing is left for the poets but to sing. "It is not their function to conceive things truly but to live them vividly." But while ignoring completely the role of poetry in "articulating contemporary human consciousness" and giving form to it, Mr. Eastman disregards an almost equally important function of the poet. Science does not and cannot make men feel, much less act. Nor does science as such, any more than sociology as such, give modern man that confidence in his own dignity and essential nobility which is necessary for the translation of mere animal energy into aspirations, aspirations into deeds. A great scientist must be a poet also. He must have vision to exceed precepts and conceive what never was. But a poet need not be a scientist, though his mind must have equal integrity, daring and orderliness. "No amount of psychological experimentation," a leading modern biologist has said, "can reveal the profundities of an emotional situation like a single poem."

A great scientist or a great prophet or a great revolutionary must be singleminded. For the success of his enterprise, his dedication must be complete. When Millikan writes of religion or politics he writes as a child. Lenin, according to Maxim Gorky, listened to a Beethoven sonata with a feeling of guilt—"It affects your nerves, makes you want to say stupid, nice things and stroke the heads of people who could create such beauty while living in this vile hell."

But a poet must be a whole man, else he will never see the relationship between things, the dualities and incongruities, yes, and the permanencies that makes sonnets and sonatas. Imagine this scene. An old man, poorly clad, totters down the steps of a library with his eyes fixed ahead of him. Our three "doers"—the scientist, statesman and priest—will want to do something about him, and rightly. They will prescribe medicine, old-age pensions or prayer, as the case may be. But the poet, while acknowledging the necessity for some of these remedies, is not looking primarily for a "cure." His poem may end with an exhortation, bidding the old man shake his fist as he did in his youth, but he will see the situation symbolically. He may see the futility of years of knowledge that have left the old man still staring blankly into the void. He may see the unconquerable impulse that sends him to the library with his remaining strength. Or he may see him as one in whose veins, quickened by the passionate lines of some other poet, blossom again dimly remembered Springs.

In any case one may be sure that the poet who captures the incident in any one of its symbolic relationships will, if he does so intensely, communicate something to the reader that the reader will never get from a description conceived in terms of its "cure." The cure, if there is one, comes afterward. If the reader's sensibilities have been moved, his will may be charged also. At the very least, the lens of his eye will have been adjusted to receive more light. For art, along with science, is one of the valid ways of communicating knowledge about reality. And it is even quite possible, as one scientist has suggested, that tomorrow, following this era in which materialistic conceptions have proven inadequate in the very fields where they achieved their greatest triumphs, "values will be regarded as inherent in reality."

VIII. DOES PROPAGANDA CANCEL IT?

Shall we infer from this that "propaganda" has no place in poetry? That aesthetic values are independent of all other values? That because the poem often grows out of no more than an abstract rhythmical impulse, the idea which it later embodies is not a product of the whole man? Shall we agree with the early T. S. Eliot, for instance, that moral, didactic, emotional, religious, historical and political purposes are the spheres of prose alone—purposes *in spite of which* "poetry" has sometimes emerged and survived? Shall we concur in his pedantic definition of poetry as "not a turning loose of emotion, but an escape from emotion; not an expression of personality, but an escape from personality?"

I think we are getting away from this most unhistorical view of poetry today. We acknowledge, to be sure, that religious fervor and "sound" politics do not necessarily produce poetry. But we observe that the very greatest poetry, and certainly the most monumental, was written by men who vaunted their extra-aesthetic intentions and who, if they were not actually out to instruct, were certainly anxious to expound.

It is even possible that we are returning to Matthew Arnold's rather heavy view of poetry as "criticism of life in which our race, as time goes on, will find an ever surer and surer stay"—but I think not. This definition is as narrow on the moral side as Eliot's is on the aesthetic. For though it is true, as Spender says, that the greatest art is moral "even when the artist has no particular axe to grind," and that in revolutionary times issues of war and peace and social justice tend to make issues of private morality and manners seem almost insignificant—poetry, to remain poetry, must deal with all of these larger questions in terms of the emotions generated

[*xli*]

by the smaller, in terms of human values rather than "party lines"; it must stand on the plane of *choice* where tragedy or acceptance are the alternatives, rather than on the plane of *conversion* where the poles are heresy or conformity only.

Propaganda is concerned with telling people what to do; poetry, at least the social poetry generated in times like ours, with "extending our knowledge of good and evil, perhaps making the necessity for action more urgent, and its nature more clear." Where the mind is still free, neither complacent nor shackled to the past nor servile to the discipline of the future, there will poetry flourish.

IX. THE POET'S PLACE

The most demanding, but the most rewarding view of the poet's function that we have is Emerson's. The poet, he said, is the "complete man" who "apprises us not of his wealth, but of the commonwealth." In recent years we have strayed far from this definition— to poetry's loss and the poet's, as well as the public's. If we have come to regard poetry as something to be taken with breathless ceremony on the rarest of occasions, it is because we have ceased to think of the poet as "the utterer of the necessary and the casual."

Poetry is the greatest of the arts because everyone can—and does—practise it. The ad-man and the gag-man, the housewife and the corner grocer are latent poets. The poetry of Carl Sandburg is memorable not because it gives words and ideas imperishable shape (it rarely does), but because it captures and records lovingly the poetry in the common speech, attitudes and aspirations of the people. It is hardly surprising that in a young civilization like America's the most original and indigenous art is to be found in the anonymous outpourings of the oppressed Negro. Or that in a nation of immigrants a new tongue is being constantly enriched by the overtones of diverse cultures. The last speech of Vanzetti, eloquent with compassion and anguish, falls into lines as easily as the frost into crystals. Thomas Wolfe, the novelist who wanted above all else to be a poet, wrote naturally and unconsciously *in verse*. Peter Bowman, who writes in unrhymed metres the first soldier's account of Pacific combat in World War II, insists that he is producing "sprung prose"! A confusion exists, but it bespeaks health: form is not frozen and refuses to freeze while the poet remains a whole man, exercising his heart.

"The experience of each new age requires a new confession," and the utterance of that confession in such an unequivocal medium as language requires every instrument in expression's orchestra. "It is not metres," said Emerson, "but a metre-making argument that makes a poem." And never in history has a people been faced with more urgent matters for argument. If anybody should be above the battle, it is the poet. If anybody should be *in* the battle, it is he. He alone must take sides and still reserve half his sympathy for the enemy. His heart must be involved, but his mind clear as spring water.

Nothing can be too ugly, too sordid, too brutal, too immediate, too mean to evoke the poet's interest. Yet his own sensibilities must be incorruptible; he must be virtuous, if not chaste; devout without subscribing to creeds; humble, but not pious. "On the brink of the waters of life and truth" we may be miserably dying, but the poet, if he comes down, as Milton urged, from the wine and generous living of his natural state to drink water out of a wooden bowl, may impart life to a whole generation. . . .

X. THE FUTURE

We Americans should be proud of our poetry, but we are not. Poe and Emerson, Whitman, Emily Dickinson and Frost, Vachel Lindsay and Eliot, the anonymous authors of the spirituals and chanteys, have contributed to the literature of the world. What other art in America has as much to show? Yet we honor poetry, if at all, with a jingling column in the morning paper, stuff it in the cracks of a magazine as a space-filler, at best pay perfunctory homage once a year with a professors' prize.

The poet himself is looked at askance; we are not quite sure it is a man's job he is doing. It is safe enough to admire the professional rabbit-poetry of the prize-winners. But a Hemingway or a Sandburg, who has been photographed with a fishing-tackle or a guitar, is accepted almost in spite of his literary accomplishments. It would be an almost insurmountable handicap if a man in public life were discovered, like a Milton or a Lorenzo de' Medici, to write good poetry.

Our poets themselves take refuge from notoriety in a double life, or, like Jeffers, seal themselves away from the people in some "tower beyond tragedy." The communication and integration of ideas that New England knew in Emerson's time is a long way from us. Yet this community of experience has been a phenomenon of every creative epoch from Athens and Rome to Florence, Weimar, Paris and London.

In the thirties, in the brotherhood of the younger English poets, there was a portent of change. Its immediate effect was not only to stimulate the leaders of this group themselves, but to attract to their standard a number of lesser talents, quickening their production, quantitatively and qualitatively, increasing their self-confidence. In Madrid, during the Spanish Civil War, where these sophisticated poets enjoyed a brief encounter with the more naïve and earthy writers of Eastern Europe and Latin America, it seemed possible for a moment that folk art and Western symbolism would enrich each other. Such a transfusion does appear in some measure to have been effected during the occupation of France in the early forties.

We have greater potentialities for a vital national literature in America. Our manner of speech is necessarily more "public." Our traditions are less smothering, the very resources of our land are more promising. The country that was big enough for Poe and Whitman at the same time is still big enough.

Our younger poets have taken the first steps. They were beginning in the thirties, as I believe the fourth part of this anthology indicated, to fuse the naturalistic and the symbolic in a new synthesis. They knew that neither science nor sociology could be rejected. They knew, too, that they could not become the slaves of either of these. The dilemma in another form had been faced successfully before, and it could be again. And the synthesis might be broadened to include the integration of conscious and unconscious experience, of man and machine, but above all the creative individual life balanced with the constant effort to help shape the face of the world in which the poet, like everyone else, must live.

Now in the forties the revolt against intellectualism promises to go much further, sweeping away in its wake even the rational determinism to which so many of the poets of the thirties clung. We have lived, John Heath-Stubbs reminds us (comparing unfavorably the age of Congreve to that of Pope):

> ". . . in a rounded time, rounded
> With a low horizon of feeling . . .
> We have forgotten the old high modes of loving,
> And the song's poise is gone.
> The intellect squats twisted like a spider,
> A tortured, hunch-backed poet."

By those who resent the revolt against our own "low horizon of feeling," Karl Shapiro has been severely criticized for deploring the isolated supremacy of the intellectual. Auden has been accused of feeling guilty over "the primary fission of the germ-cell instead of over that primary fission of the atom which produced in a few minutes half a million casualties." The French poet Aragon has been vilified for mixing his poems of the Resistance with poems of sensuous love.

Eliot, whose recent work like Auden's has sung the virtues of humility, has tried to match that theme with a like simplicity of utterance. But, as Louise Bogan remarks, "while a Browning or a Tennyson could go blustering back to feeling after war, the modern poet must break down the defenses that exist from top to bottom of our culture against the 'soft' and the 'corny.' He must skirt deeper bogs and darker thickets than his nineteenth-century brothers in order to get himself and his audience out into open emotional territory." The social poet who identifies himself with his audience, no matter how critically, will be called an opportunist. The war poet who refuses to see war as a simple dichotomy but as a universal tragedy has in every age had to wait until the partisans were in their shallow graves. The poet of feeling can expect to be branded a philistine. And the religious poet, if he is not accused of merely escaping into the church, will be charged with resuscitating a forgotten language and encouraging still another confusion in belief.

The fact remains, notwithstanding, that the new poets, whether concerned with the state, with war, with feeling or with God, seem guided by a sense of responsibility toward their readers and a taking-for-granted of the immediacy of poetry to contemporary speech [4] that sets them apart from their predecessors. It is becoming possible, we note for example, to write 'modern' poetry in forms recently discarded as outworn. Perhaps what we sense is that a revolution was accomplished in the twenties and that the new poets are legitimately at work in fields that had been too freshly ploughed for the ground-breakers to cultivate.

[4] "Every revolution in poetry," writes T. S. Eliot in *The Music of Poetry*, "is apt to be, and sometimes announces itself as, a return to common speech . . . No poetry, of course, is ever exactly the same speech as the poet talks and hears: but it has to be in such a relation to the speech of his time that the listener or reader can say 'that is how I should talk if I could write poetry.' This is the reason why the very best contemporary poetry can give us a feeling of excitement and a sense of fulfilment different from any sentiment aroused by even very much greater poetry of a past age."

PART ONE

POETRY

I TOO, dislike it: there are things that are important
  beyond all this fiddle.
Reading it, however, with a perfect contempt for it,
  one discovers in
it after all, a place for the genuine.
    Hands that can grasp, eyes
    that can dilate, hair that can rise
      if it must, these things are important not because a

high sounding interpretation can be put upon them
  but because they are
useful. When they become so derivative
    as to become unintelligible,
the same thing may be said for all of us, that we
    do not admire what
    we cannot understand: the bat,
      holding on upside down or in quest of something to

eat, elephants pushing, a wild horse taking a roll,
  a tireless wolf under

a tree, the immovable critic twitching his skin
    like a horse that feels a flea, the base-
ball fan, the statistician—
        nor is it valid
           to discriminate against 'business documents and

school-books'; all these phenomena are important.
    One must make a distinction
however: when dragged into prominence by half-poets,
    the result is not poetry,
nor till the poets among us can be
    'literalists of
    the imagination'—above
        insolence and triviality and can present

for inspection, imaginary gardens with real toads in
        them, shall we have
it. In the meantime, if you demand on the one hand,
the raw material of poetry in
    all its rawness and
    that which is on the other hand
        genuine, then you are interested in poetry.

MARIANNE MOORE

AFTERWARDS

WHEN the Present has latched its postern behind my
  tremulous stay,
  And the May month flaps its glad green leaves like
    wings,
Delicate-filmed as new-spun silk, will the neighbors say,
  "He was a man who used to notice such things"?

If it be in the dusk when, like an eyelid's soundless blink,
  The dewfall-hawk comes crossing the shades to alight
Upon the wind-warped upland thorn, a gazer may think,
  "To him this must have been a familiar sight."

If I pass during some nocturnal blackness, mothy and
    warm,
  When the hedgehog travels furtively over the lawn,
One may say, "He strove that such innocent creatures
    should come to no harm,
  But he could do little for them; and now he is gone."

If, when hearing that I have been stilled at last, they
    stand at the door,
  Watching the full-starred heavens that winter sees,
Will this thought rise on those who will meet my face
    no more,
  "He was one who had an eye for such mysteries"?

And will any say when my bell of quittance is heard in
      the gloom,
   And a crossing breeze cuts a pause in its out-rollings,
Till they rise again, as they were a new bell's boom,
    "He hears it not now, but used to notice such things"?

CHANNEL FIRING

THAT night your great guns, unawares,
  Shook all our coffins as we lay,
And broke the chancel window-squares,
We thought it was the Judgment-day

And sat upright. While drearisome
Arose the howl of wakened hounds:
The mouse let fall the altar-crumb,
The worms drew back into the mounds,

The glebe cow drooled. Till God called, "No;
It's gunnery practice out at sea
Just as before you went below;
The world is as it used to be:

"All nations striving strong to make
Red war yet redder. Mad as hatters
They do no more for Christés sake
Than you who are helpless in such matters.

"That this is not the judgment-hour
For some of them's a blessed thing,
For if it were they'd have to scour
Hell's floor for so much threatening.

"Ha, ha. It will be warmer when
I blow the trumpet (if indeed
I ever do; for you are men,
And rest eternal sorely need)."

So down we lay again. "I wonder,
Will the world ever saner be,"
Said one, "than when He sent us under
In our indifferent century!"

And many a skeleton shook his head.
"Instead of preaching forty year,"
My neighbor Parson Thirdly said,
"I wish I had stuck to pipes and beer."

Again the guns disturbed the hour,
Roaring their readiness to avenge,
As far inland as Stourton Tower,
And Camelot, and starlit Stonehenge.
April 1914.

* L E W I S   C A R R O L L *

JABBERWOCKY

'TWAS brillig, and the slithy toves
    Did gyre and gimble in the wabe;
All mimsy were the borogoves,
    And the mome raths outgrabe.

"Beware the Jabberwock, my son!
    The jaws that bite, the claws that catch!
Beware the Jubjub bird, and shun
    The frumious Bandersnatch!"

He took his vorpal sword in hand:
    Long time the manxome foe he sought—]
So rested he by the Tumtum tree,
    And stood awhile in thought.

And as in uffish thought he stood,
    The Jabberwock with eyes of flame,
Came whiffling through the tulgey wood,
    And burbled as it came!

One, two! One, two! And through and through
    The vorpal blade went snicker-snack!
He left it dead, and with its head
    He went galumphing back.

"And hast thou slain the Jabberwock?
   Come to my arms, my beamish boy!
O frabjous day! Callooh! Callay!"
   He chortled in his joy.

'Twas brillig, and the slithy toves
Did gyre and gimble in the wabe;
All mimsy were the borogoves,
   And the mome raths outgrabe.

PIED BEAUTY

GLORY be to God for dappled things—
　　For skies of couple-colour as a brinded cow;
　　　　For rose-moles all in stipple upon trout that swim;
Fresh-firecoal chestnut-falls; finches' wings;
　　　　Landscape plotted and pieced—fold, fallow, and
　　　　　　plough;
　　　　And áll trádes, their gear and tackle and trim.
All things counter, original, spare, strange;
　　　　Whatever is fickle, freckled (who knows how?)
　　　　　　With swift, slow; sweet, sour; adazzle, dim;
He fathers-forth whose beauty is past change:
　　　　　　Praise him.

DUNS SCOTUS'S OXFORD

Towery city and branchy between towers;
  Cuckoo-echoing, bell-swarméd, lark-charméd, rook-
    racked, river-rounded;
The dapple-eared lily below thee; that country and town
    did
Once encounter in, here coped and poiséd powers;

Thou hast a base and brickish skirt there, sours
That neighbour-nature thy grey beauty is grounded
Best in; graceless growth, thou hast confounded
Rural rural keeping—folk, flocks and flowers.

Yet ah! this air I gather and I release
He lived on; these weeds and waters, these walls are
    what
He haunted who of all men most sways my spirits to
    peace;
Of realty the rarest-veinéd unraveller; a not
Rivalled insight, be rival Italy or Greece;
Who fired France for Mary without spot.

FRAGMENT

STRIKE, churl; hurl, cheerless wind, then; heltering hail
May's beauty massacre and wispéd wild clouds grow
Out on the giant air; tell Summer No,
Bid joy back, have at the harvest, keep Hope pale.

FELIX RANDAL

FELIX RANDAL the farrier, O he is dead then? my duty all ended,
Who have watched his mould of man, big-boned and hardy-
handsome
Pining, pining, till time when reason rambled in it and some
Fatal four disorders, fleshed there, all contended?

Sickness broke him. Impatient he cursed at first, but mended
Being anointed and all; though a heavenlier heart began some
Months earlier, since I had our sweet reprieve and ransom
Tendered to him. Ah well, God rest him all road ever he offended!

This seeing the sick endears them to us, us too it endears.
My tongue had taught thee comfort, touch had quenched thy tears,
Thy tears that touched my heart, child, Felix, poor Felix Randal;

How far from then forethought of, all thy more boisterous years,
When thou at the random grim forge, powerful amidst peers,
Didst fettle for the great grey drayhorse his bright and battering
sandal!

✳ J O H N   M A S E F I E L D ✳

From REYNARD THE FOX

FROM the Gallows Hill to the Tineton Copse
There were ten ploughed fields, like ten full-stops,
All wet red clay, where a horse's foot
Would be swathed, feet thick, like an ash-tree root.
The fox raced on, on the headlands firm,
Where his swift feet scared the coupling worm;
The rooks rose raving to curse him raw,
He snarled a sneer at their swoop and caw.
Then on, then on, down a half-ploughed field
Where a ship-like plough drove glitter-keeled,
With a bay horse near and a white horse leading,
And a man saying "Zook," and the red earth bleeding.
He gasped as he saw the ploughman drop
The stilts and swear at the team to stop.
The ploughman ran in his red clay clogs,
Crying, "Zick un, Towzer; zick, good dogs!"
A couple of wire-haired lurchers lean
Arose from his wallet, nosing keen;
With a rushing swoop they were on his track,
Putting chest to stubble to bite his back.
He swerved from his line with the curs at heel,
The teeth as they missed him clicked like steel.
With a worrying snarl, they quartered on him,
While the ploughman shouted, "Zick; upon him."

✳

The fox raced on, up the Barton Balks,
With a crackle of kex in the nettle stalks,
Over Hammond's grass to the dark green line
Of the larch-wood smelling of turpentine.
Scratch Steven Larches, black to the sky,
A sadness breathing with one long sigh,
Grey ghosts of trees under funeral plumes,
A mist of twig over soft brown glooms.
As he entered the wood he heard the smacks,
Chip-jar, of the fir-pole feller's axe.
He swerved to the left to a broad green ride,
Where a boy made him rush for the farther side.
He swerved to the left, to the Barton Road,
But there were the timerers come to load—
Two timer carts and a couple of carters
With straps round their knees instead of garters.
He swerved to the right, straight down the wood,
The carters watched him, the boy hallooed.
He leaped from the larch-wood into tillage,
The cobbler's garden of Barton village.

✳

The cobbler bent at his wooden foot,
Beating sprigs in a broken boot;
He wore old glasses with thick horn rim,
He scowled at his work for his sight was dim.
His face was dingy, his lips were grey,
From primming sparrowbills day by day.
As he turned his boot he heard a noise
At his garden-end, and he thought, "It's boys."
Like a rocket shot to a ship ashore
The lean red bolt of his body tore,
Like a ripple of wind running swift on grass;
Like a shadow on wheat when a cloud blows past,

Like a turn at the buoy in a cutter sailing
When the bright green gleam lips white at the railing,
Like the April snake whipping back to sheath,
Like the gannets' hurtle on fish beneath,
Like a kestrel chasing, like a sickle reaping,
Like all things swooping, like all things sweeping,
Like a hound for stay, like a stag for swift,
With his shadow beside like spinning drift.

*

Past the gibbet-stock all stuck with nails,
Where they hanged in chains what had hung at jails,
Past Ashmundshowe where Ashmund sleeps,
And none but the tumbling peewit weeps,
Past Curlew Calling, the gaunt grey corner
Where the curlew comes as a summer mourner,
Past Blowbury Beacon, shaking his fleece,
Where all winds hurry and none brings peace;
Then down on the mile-long green decline,
Where the turf's like spring and the air's like wine,
Where the sweeping spurs of the downland spill
Into Wan Brook Valley and Wan Dyke Hill.

*

On he went with a galloping rally
Past Maesbury Clump for Wan Brook Valley.
The blood in his veins went romping high,
"Get on, on, on, to the earth or die."
The air of the downs went purely past
Till he felt the glory of going fast,
Till the terror of death, though there indeed,
Was lulled for a while by his pride of speed.
He was romping away from the hounds and hunt,
He had Wan Dyke Hill and his earth in front,

In a one mile more when his point was made
He would rest in safety from dog or spade;
Nose between paws he would hear the shout
Of the "Gone to earth!" to the hounds without,
The whine of the hounds, and their cat-feet gadding
Scratching the earth, and their breath pad-padding;
He would hear the horn call hounds away,
And rest in peace till another day.

* A. E. HOUSMAN *

OTHERS, I AM NOT THE FIRST

OTHERS, I am not the first,
  Have willed more mischief than they durst:
If in the breathless night I too
Shiver now, 'tis nothing new.

More than I, if truth were told,
Have stood and sweated hot and cold,
And through their reins in ice and fire
Fear contended with desire.

Agued once like me were they,
But I like them shall win my way
Lastly to the bed of mould
Where there's neither heat nor cold.

But from my grave across my brow
Plays no wind of healing now,
And fire and ice within me fight
Beneath the suffocating night.

1887

FROM Clee to heaven the beacon burns,
    The shires have seen it plain,
From north and south the sign returns
    And beacons burn again.

Look left, look right, the hills are bright,
    The dales are light between,
Because 'tis fifty years tonight
    That God has saved the Queen.

Now, when the flame they watch not towers
    Above the soil they trod,
Lads, we'll remember friends of ours
    Who shared the work with God.

To skies that knit their heartstrings right,
    To fields that bred them brave,
The saviours come not home tonight:
    Themselves they could not save.

It dawns in Asia, tombstones show
    And Shropshire names are read;
And the Nile spills his overflow
    Beside the Severn's dead.

We pledge in peace by farm and town
    The Queen they served in war,
And fire the beacons up and down
    The land they perished for.

'God save the Queen' we living sing,
　　From height to height 'tis heard;
And with the rest your voices ring,
　　Lads of the Fifty-third.

Oh, God will save her, fear you not:
　　Be you the men you've been
Get you the sons your fathers got,
　　And God will save the Queen.

TERENCE, THIS IS STUPID STUFF

TERENCE, this is stupid stuff:
  You eat your victuals fast enough;
There can't be much amiss, 'tis clear,
To see the rate you drink your beer.
But oh, good Lord, the verse you make
It gives a chap the belly-ache.
The cow, the old cow, she is dead;
It sleeps well, the horned head:
We poor lads, 'tis our turn now
To hear such tunes as killed the cow.
Pretty friendship 'tis to rhyme
Your friends to death before their time
Moping melancholy mad:
Come, pipe a tune to dance to, lad.'

Why, if 'tis dancing you would be,
There's brisker pipes than poetry.
Say, for what were hop-yards meant,
Or why was Burton built on Trent?
Oh many a peer of England brews
Livelier liquor than the Muse,
And malt does more than Milton can
To justify God's ways to man.
Ale, man, ale's the stuff to drink
For fellows whom it hurts to think:

Look into the pewter pot
To see the world as the world's not.
And faith, 'tis pleasant till 'tis past:
The mischief is that 'twill not last.

Oh I have been to Ludlow fair
And left my necktie God knows where,
And carried half way home, or near,
Pints and quarts of Ludlow beer:
Then the world seemed none so bad,
And I myself a sterling lad;
And down in lovely muck I've lain,
Happy till I woke again.
Then I saw the morning sky:
Heigho, the tale was all a lie;
The world, it was the old world yet,
I was I, my things were wet,
And nothing now remained to do
But begin the game anew.

Therefore, since the world has still
Much good, but much less good than ill,
And while the sun and moon endure
Luck's a chance, but trouble's sure,
I'd face it as a wise man would,
And train for ill and not for good.
'Tis true, the stuff I bring for sale
Is not so brisk a brew as ale:
Out of a stem that scored the hand
I wrung it in a weary land.
But take it: if the smack is sour,
The better for the embittered hour;
It should do good to heart and head
When your soul is in my soul's stead;
And I will friend you, if I may
In the dark and cloudy day.

There was a king reigned in the East:
There, when kings will sit to feast,

They get their fill before they think
With poisoned meat and poisoned drink.
He gathered all that springs to birth
From the many-venomed earth;
First a little, thence to more,
He sampled all her killing store;
And easy, smiling, seasoned sound,
Sate the king when healths went round.
They put arsenic in his meat
And stared aghast to watch him eat;
They poured strychnine in his cup
And shook to see him drink it up:
They shook, they stared as white's their shirt;
Them it was their poison hurt.
—I tell the tale that I heard told.
Mithridates, he died old.

THE LISTENERS

IS THERE anybody there?' said the Traveller,
  Knocking on the moonlit door;
And his horse in the silence champed the grasses
    Of the forest's ferny floor:
And a bird flew up out of a turret,
    Above the Traveller's head:
And he smote upon the door again a second time;
    'Is there anybody there?' he said.
But no one descended to the Traveller;
    No head from the leaf-fringed sill
Leaned over and looked into his grey eyes,
    Where he stood perplexed and still.
But only a host of phantom listeners
    That dwelt in the lone house then
Stood listening in the quiet of the moonlight
    To that voice from the world of men:
Stood thronging the faint moonbeams on the dark stair,
    That goes down to the empty hall,
Hearkening in an air stirred and shaken
    By the lonely Traveller's call.
And he felt in his heart their strangeness,
    Their stillness answering his cry,
While his horse moved, cropping the dark turf,
    'Neath the starred and leafy sky;

For he suddenly smote on the door, even
    Louder, and lifted his head:—
'Tell them I came, and no one answered,
    That I kept my word,' he said.
Never the least stir made the listeners,
    Though every word he spake
Fell echoing through the shadowiness of the still house
    From the one man left awake:
Aye, they heard his foot upon the stirrup,
    And the sound of iron on stone,
And how the silence surged softly backward,
    When the plunging hoofs were gone.

JOHANNES MILTON, SENEX

SINCE I believe in God the Father Almighty
Man's Maker and Judge, Overruler of Fortune,
'Twere strange should I praise anything and refuse Him
  praise,
Should love the creature forgetting the Creator,
Nor unto Him in suff'ring and sorrow turn me:
Nay how cou'd I withdraw me from His embracing?

But since that I have seen not, and cannot know Him,
Nor in my earthly temple apprehend rightly
His wisdom and the heav'nly purpose eternal;
Therefore will I be bound to no studied system
Nor argument, nor with delusion enslave me,
Nor seek to please Him in any foolish invention
Which my spirit within me, that loveth beauty
And hateth evil, hath reprov'd as unworthy:

But I cherish my freedom in loving service,
Gratefully adoring for delight beyond asking
Or thinking, and in hours of anguish and darkness
Confiding always on His excellent greatness.

* R O B E R T G R A V E S *

THE EREMITES

WE MAY well wonder at those froward hermits
Who like the scorpion and the basilisk
Crouched in the desert sands, to undo
Their scurfy flesh with tortures.

They drank from pools fouled by the ass and camel,
Chewed uncooked millet pounded between stones,
Wore but a shame-rag, dusk or dawn,
And rolled in thorny places.

In the wilderness there are no women;
Yet hermits harbour in their shrunken loins
A penetential paradise,
A leaping-house of glory.

Solomons of a thousand lusty love-chants,
These goatish men, burned Aethiopian black,
Kept vigil till the angelic whores
Should lift the latch of pleasure.

And what Atellan orgies of the soul
Were celebrated then among the rocks
They testify themselves in books
That rouse Atellan laughter.

Haled back at last to wear the ring and mître,
They clipped their beards and, for their stomachs' sake,
Drank now and then a little wine,
And tasted cakes and honey.

Observe then how they disciplined the daughters
Of noble widows, who must fast and thirst,
Abjure down-pillows, rouge and curls,
Deform their delicate bodies:

Whose dreams were curiously beset with visions
Of stinking hermits in a wilderness
Pressing unnatural lusts on them
Until they wakened screaming.

Such was the virtue of our pious fathers:
To refine pleasure in the hungry dream.
Pity for them, but pity too for us—
Our beds by their leave lain in.

THE LAUREATE

L IKE a lizard in the sun, though not scuttling
When men approach, this wretch, this thing of rage,
Scowls and sits rhyming in his horny age.

His time and truth he has not bridged to ours,
But shrivelled by long heliotropic idling
He croaks at us his out-of-date humours.

Once long ago here was a poet; who died.
See how remorse twitching his mouth proclaims
It was no natural death, but suicide.

Arrogant, lean, unvenerable, he
Still turns for comfort to the western flames
That glitter a cold span above the sea.

WILD PEACHES

1

WHEN the world turns completely upside down
You say we'll emigrate to the Eastern Shore
Aboard a river-boat from Baltimore;
We'll live among wild peach trees, miles from town,
You'll wear a coonskin cap, and I a gown
Homespun, dyed butternut's dark gold colour.
Lost, like your lotus-eating ancestor,
We'll swim in milk and honey till we drown.

The winter will be short, the summer long,
The autumn amber-hued, sunny and hot,
Tasting of cider and of scuppernong;
All seasons sweet, but autumn best of all.
The squirrels in their silver fur will fall
Like falling leaves, like fruit, before your shot.

The autumn frosts will lie upon the grass
Like bloom on grapes of purple-brown and gold.
The misted early mornings will be cold;
The little puddles will be roofed with glass.
The sun, which burns from copper into brass,
Melts these at noon, and makes the boys unfold
Their knitted mufflers; full as they can hold,
Fat pockets dribble chestnuts as they pass.

Peaches grow wild, and pigs can live in clover;
A barrel of salted herrings lasts a year;
The spring begins before the winter's over.
By February you may find the skins
Of garter snakes and water moccasins
Dwindled and harsh, dead-white and cloudy-clear.

3

When April pours the colours of a shell
Upon the hills, when every little creek
Is shot with silver from the Chesapeake
In shoals new-minted by the ocean swell,
When strawberries go begging, and the sleek
Blue plums lie open to the blackbird's beak,
We shall live well—we shall live very well.

The months between the cherries and the peaches
Are brimming cornucopias which spill
Fruits red and purple, sombre-bloomed and black;
Then, down rich fields and frosty river beaches
We'll trample bright persimmons, while you kill
Bronze partridge, speckled quail, and canvasback.

4

Down to the Puritan marrow of my bones
There's something in this richness that I hate.
I love the look, austere, immaculate,
Of landscapes drawn in pearly monotones.
There's something in my very blood that owns
Bare hills, cold silver on a sky of slate,
A thread of water, churned to milky spate
Streaming through slanted pastures fenced with stones.

I love those skies, thin blue or snowy gray
Those fields sparse-planted, rendering meagre sheaves;
That spring, briefer than apple-blossom's breath,
Summer, so much too beautiful to stay,
Swift autumn, like a bonfire of leaves,
And sleepy winter, like the sleep of death.

CASTILIAN

Velasquez took a pliant knife
And scraped his palette clean;
He said, "I lead a dog's own life
Painting a king and queen."

He cleaned his palette with oil rags
And oakum from Seville wharves;
"I am sick of painting painted hags
And bad ambiguous dwarves.

"The sky is silver, the clouds are pearl,
Their locks are looped with rain.
I will not paint Maria's girl
For all the money in Spain."

He washed his face in water cold,
His hands in turpentine;
He squeezed out colour like coins of gold
And colour like drops of wine.

Each colour lay like a little pool
On the polished cedar wood;
Clear and pale and ivory-cool
Or dark as solitude.

He burnt the rags in the fireplace
And leaned from the window high;
He said, "I like that gentleman's face
Who wears his cap awry."

This is the gentleman, there he stands,
Castilian, sombre-caped,
With arrogant eyes, and narrow hands
Miraculously shaped.

* EDNA ST. VINCENT MILLAY *

MORITURUS

I<small>F</small> I could have
    Two things in one:
The peace of the grave,
    And the light of the sun;

My hands across
    My thin breast-bone,
But aware of the moss
    Invading the stone,

Aware of the flight
    Of the golden flicker
With his wing to the light;
    To hear him nicker

And drum with his bill
    On the rotted window;
Snug and still
    On a gray pillow

Deep in the clay
    Where digging is hard,
Out of the way,—
    The blue shard

Of a broken platter—
 If I might be
Insensate matter
 With sensate me

Sitting within,
 Harking and prying,
I might begin
 To dicker with dying.

For the body at best
 Is a bundle of aches,
Longing for rest;
 It cries when it wakes

"Alas, 'tis light!"
 At set of sun
"Alas, 'tis night,
 And nothing done!"

Death, however,
 Is a spongy wall,
Is a sticky river,
 Is nothing at all.

Summon the weeper,
 Wail and sing;
Call him Reaper,
 Angel, King;

Call him Evil
 Drunk to the lees,
Monster, Devil,—
 He is less than these.

Call him Thief,
    The Maggot in the Cheese,
The Canker in the Leaf—
    He is less than these.

Dusk without sound,
    Where the spirit by pain
Uncoiled, is wound
    To spring again;

The mind enmeshed
    Laid straight in repose,
And the body refreshed
    By feeding the rose—

These are but visions;
    These would be
The grave's derisions,
    Could the grave see.

Here is the wish
    Of one that died
Like a beached fish
    On the ebb of the tide:

That he might wait
    Till the tide came back,
To see if a crate,
    Or a bottle, or a black

Boot, or an oar,
    Or an orange peel
Be washed ashore. . . .
    About his heel

The sand slips;
 The last he hears
From the world's lips
 Is the sand in his ears.

What thing is little?—
 The aphis hid
In a house of spittle?
 The hinge of the lid

Of the spider's eye
 At the spider's birth?
"Greater am I
 By the earth's girth

"Than Mighty Death!"
 All creatures cry
That can summon breath—
 And speak no lie.

For he is nothing;
 He is less
Than Echo answering
 "Nothingness!"—

Less than the heat
 Of the furthest star
To the ripening wheat;
 Less by far,

When all the lipping
 Is said and sung,
Than the sweat dripping
 From a dog's tongue.

This being so,
  And I being such,
I would liever go
  On a cripple's crutch,

Lopped and felled:
  Liever be dependent
On a chair propelled
  By a surly attendant

With a foul breath,
  And be spooned my food
Than go with Death
  Where nothing good,

Not even the thrust
  Of the summer gnat,
Consoles the dust
  For being that.

Needy, lonely,
  Stitched by pain,
Left with only
  The drip of the rain

Out of all I had;
  The books of the wise,
Badly read
  By other eyes,

Lewdly bawled
  At my closing ear;
Hated, called
  A lingerer here—

Withstanding Death
    Till Life be gone,
I shall treasure my breath,
    I shall linger on.

I shall bolt my door
    With a bolt and a cable;
I shall block my door
    With a bureau and a table;

With all my might
    My door shall be barred.
I shall put up a fight,
    I shall take it hard.

With his hand on my mouth
    He shall drag me forth,
Shrieking to the south
    And clutching at the north.

* ROBINSON JEFFERS *

PRACTICAL PEOPLE

PRACTICAL people, I have been told,
    Weary of the sea for his waves go up and down
Endlessly to no visible purpose;
Tire of the tides, for the tides are tireless, the tides
Are well content with their own march-tune
And nothing accomplished is no matter to them.
It seems wasteful to practical people.
And that the nations labor and gather and dissolve
Into destruction; the stars sharpen
Their spirit of splendor, and then it dims, and the stars
Darken; and that the spirit of man
Sharpens up to maturity and cools dull
With age, dies, and rusts out of service;
And all these tidal gatherings, growth and decay,
Shining and darkening, are forever
Renewed; and the whole cycle impenitently
Revolves, and all the past is future:—
Make it a difficult world . . . for practical people.

SHINE, PERISHING REPUBLIC

While this America settles in the mould of its vulgarity,
heavily thickening to empire,
And protest, only a bubble in the molten mass, pops and
sighs out, and the mass hardens,

I sadly remember that the flower fades to make fruit,
the fruit rots to make earth.
Out of the mother; and through the spring exultances,
ripeness and decadence; and home to the mother.

You making haste haste on decay: not blameworthy;
life is good, be it stubbornly long or suddenly
A mortal splendor: meteors are not needed less than
mountains: shine, perishing republic.

But for my children, I would rather have them keep their
distance from the thickening center; corruption
Never has been compulsory, when the cities lie at the
monster's feet there are left the mountains.

And boys, be in nothing so moderate as in love of man, a
clever servant, insufferable master.
There is the trap that catches noblest spirits, that caught—
they say—God, when he walked on earth.

NIGHT

THE ebb slips from the rock, the sunken
Tide-rocks lift streaming shoulders
Out of the slack, the slow west
Sombering its torch; a ship's light
Shows faintly, far out,
Over the weight of the prone ocean
On the low cloud.

Over the dark mountain, over the dark pinewood,
Down the long dark valley along the shrunken river,
Returns the splendor without rays, the shining of shadow,
Peace-bringer, the matrix of all shining and quieter of shining.
Where the shore widens on the bay she opens dark wings
And the ocean accepts her glory. O soul worshipful of her
You like the ocean have grave depths where she dwells always,
And the film of waves above that takes the sun takes also
Her, with more love. The sun-lovers have a blond favorite,
A father of lights and noises, wars, weeping and laughter,
Hot labor, lust and delight and the other blemishes. Quietness
Flows from her deeper fountain; and he will die; and she is im-
    mortal.

Far off from here the slender
Flocks of the mountain forest
Move among stems like towers
Of the old redwoods to the stream,
No twig crackling; dip shy
Wild muzzles into the mountain water
Among the dark ferns.

O passionately at peace you being secure will pardon
The blasphemies of glowworms, the lamp in my tower, the fret,
    fulness
Of cities, the cressets of the planets, the pride of the stars.
This August night in a rift of cloud Antares reddens,
The great one, the ancient torch, a lord among lost children,
The earth's orbit doubled would not girdle his greatness, one fire
Globed, out of grasp of the mind enormous; but to you O Night
What? Not a spark? What flicker of a spark in the faint far glimmer
Of a lost fire dying in the desert, dim coals of a sand-pit the
    Bedouins
Wandered from at dawn . . . Ah singing prayer to what gulfs
    tempted
Suddenly are you more lost? To us the near-hand mountain
Be a measure of height, the tide-worn cliff at the sea-gate a
    measure of continuance.

The tide, moving the night's
Vastness with lonely voices,
Turns, the deep dark-shining
Pacific leans on the land,
Feeling his cold strength
To the outmost margins: you Night will resume
The stars in your time.

O passionately at peace when will that tide draw shoreward?
Truly the spouting fountains of light, Antares, Arcturus,
Tire of their flow, they sing one song but they think silence.
The striding winter giant Orion shines, and dreams darkness.
And life, the flicker of men and moths and the wolf on the hill,
Though furious for continuance, passionately feeding, passion-
    ately
Remaking itself upon its mates, remembers deep inward

The calm mother, the quietness of the womb and the egg,
The primal and the latter silences: dear Night it is memory
Prophesies, prophecy that remembers, the charm of the dark.
And I and my people, we are willing to love the four-score years
Heartily; but as a sailor loves the sea, when the helm is for harbor.

Have men's minds changed,
Or the rock hidden in the deep of the waters of the soul
Broken the surface? A few centuries
Gone by, was none dared not to people
The darkness beyond the stars with harps and habitations.
But now, dear is the truth. Life is grown sweeter and lonelier,
And death is no evil.

THE BEAKS OF EAGLES

A N EAGLE's nest on the head of an old redwood on one of the
precipice-footed ridges
Above Ventana Creek, that jagged country which nothing but a
falling meteor will ever plow; no horseman
Will ever ride there, no hunter cross this ridge but the winged
ones, no one will steal the eggs from this fortress.
The she-eagle is old, her mate was shot long ago, she is now mated
with a son of hers.
When lightning blasted her nest she built it again on the same
tree, in the splinters of the thunderbolt.
The she-eagle is older than I; she was here when the fires of
eighty-five raged on these ridges,
She was lately fledged and dared not hunt ahead of them but ate
scorched meat. The world has changed in her time;
Humanity has multiplied, but not here; men's hopes and thoughts
and customs have changed, their powers are enlarged,
Their powers and their follies have become fantastic,
The unstable animal never has been changed so rapidly. The
motor and the plane and the great war have gone over him,
And Lenin has lived and Jehovah died: while the mother-eagle
Hunts her same hills, crying the same beautiful and lonely cry and
is never tired; dreams the same dreams,
And hears at night the rock-slides rattle and thunder in the throats
of these living mountains.
                                        It is good for man
To try all changes, progress and corruption, powers, peace and
anguish, not to go down the dinosaur's way
Until all his capacities have been explored: and it is good for him
To know that his needs and nature are no more changed in fact
in ten thousand years than the beaks of eagles.

* J A M E S   J O Y C E *

I HEAR AN ARMY CHARGING UPON THE LAND

I HEAR an army charging upon the land,
　　And the thunder of horses plunging, foam about their
　　　　knees:
Arrogant, in black armour, behind them stand,
　　Disdaining the reins, with fluttering whips, the
　　　　charioteers.

They cry unto the night their battle-name:
　　I moan in sleep when I hear afar their whirling
　　　　laughter.
They cleave the gloom of dreams a blinding flame,
　　Clanging, clanging upon the heart as upon an anvil.

They come shaking in triumph their long, green hair:
　　They come out of the sea and run shouting by the
　　　　shore.
My heart, have you no wisdom thus to despair?
　　My love, my love, my love, why have you left me
　　　　alone?

From NOT SO DEEP AS A WELL

1. FIGHTING WORDS

SAY my love is easy had,
 Say I'm bitten raw with pride,
Say I am too often sad—
 Still behold me at your side.

Say I'm neither brave nor young,
 Say I woo and coddle care,
Say the devil touched my tongue—
 Still you have my heart to wear.

But say my verses do not scan,
 And I get me another man!

2. BOHEMIA

Authors and actors and artists and such
Never know nothing, and never know much.
Sculptors and singers and those of their kidney
Tell their affairs from Seattle to Sydney.
Playwrights and poets and such horses' necks
Start off from anywhere, end up at sex.
Diarists, critics and similar roe
Never say nothing, and never say no.
People who do things exceed my endurance;
God, for a man that solicits insurance!

[47]

* MARIANNE MOORE *

THE MONKEYS

WINKED too much and were afraid of snakes. The zebras,
    supreme in
their abnormality; the elephants with their fog-coloured skin
    and strictly practical appendages
        were there, the small cats; and the parrakeet—
            trivial and humdrum on examination, destroying
        bark and portions of the food it could not eat.

I recall their magnificence, now not more magnificent
than it is dim. It is difficult to recall the ornament,
    speech, and precise manner of what one might
        call the minor acquaintances twenty
            years back; but I shall not forget him—that
                Gilgamesh among
        the hairy carnivora—that cat with the

wedge-shaped, slate-gray marks on its forelegs and the resolute
                tail,
astringently remarking, 'They have imposed on us with their
                pale
    half-fledge protestations, trembling about
        in inarticulate frenzy, saying
            it is not for us to understand art; finding it
        all so difficult, examining the thing

as if it were inconceivably arcanic, as symmet-
rically frigid as if it had been carved out of chrysophrase
   or marble—strict with tension, malignant
      in its power over us and deeper
         than the sea when it proffers flattery in exchange
           for hemp,
         rye, flax, horses, platinum, timber, and fur.'

* D . H . L A W R E N C E *

THE SEA

You, you are all unloving, loveless, you;
   Restless and lonely, shaken by your own moods,
You are celibate and single, scorning a comrade even,
Threshing your own passions with no woman for the
      threshing-floor,
Finishing your dreams for your own sake only,
Playing your great game around the world, alone,
Without playmate, or helpmate, having no one to cherish,
No one to comfort, and refusing any comforter.

Not like the earth, the spouse all full of increase
Moiled over with the rearing of her many-mouthed
      young;
You are single, you are fruitless, phosphorescent, cold
      and callous,
Naked of worship, of love or of adornment,
Scorning the panacea even of labour,
Sworn to a high and splendid purposelessness
Of brooding and delighting in the secret of life's goings,
Sea, only you are free, sophisticated.

You who toil not, you who spin not,
Surely but for you and your like, toiling
Were not worth while, nor spinning worth the effort!
You who take the moon as in a sieve, and sift

Her flake by flake and spread her meaning out;
You who roll the stars like jewels in your palm,
So that they seem to utter themselves aloud;
You who steep from out the days their colour,
Reveal the universal tint that dyes
Their web; who shadow the sun's great gestures and
    expressions
So that he seems a stranger in his passing;
Who voice the dumb night fittingly;
Sea, you shadow of all things, now mock us to death
    with your shadowing.

THE ELEPHANT IS SLOW TO MATE

THE elephant, the huge old beast
    is slow to mate;
he finds a female, they show no haste
    they wait

for the sympathy in their vast shy hearts
    slowly, slowly to rouse
as they loiter along the river-beds
    and drink and browse

and dash in panic through the brake
    of forest with the herd,
and sleep in massive silence, and wake
    together, without a word.

So slowly the great hot elephant hearts
    grow full of desire,
and the great beasts mate in secret at last,
    hiding their fire.

Oldest they are and the wisest of beasts
    so they know at last
how to wait for the loneliest of feasts
    for the full repast.

They do not snatch, they do not tear;
    their massive blood
moves as the moon-tides, near, more near
    till they touch in flood.

SNAKE

A SNAKE came to my water-trough
On a hot, hot day, and I in pyjamas for the heat,
To drink there.

In a deep, strange-scented shade of the great dark carob-tree
I came down the steps with my pitcher
And must wait, must stand and wait, for there he was at the
    trough before me.

He reached down from a fissure in the earth-wall in the gloom
And trailed his yellow-brown slackness soft-bellied down, over
    the edge of the stone trough
And rested his throat upon the stone bottom,
And where the water had dripped from the tap, in a small clearness,
He sipped with his straight mouth,
Softly drank through his straight gums, into his slack long body,
Silently.

Someone was before me at my water-trough,
And I, like a second comer, waiting.

He lifted his head from his drinking, as cattle do,
And looked at me vaguely, as drinking cattle do,
And flickered his two-forked tongue from his lips, and mused a
    moment,
And stooped and drank a little more,
Being earth-brown, earth-golden from the burning bowels of the
    earth
On the day of Sicilian July, with Etna smoking.

The voice of my education said to me
He must be killed,
For in Sicily the black, black snakes are innocent, the gold are
    venomous.

And voices in me said, If you were a man
You would take a stick and break him now, and finish him off.

But must I confess how I liked him,
How glad I was he had come like a guest in quiet, to drink at
    my water-trough
And depart peaceful, pacified, and thankless,
Into the burning bowels of this earth?

Was it cowardice, that I dared not kill him?
Was it perversity, that I longed to talk to him?
Was it humility, to feel so honoured?
I felt so honoured.

And yet those voices:
If you were not afraid, you would kill him!
And truly I was afraid, I was most afraid,
But even so, honoured still more
That he should seek my hospitality
From out the dark door of the secret earth.

He drank enough
And lifted his head, dreamily, as one who has drunken,
And flickered his tongue like a forked night on the air, so black,
Seeming to lick his lips,
And looked around like a god, unseeing, into the air,
And slowly turned his head,
And slowly, very slowly, as if thrice adream,
Proceeded to draw his slow length curving round
And climb again the broken bank of my wall-face.

And as he put his head into that dreadful hole,
And as he slowly drew up, snake-easing his shoulders, and entered
    farther,
A sort of horror, a sort of protest against his withdrawing into
    that horrid black hole,
Deliberately going into the blackness, and slowly drawing himself
    after,
Overcame me now his back was turned.

I looked round, I put down my pitcher,
I picked up a clumsy log
And threw it at the water-trough with a clatter.

I think it did not hit him,
But suddenly that part of him that was left behind convulsed in
    undignified haste,
Writhed like lightning, and was gone
Into the black hole, the earth-lipped fissure in the wall-front,
At which, in the intense still noon, I stared with fascination.

And immediately I regretted it.
I thought how paltry, how vulgar, what a mean act!
I despised myself and the voices of my accursed human education.

And I thought of the albatross,
And I wished he would come back, my snake.

For he seemed to me again like a king,
Like a king in exile, uncrowned in the underworld,
Now due to be crowned again.

And so, I missed my chance with one of the lords
Of life.
And I have something to expiate;
A pettiness.

Taormina.

From THE SHIP OF DEATH

I SING of autumn and the falling fruit
  and the long journey toward oblivion.

The apples falling like great drops of dew
to bruise themselves and exit from themselves.

Have you built your ship of death, oh, have you?

Build then your ship of death, for you will need it!

And if tonight my soul may find her peace
in sleep, and sink in good oblivion,
and in the morning wake like a new-opened flower
then I have been dipped again in God, and new-created.

And if, as weeks go round, in the dark of the moon
my spirit darkens and goes out, and soft strange gloom
pervades my movements and my thoughts and words
then I shall know that I am walking still
with God, we are close together now the moon's in shadow.

And if, as autumn deepens and darkens
I feel the pain of falling leaves, and stems that break in
        storms
and trouble and dissolution and distress
and then the softness of deep shadows folding, folding
around my soul and spirit, around my lips
so sweet, like a swoon, or more like the drowse of a low,
        sad song

singing darker than the nightingale, on, on to the solstice
and the silence of short days, the silence of the year, the
    shadow,
then I shall know that my life is moving still
with the dark earth, and drenched
with the deep oblivion of earth's lapse and renewal.

And if, in the changing phases of man's life
I fall in sickness and in misery
my wrists seem broken and my heart seems dead
and strength is gone, and my life
is only the leavings of a life:

and still, among it all, snatches of lovely oblivion, and
    snatches of renewal
odd, wintry flowers upon the withered stem, yet new,
    strange flowers
such as my life has not brought forth before, new blos-
    soms of me—

then I must know that still
I am in the hands of the unknown God,
he is breaking me down to his own oblivion
to send me forth on a new morning, a new man.
Drift on, drift on, my soul, toward the most pure
most dark oblivion.
And at the penultimate porches, the dark-red mantle
of the body's memories slips and is absorbed
into the shell-like, womb-like convoluted shadow.

And round the great final bend of unbroken dark
the skirt of the spirit's experience has melted away
the oars have gone from the boat, and the little dishes
gone, gone, and the boat dissolves like pearl

as the soul at last slips perfect into the goal, the core
of sheer oblivion and of utter peace,
the womb of silence in the living night.

Ah peace, ah lovely peace, most lovely lapsing
of this my soul into the plasm of peace.

Oh lovely last, last lapse of death, into pure oblivion
at the end of the longest journey
peace, complete peace!
But can it be that also it is procreation?

*

Ah, if you want to live in peace on the face of the earth
Then build your ship of death, in readiness
For the longest journey, over the last of seas.

OLD COUNTRYSIDE

BEYOND the hour we counted rain that fell
On the slant shutter, all has come to proof.
The summer thunder, like a wooden bell,
Rang in the storm above the mansard roof,

And mirrors cast the cloudy day along
The attic floor; wind made the clapboards creak.
You braced against the wall to make it strong,
A shell against your cheek.

Long since, we pulled brown oak-leaves to the ground
In a winter of dry trees; we heard the cock
Shout its unplaceable cry, the axe's sound
Delay a moment after the axe's stroke.

Far back, we saw, in the stillest of the year,
The scrawled vine shudder, and the rose-branch show
Red to the thorns, and, sharp as sight can bear,
The thin hound's body arched against the snow.

BAROQUE COMMENT

FROM loud sound and still chance;
From mindless earth, wet with a dead million leaves;
From the forest, the empty desert, the tearing beasts,
The kelp-disordered beaches;
Coincident with the lie, anger, lust, oppression and death
    in many forms:

Ornamental structures, continents apart, separated by seas;
Fitted marble, swung bells; fruit in garlands as well as on
    the branch;
The flower at last in bronze, stretched backward, or curled
    within;
Stone in various shapes: beyond the pyramid, the contrived
    arch and the buttress;
The named constellations;
Crown and vesture; palm and laurel chosen as noble and
    enduring;
Speech proud in sound; death considered sacrifice;
Mask, weapon, urn; the ordered strings;
Fountains; foreheads under weather-bleached hair;
The wreath, the oar, the tool,
The prow·
The turned eyes and the opened mouth of love.

WAR EXPERIENCE

DEGREES of groping thought have taught me to conclude
That when a man began in youth to learn truth crude
From life in the demented strife and ghastly glooms
Of soul-conscripting war, mechanic and volcanic,—
Not much remains, twelve winters later, of the hater
Of purgatorial pains. And somewhat softly booms
A Somme bombardment: almost unbelieved-in looms
The day-break sentry staring over Kiel Trench crater.

AT THE GRAVE OF HENRY VAUGHAN

A BOVE the voiceful windings of a river
An old green slab of simply graven stone
Shuns notice, overshadowed by a yew.
Here Vaughan lies dead, whose name flows on for ever
Through pastures of the spirit washed with dew
And starlit with eternities unknown.

Here sleeps the Silurist; the loved physician;
The face that left no portraiture behind;
The skull that housed white angels and had vision
Of day-break through the gateways of the mind.
 Here faith and mercy, wisdom and humility
 (Whose influence shall prevail for evermore)
 Shine. And the lowly grave tells Heaven's tranquility.
 And here stand I, a suppliant at the door.

I AM OF IRELAND

I AM *of Ireland,*
And the Holy Land of Ireland,
And time runs on," cried she.
"Come out of charity,
Come dance with me in Ireland."

One man, one man alone
In that outlandish gear,
One solitary man
Of all that rambled there
Had turned his stately head.
"That is a long way off,
And time runs on," he said,
"And the nigh grows rough."

"I am of Ireland,
And the Holy Land of Ireland,
And time runs on," cried she,
"Come out of charity
And dance with me in Ireland."

"The fiddlers are all thumbs,
Or the fiddle-strings accursed,
The drums and the kettle-drums
And the trumpets all are burst.

And the trombone," cried he,
"The trumpet and trombone,"
And cocked a malicious eye,
"But time runs on, runs on."

"I am of Ireland,
And the Holy Land of Ireland,
And time runs on," cried she.
"Come out of charity
And dance with me in Ireland."

THE COLD HEAVEN

SUDDENLY I saw the cold and rook-delighting **Heaven**
That seemed as though ice burned and was but the **more**
    ice,
And thereupon imagination and heart were driven
So wild that every casual thought of that and this
Vanished, and left but memories, that should be out of
    season
With the hot blood of youth, of love crossed long ago;
And I took all the blame out of all sense and reason,
Until I cried and trembled and rocked to and fro,
Riddled with light. Ah! when the ghost begins to
        quicken,
Confusion of the death-bed over, is it sent
Out naked on the roads, as the books say, and stricken
By the injustice of the skies for punishment?

SAILING TO BYZANTIUM

1

THAT is no country for old men. The young
In one another's arms; birds in the trees,
—Those dying generations—at their song;
The salmon-falls, the mackerel-crowded seas,
Fish, flesh, or fowl, commend all summer long
Whatever is begotten, born, and dies.
Caught in that sensual music all neglect
Monuments of unageing intellect.

2

An aged man is but a paltry thing,
A tattered coat upon a stick, unless
Soul clap its hands and sing, and louder sing
For every tatter in its mortal dress,
Nor is there singing school but studying
Monuments of its own magnificence;
And therefore I have sailed the seas and come
To the holy city of Byzantium.

3

O sages standing in God's holy fire
As in the gold mosaic of a wall,
Come from the holy fire, perne in a gyre,
And be the singing masters of my soul.
Consume my heart away; sick with desire
And fastened to a dying animal
It knows not what it is; and gather me
Into the artifice of eternity.

4

Once out of nature I shall never take
My bodily form from any natural thing,
But such a form as Grecian goldsmiths make
Of hammered gold and gold enamelling
To keep a drowsy emperor awake;
Or set upon a golden bough to sing
To lords and ladies of Byzantium
Of what is past, or passing, or to come.

THE SECOND COMING

TURNING and turning in the widening gyre
The falcon cannot hear the falconer;
Things fall apart; the centre cannot hold;
Mere anarchy is loosed upon the world,
The blood-dimmed tide is loosed, and everywhere
The ceremony of innocence is drowned;
The best lack all conviction, while the worst
Are full of passionate intensity.

Surely some revelation is at hand;
Surely the Second Coming is at hand.
The Second Coming! Hardly are those words out
When a vast image out of *Spiritus Mundi*
Troubles my sight: somewhere in sands of the desert
A shape with lion body and the head of a man,
A gaze blank and pitiless as the sun,
Is moving its slow thighs, while all about it
Reel shadows of the indignant desert birds.
The darkness drops again; but now I know
That twenty centuries of stony sleep
Were vexed to nightmare by a rocking cradle,
And what rough beast, its hour come round at last,
Slouches towards Bethlehem to be born?

AN ACRE OF GRASS

Picture and book remain,
  An acre of green grass
For air and exercise,
Now strength of body goes;
Midnight, an old house
Where nothing stirs but a mouse.

My temptation is quiet.
Here at life's end
Neither loose imagination,
Nor the mill of the mind
Consuming its rag and bone,
Can make the truth known.

Grant me an old man's frenzy,
Myself must I remake
Till I am Timon and Lear
Or that William Blake
Who beat upon the wall
Till Truth obeyed his call;

A mind Michael Angelo knew
That can pierce the clouds,
Or inspired by frenzy
Shake the dead in their shrouds;
Forgotten else by mankind,
An old man's eagle mind.

∗ PART TWO ∗

WHO *can make a poem of the depths of weariness*
bringing meaning to those never in the depths?
 Those who order what they please
 when they choose to have it—
 can they understand the many down under
who come home to their wives and children at night
and night after night as yet too brave and unbroken
 to say, "I ache all over"?
 How can a poem deal with production cost
 and leave out definite misery paying
a permanent price in shattered health and early old age?
 When will the efficiency engineers and the poets
 get together on a program?
Will that be a cold day? will that be a special hour?
 Will somebody be coocoo then?
 And if so, who?
 And what does the Christian Bible say?
And the Mohammedan Koran and Confucius and the
 Shintoists
 and the Encyclicals of the Popes?
 Will somebody be coocoo then?
 And if so, who??

CARL SANDBURG

A GROUP OF NEGRO SONGS

1

I KNOW moon-rise, I know star-rise,
  I lay dis body down.
I walk in de moonlight, I walk in de starlight
    To lay dis body down.
I walk in de graveyard, I walk through the graveyard
    To lay dis body down.
I lie in de grave an' stretch out my arms;
    Lay dis body down.
I go to de judgement in de evenin' of de day
    When I lay dis body down
An' my soul and your soul will meet in de day
    When I lay dis body down.

2

    Joshua fit de battle ob Jerico,
      Jerico, Jerico,—
    Joshua fit de battle ob Jerico
      An' de walls come tumblin' down

  You may talk about yo' king ob Gideon,
  You may talk about yo' man ob Saul:
  Dere's none like good ole Josh-ua
  At de battle ob Jerico.

Up to de walls ob Jerico
He marched with spear in han';
"Go blow dem ram horns," Joshua cried,
"Kase de battle am in my han'."

Den de lam' ram sheep horns begin to blow,
Trumpets begin to soun';
Josh-u-a commanded de chillun to shout
An' de walls come tumblin' down;

      Dat mornin'
      Joshua fit de battle ob Jerico,
         Jerico, Jerico;
      Joshua fit de battle ob Jerico
         An' de walls come tumblin' down.

3

Dark was de night an' col' was de groun'
In which de Lawd was laid,
Sweat like blood run down in drops
An' in agony he prayed.

4

Yes, de book of Revelations will be brought forth dat
    day,
An' every leaf unfolded, de book of de seven seals.

An' I went down to Egypt, I camped upon de groun'
At de soundin' of de trumpet de Holy Ghost came down.

And when de seals were opened, de voice said, "Come
    an' see,"
I went an' stood a-looking to see de mystery.

De red horse came a-gallopin', and de black horse he
  came too,
An' de pale horse he came down de road, an' stole my
  father away.

An' den I see ole Satan, an' dey bound him wid a chain,
An' dey put him in de fi-ar an' I see de smoke arise.

Dey bound him in de fi-ar, where he wanted to take my
  soul,
Ole Satan gnashed his teeth and howled, he missed po'
  sinner man's soul.

Den I see de dead arisin', and stan' before de Lamb
And de wicked call on de mountains to hide dem f'om
  His face,

An' den I see de Christians, standin' on God's right hand
A-shoutin' "Hallelujah!" singing praises to de Lord.

5

When de golden trumpets sound
Where will yo' soul be found?
Standin' aroun', standin' around
When de golden trumpets sound.

When de golden trumpets sound
Where will my soul be found?
With de crowned, with de crowned
When de golden trumpets sound.

6

I wrastled wid Satan, I wrastled wid sin,
Stepped over hell, an' come back ag'in.

[75]

Isaiah mounted on de wheel of time,
Spoke to God A-mighty way down de line.

O hear dat lumberin' thunder
A-roll f'om door to door,
A-callin' de people home to God,
Dey'll git home bime-by.

O see dat forkéd lightnin'
A-jump f'om cloud to cloud,
A-pickin' up God's chillun,
Dey'll git home bime-by.

7

Sometimes I feel like an eagle in de air
Some-a dese mornin's bright an' fair
I'm goin' to lay down my heavy load;
Goin' to spread my wings an' cleave de air.
You may bury me in de east,
You may bury me in de west,
But I'll hear de trumpet sound
In-a dat mornin'.

8

John Henry tol' his Cap'n
That a man was a natch'al man:
And before he'd let that steam drill beat him down
He'd fall dead wid his hammer in his han'
He'd fall dead wid his hammer in his han'.

John Henry says to his Cap'n
"Send me a twelve-poun' hammer aroun',
A twelve-poun' wid a four-foot handle
And I beat yo' steam drill down
And I beat yo' steam drill down."

John Henry says to his shaker
"Look hear, man, why don't you sing?
I'm throwin' twelve-poun' from my hips on **down,**
Jes' you lis'en to de col' steel ring,
Jes' you lis'en to de col' steel ring."

John Henry went down on de railroad
Wid a twelve-poun' hammer by his side,
He walked down de track but he never come **back,**
'Cause he laid down his hammer an' he died,
'Cause he laid down his hammer an' he died.

John Henry had a good woman,
Her name was Polly Ann.
On de day John Henry he dropped dead
Polly Ann hammered steel like a man,
Polly Ann hammered steel like a man.

9
W. C. Handy

I've put some
ASHES in my sweet papa's bed,
So that he can't slip out—
HOODOO in his bread,
Goopher-dust all about—I'll fix him!
CON-JU-RA-TION
Is in his socks and shoes;
Tomorrow he will have those
Mean Sundown Blues!

10
W. C. Handy

Ah hate to see de evenin' sun go down,
Hate to see de evenin' sun go down,—

'Cause my baby,—he done lef' dis town
Feelin' tomorrow lak Ah feel today,
Feel tomorrow lak Ah feel today,
Ah'll pack my trunk, make mah get away.
St. Louis woman wid her diamon' rings
Pulls dat man 'roun' by her apron strings;
'Twa'nt for powder and for store-bought hair
De man I love would not gone nowhere.

You ought to see dat stove-pipe brown of mine
Lak he own de Diamon' Joseph line;
He'd make a cross-eyed 'oman go stone blind
Blacker than midnight, teeth lak flags of truce,—
Blackest man in de whole St. Louis
(Blacker de berry—sweeter is de juice)
About a crap game he knows a pow'ful lot
But when work-time comes he's on de dot;
Gwine to ask him for a cold ten spot:
What it takes to git it, he's cert'nly got.

Got de St. Louis Blues jes' as blue as Ah can be
Dat man got a heart lak a rock cast in de sea
Or else he wouldn't have gone so far from me,
Dog-gone it!

✳ E D W I N   M A R K H A M ✳

THE MAN WITH THE HOE

God made man in his own image
in the image of God he made him.

GENESIS.

Bowed by the weight of centuries he leans
Upon his hoe and gazes on the ground,
The emptiness of ages in his face,
And on his back the burden of the world.
Who made him dead to rapture and despair,
A thing that grieves not and that never hopes,
Stolid and stunned, a brother to the ox?
Who loosened and let down this brutal jaw?
Whose was the hand that slanted back this brow?
Whose breath blew out the light within this brain?

Is this the Thing the Lord God made and gave
To have dominion over sea and land?
To trace the stars and search the heavens for power;
To feel the passion of Eternity?
Is this the dream He dreamed who shaped the suns
And markt their ways upon the ancient deep?
Down all the caverns of Hell to their last gulf
There is no shape more terrible than this—
More tongued with censure of the world's blind greed—
More filled with signs and portents for the soul—
More packt with danger to the universe.

What gulfs between him and the seraphim!
Slave of the wheel of labor, what to him
Are Plato and the swing of Pleiades?
What the long reaches of the peaks of song,
The rift of dawn, the reddening of the rose?
Through this dread shape the suffering ages look;
Time's tragedy is in that aching stoop;
Through this dread shape humanity betrayed,
Plundered, profaned and disinherited,
Cries protest to the Powers that made the world,
A protest that is also prophecy.

O masters, lords and rulers in all lands,
Is this the handiwork you give to God,
This monstrous thing distorted and soul-quencht?
How will you ever straighten up this shape;
Touch it again with immortality;
Give back the upward looking and the light;
Rebuild in it the music and the dream;
Make right the immemorial infamies,
Perfidious wrongs, immedicable woes?

O masters, lords and rulers in all lands,
How will the future reckon with this Man?
How answer his brute question in that hour
When whirlwinds of rebellion shake all shores?
How will it be with kingdoms and with kings—
With those who shaped him to the thing he is—
When this dumb Terror shall rise to judge the world,
After the silence of the centuries?

THROUGH THE NEEDLE'S EYE

1. COMRADE JESUS

THANKS to Saint Matthew, who had been
    At mass meetings in Palestine,
We know whose side was spoken for
When Comrade Jesus had the floor.

"Where sore they toil and hard they lie,
Among the great unwashed, dwell I.
The tramp, the convict, I am he;
Cold-shoulder him, cold-shoulder me."

By Dives' door, with thoughtful eye,
He did tomorrow prophesy.
"The kingdom's gate is low and small;
The rich can scarce wedge through at all."

"A dangerous man," said Caiaphas,
"An ignorant demagogue, alas,
Friend of low women, it is he
Slanders the upright Pharisee."

For law and order, it was plain
For holy church, he must be slain.
The troops were there to awe the crowd
And "violence" was not allowed.

The clumsy force with force to foil
His strong, clean hands he would not soil.
He saw their childishness quite plain
Between the lightnings of his pain.

Between the twilights of his end
He made his fellow-felon friend;
With swollen tongue and blinding eyes
Invited him to paradise.

2. QUATRAIN

The golf links lie so near the mill
    That almost every day
The laboring children can look out
    And see the men at play.

From SPOON RIVER

1. MRS. WILLIAMS

I WAS the milliner
Talked about, lied about,
Mother of Dora,
Whose strange disappearance
Was charged to her rearing.
My eye quick to beauty
Saw much beside ribbons
And buckles and feathers
And leghorns and felts,
To set off sweet faces,
And dark hair and gold.
One thing I will tell you
And one I will ask:
The stealers of husbands
Wear powder and trinkets,
And fashionable hats.
Wives, wear them yourselves.
Hats may make divorces—
They also prevent them.
Well now, let me ask you:
If all of the children, born here in Spoon River
Had been reared by the County, somewhere on a farm;
And the fathers and mothers had been given their freedom

To live and enjoy, change mates if they wished,
Do you think that Spoon River
Had been any the worse?

2. CHANDLER NICHOLAS

Every morning bathing myself and shaving myself,
And dressing myself.
But no one in my life to take delight
In my fastidious appearance.
Every day walking, and deep breathing
For the sake of my health.
But to what use vitality?
Every day improving my mind
With meditation and reading,
But no one with whom to exchange wisdoms.
No agora, no clearing house
For ideas, Spoon River.
Seeking, but never sought;
Ripe, companionable, useful, but useless.
Chained here in Spoon River,
My liver scorned by the vultures,
And self-devoured!

3. HOWARD LAMSON

Ice cannot shiver in the cold,
Nor stones shrink from the lapping flame.
Eyes that are sealed no more have tears;
Ears that are stopped hear nothing ill;
Hearts turned to silt are strange to pain;
Tongues that are dumb report no loss;
Hands stiffened, well may idle be;
No sigh is from a breathless breast.
Beauty may fade, but closed eyes see not;

Sorrow may wail, but stopped ears hear not;
Nothing to say is for dumb tongues.
The rolling earth rolls on and on
With trees and stones and winding streams—
My dream is what the hillside dreams!

* EDWIN ARLINGTON ROBINSON *

MINIVER CHEEVY

MINIVER CHEEVY, child of scorn
    Grew lean while he assailed the seasons;
He wept that he was ever born,
    And he had reasons.

Miniver loved the days of old
    When swords were bright and steeds were
        prancing;
The vision of a warrior bold
    Would set him dancing.

Miniver sighed for what was not,
    And dreamed, and rested from his labors;
He dreamed of Thebes and Camelot,
    And Priam's neighbors.

Miniver mourned the ripe renown
    That made so many a name so fragrant;
He mourned Romance, now on the town,
    And Art, a vagrant.

Miniver loved the Medici,
    Albeit he had never seen one;
He would have sinned incessantly
    Could he have been one.

Miniver cursed the commonplace
    And eyed a khaki suit with loathing;
He missed the medieval grace
    Of iron clothing.

Miniver scorned the gold he sought,
    But sore annoyed was he without it;
Miniver thought, and thought, and thought
    And thought about it.

Miniver Cheevy, born too late,
    Scratched his head and kept on thinking;
Miniver coughed, and called it fate,
    And kept on drinking.

GEORGE CRABBE

G IVE him the darkest inch your shelf allows,
Hide him in lonely garrets, if you will,—
But his hard, human pulse is throbbing still
With the sure strength that fearless truth endows.
In spite of all fine science disavows,
Of his plain excellence and stubborn skill
There yet remains what fashion cannot kill,
Though years have thinned the laurel from his brows

Whether or not we read him, we can feel
From time to time the vigor of his name
Against us like a finger for the shame
And emptiness of what our souls reveal
In books that are as altars where we kneel
To consecrate the flicker, not the flame.

TWO TRAMPS IN MUD TIME

Out of the mud two strangers came
      And caught me splitting wood in the yard.
And one of them put me off my aim
By hailing cheerily "Hit them hard!"
I knew pretty well why he dropped behind
And let the other go on a way.
I knew pretty well what he had in mind:
He wanted to take my job for pay.

Good blocks of beech it was I split,
As large around as the chopping block;
And every piece I squarely hit
Fell splinterless as a cloven rock.
The blows that a life of self-control
Spares to strike for the common good
That day, giving a loose to my soul,
I spent on the unimportant wood.

The sun was warm but the wind was chill.
You know how it is with an April day
When the sun is out and the wind is still,
You're one month on in the middle of May.
But if you so much as dare to speak,
A cloud comes over the sunlit arch,
A wind comes off a frozen peak,
And you're two months back in the middle of March.

A bluebird comes tenderly up to alight
And fronts the wind to unruffle a plume,
His song so pitched as not to excite
A single flower as yet to bloom.
It is snowing a flake: and he half knew
Winter was only playing possum.
Except in color he isn't blue,
But he wouldn't advise a thing to blossom.

The water for which we may have to look
In summertime with a witching-wand,
In every wheelrut's now a brook,
In every print of a hoof a pond.
Be glad of water, but don't forget
The lurking frost in the earth beneath
That will steal forth after the sun is set
And show on the water its crystal teeth.

The time when most I loved my task
These two must make me love it more
By coming with what they came to ask.
You'd think 1 never had felt before
The weight of an ax-head poised aloft,
The grip on earth of outspread feet,
The life of muscles rocking soft
And smooth and moist in vernal heat.

Out of the woods two hulking tramps
(From sleeping God knows where last night,
But not long since in the lumber camps).
They thought all chopping was theirs of right.
Men of the woods and lumberjacks,
They judged me by their appropriate tool.

Except as a fellow handled an ax,
They had no way of knowing a fool.

Nothing on either side was said.
They knew they had but to stay their stay
And all their logic would fill my head:
As that I had no right to play
With what was another man's work for gain.
My right might be love but theirs was need.
And where the two exist in twain
Theirs was the better right—agreed.

But yield who will to their separation,
My object in living is to unite
My avocation and my vocation
As my two eyes make one in sight.
Only where love and need are one,
And the work is play for mortal stakes,
Is the deed ever really done
For Heaven and the future's sakes.

* V A C H E L   L I N D S A Y *

SIMON LEGREE—A NEGRO SERMON

(To be read in your own variety of Negro dialect)

L EGREE's big house was white and green,
  His cotton fields were the best to be seen.
He had strong horses and opulent cattle,
And bloodhounds bold, with chains that would rattle.
His garret was full of curious things:
Books of magic, bags of gold,
And rabbits' feet on long twine strings.
But he went down to the Devil.

Legree he sported a brass-buttoned coat,
A snake-skin necktie, a blood-red shirt,
Legree he had a beard like a goat,
And a thick hairy neck, and eyes like dirt.
His puffed-out cheeks were fish-belly white,
He had great long teeth, and an appetite.
He ate raw meat, 'most every meal,
And rolled his eyes till the cat would squeal.

His fist was an enormous size
To mash poor niggers that told him lies:
He was surely a witch-man in disguise.
But he went down to the Devil.

He wore hip-boots and would wade all day,
To capture his slaves that had fled away.
But he went down to the Devil.

He beat poor Uncle Tom to death
Who prayed for Legree with his last breath.
Then Uncle Tom to Eva flew,
To the high sanctoriums bright and new;
And Simon Legree stared up beneath,
And cracked his heels, and ground his teeth:
And went down to the Devil.

He crossed the yard in the storm and gloom;
He went into his grand front room.
He said, "I killed him, and I don't care."
He kicked a hound, he gave a swear;
He tightened his belt, he took a lamp,
Went down cellar to the webs and damp.
There in the middle of the mouldy floor
He heaved up a slab, he found a door—
And went down to the Devil.

His lamp blew out, but his eyes burned bright.
Simon Legree stepped down all night—
Down, down to the Devil.
Simon Legree he reached the place,
He saw one half of the human race,
He saw the Devil on a wide green throne,
Gnawing the meat from a big ham-bone,
And he said to Mister Devil:

> "I see that you have much to eat—
> A red ham-bone is surely sweet.
> I see that you have lion's feet;

I see your frame is fat and fine,
I see you drink your poison wine—
Blood and burning turpentine."

And the Devil said to Simon Legree:

"I like your style, so wicked and free.
Come sit and share my throne with me,
And let us bark and revel."

And there they sit and gnash their teeth,
And each one wears a hop-vine wreath.
They are matching pennies and shooting craps,
They are playing poker and taking naps.
And old Legree is fat and fine:
He eats the fire, he drinks the wine—
Blood and burning turpentine—
   Down, down with the Devil;
         Down, down with the Devil;
               Down, down with the Devil.

THE LEADEN-EYED

L ET not young souls be smothered out before
They do quaint deeds and fully flaunt their pride.
It is the world's one crime its babes grow dull,
Its poor are ox-like, limp and leaden-eyed.

Not that they starve, but starve so dreamlessly,
Not that they sow, but that they seldom reap,
Not that they serve, but have no gods to serve,
Not that they die but that they die like sheep.

ON THE BUILDING OF SPRINGFIELD

L ET not our town be large, remembering
  That little Athens was the Muses' home,
That Oxford rules the heart of London still,
That Florence gave the Renaissance to Rome.

Record it for the grandson of your son—
A city is not builded in a day:
Our little town cannot complete her soul
Till countless generations pass away.

Now let each child be joined as to a church
To her perpetual hopes, each man ordained:
Let every street be made a reverent aisle
Where Music grows and Beauty is unchained.

Let Science and Machinery and Trade
Be slaves of her, and make her all in all,
Building against our blatant, restless time
An unseen, skilful, medieval wall.

Let every citizen be rich toward God.
Let Christ the beggar, teach divinity.
Let no man rule who holds his money dear.
Let this, our city, be our luxury.

We should build parks that students from afar
Would choose to starve in, rather than go home,
Fair little squares, with Phidian ornament,
Food for the spirit, milk and honeycomb.

Songs shall be sung by us in that good day,
Songs we have written, blood within the rhyme
Beating, as when Old England still was glad,—
The purple, rich Elizabethan time.

*

Say, is my prophecy too fair and far?
I only know, unless her faith be high,
The soul of this, our Nineveh, is doomed,
Our little Babylon will surely die.

Some city on the breast of Illinois
No wiser and no better at the start
By faith shall rise redeemed, by faith shall rise
Bearing the western glory in her heart.

The genius of the Maple, Elm and Oak,
The secret hidden in each grain of corn,
The glory that the prairie angels sing
At night when sons of Life and Love are born,

Born but to struggle, squalid and alone,
Broken and wandering in their early years.
When will they make our dusty streets their goal,
Within our attics hide their sacred tears?

When will they start our vulgar blood athrill
With living language, words that set us free?
When will they make a path of beauty clear
Between our riches and our liberty?

We must have many Lincoln-hearted men.
A city is not builded in a day.
And they must do their work, and come and go,
While countless generations pass away.

ABRAHAM LINCOLN WALKS AT MIDNIGHT

(In Springfield, Illinois)

IT is portentous, and a thing of state
That here at midnight, in our little town
A mourning figure walks, and will not rest,
Near the old court-house pacing up and down,

Or by his homestead, or in shadowed yards
He lingers where his children used to play,
Or through the market, on the well-worn stones
He stalks until the dawn-stars burn away.

A bronzed, lank man! His suit of ancient black,
A famous high top-hat and plain worn shawl
Make him the quaint great figure that men love,
The prairie-lawyer, master of us all.

He cannot sleep upon his hillside now.
He is among us:—as in times before!
And we who toss and lie awake for long
Breathe deep, and start, to see him pass the door.

His head is bowed. He thinks on men and kings.
Yes, when the sick world cries, how can he sleep?
Too many peasants fight, they know not why,
Too many homesteads in black terror weep.

The sins of all the war-lords burn his heart.
He sees the dreadnaughts scouring every main.
He carries on his shawl-wrapped shoulders now
The bitterness, the folly and the pain.

He cannot rest until a spirit-dawn
Shall come;—the shining hope of Europe free:
The league of sober folk, the Workers' Earth,
Bringing long peace to Cornland, Alp and Sea.

It breaks his heart that kings must murder still,
That all his hours of travail here for men
Seem yet in vain. And who will bring white peace
That he may sleep upon his hill again?

FACTORY WINDOWS ARE ALWAYS BROKEN

Factory windows are always broken.
Somebody's always throwing bricks,
Somebody's always heaving cinders,
Playing ugly Yahoo tricks.

Factory windows are always broken.
Other windows are let alone.
No one throws through the chapel-window
The bitter, snarling, derisive stone.

Factory windows are always broken.
Something or other is going wrong.
Something is rotten—I think, in Denmark.
End of the factory-window song.

* WILLIAM ROSE BENÉT *

JESSE JAMES

JESSE JAMES was a two-gun man,
   (*Roll on, Missouri!*)
Strong-arm chief of an outlaw clan.
   (*From Kansas to Illinois!*)
He twirled an old Colt forty-five,
   (*Roll on, Missouri!*)
They never took Jesse James alive.
   (*Roll on, Missouri, roll!*)
Jesse James was King of the Wes';
   (*Cataracks in the Missouri!*)
He'd a di'mon' heart in his lef' breas';
   (*Brown Missouri rolls!*)
He'd a fire in his heart no hurt could stifle;
   (*Thunder, Missouri!*)
Lion eyes an' a Winchester rifle.
   (*Missouri, roll down!*)

Jesse James rode a pinto hawse;
Come at night to a water-cawse;
Tetched with the rowel that pinto's flank;
She sprung the torrent from bank to bank.

Jesse rode through a sleepin' town;
Looked the moonlit street both up an' down;
Crack-crack-crack, the street ran flames
An' a great voice cried, "I'm Jesse James!"

Hawse an' afoot they're after Jess!
    (*Roll on, Missouri!*)
Spurrin' an' spurrin'—but he's gone Wes'.
    (*Brown Missouri rolls!*)
He was ten foot tall when he stood in his boots;
    (*Lightnin' light the Missouri!*)
More'n a match fer sich galoots.
    (*Roll, Missouri, roll!*)

Jesse James rode outa the sage;
Roun' the rocks come the swayin' stage;
Straddlin' the road a giant stan's
An' a great voice bellers, "Throw up yer han's!"

Jesse raked in the di'mon' rings,
The big gold watches an' the yuther things;
Jesse divvied 'em then an' thar
With a cryin' child had lost her mar.

The U. S. Troopers is after Jess;
    (*Roll on, Missouri!*)
Their hawses sweat foam, but he's gone Wes';
    (*Hear Missouri roar!*)
He was broad as a b'ar, he'd a ches' like a drum,
    (*Wind an' rain through Missouri!*)
An' his red hair flamed like Kingdom Come.
    (*Missouri down to the sea!*)

Jesse James all alone in the rain
Stopped an' stuck up the Eas'-boun' train;
Swayed through the coaches with horns an' a tail,
Lit out with the bullion an' the registered mail.

Jess made 'em all turn green with fright,
Quakin' in the aisles in the pitch-black night;
An' he give all the bullion to a pore ole tramp
Campin' nigh the cuttin' in the dirt an' damp.

The whole U. S. is after Jess;
    (*Roll on, Missouri!*)
The son-of-a-gun, if he ain't gone Wes';
    (*Missouri to the sea!*)
He could chaw cold iron an' spit blue flame;
    (*Cataracks down the Missouri!*)
He rode on a catamount he'd larned to tame.
    (*Hear that Missouri roll!*)

Jesse James rode into a bank;
Give his pinto a tetch on the flank;
Jumped the teller's window with an awful crash;
Heaved up the safe an' twirled his mustache;

He said, "So long, boys!" He yelped, "So long!
Feelin' porely to-day—I ain't feelin' strong!"
Rode right through the wall agoin' crack-crack-crack,—
Took the safe home to Mother in a gunny-sack.

They're creepin', they're crawlin', they're stalkin' Jess;
    (*Roll on, Missouri!*)
They's a rumor he's gone much further Wes';
    (*Roll, Missouri, roll!*)
They's word of a cayuse hitched to the bars
    (*Ruddy clouds on Missouri!*)
Of a golden sunset that busts into stars.
    (*Missouri, roll down!*)

Jesse James rode hell fer leather;
He was a hawse an' a man together;
In a cave in a mountain high up in air
He lived with a rattlesnake, a wolf, an' a bear.

Jesse's heart was as sof' as a woman;
Fer guts an' stren'th he was sooper-human;
He could put six shots through a woodpecker's eye
And take in one swaller a gallon o' rye.

They sought him here an' they sought him there,
    (*Roll on, Missouri!*)
But he strides by night through the ways of the air,
    (*Brown Missouri rolls!*)
They say he was took an' they say he is dead;
    (*Thunder, Missouri!*)
But he ain't—he's a sunset overhead!
    (*Missouri down to the sea!*)

Jesse James was a Hercules.
When he went through the woods he tore up the trees.
When he went on the plains he smoked the groun'
An' the hull lan' shuddered fer miles aroun'.

Jesse James wore a red bandanner
That waved on the breeze like the Star Spangled Banner;
In seven states he cut up dadoes.
He's gone with the buffler an' the desperadoes.

Yes, Jesse James was a two-gun man
    (*Roll on, Missouri!*)
The same as when this song began;
    (*From Kansas to Illinois!*)

An' when you see a sunset bust into flames
  (Lightnin' light the Missouri!)
Or a thunderstorm blaze—that's Jesse James!
  (Hear that Missouri roll!)

* B A R T O L O M E O   V A N Z E T T I *

LAST SPEECH TO THE COURT

I HAVE talk a great deal of myself
but I even forgot to name Sacco.
Sacco too is a worker,
from his boyhood a skilled worker, lover of work,
with a good job and pay,
a bank account, a good and lovely wife,
two beautiful children and a neat little home
at the verge of a wood, near a brook.

Sacco is a heart, a faith, a character, a man;
a man, lover of nature, and mankind;
a man who gave all, who sacrifice all
to the cause of liberty and to his love for mankind:
money, rest, mundane ambition,
his own wife, his children, himself
and his own life.

Sacco has never dreamt to steal, never to assassinate.
He and I have never brought a morsel
of bread to our mouths, from our childhood to today
which has not been gained by the sweat of our brows.
Never . . .

Oh, yes, I may be more witful, as some have put it;
I am a better babbler than he is, but many, many times

in hearing his heartful voice ringing a faith sublime,
in considering his supreme sacrifice, remembering his
    heroism,
I felt small at the presence of his greatness
and found myself compelled to fight back
from my eyes the tears,
and quanch my heart
trobling to my throat to not weep before him:
this man called thief and assassin and doomed.

But Sacco's name will live in the hearts of the people
and in their gratitude when Katzmann's bones
and yours will be dispersed by time;
when your name, his name, your laws, institutions,
and your false god are but a dim rememoring
of a cursed past in which man was wolf
to the man. . . .

If it had not been for these thing
I might have live out my life
talking at street corners to scorning men.
I might have die, unmarked, unknown, a failure.
Now we are not a failure.
This is our career and our triumph. Never
in our full life could we hope to do such work
for tolerance, for justice, for man's understanding
of man, as now we do by accident.
Our words, our lives, our pains—nothing!
The taking of our lives—lives of a good shoemaker and
    a poor fishpeddler—
all! That last moment belongs to us—
that agony is our triumph.

* M A L C O L M   C O W L E Y *

FOR ST. BARTHOLOMEW'S EVE

(August 23, 1927)

THEN die!
Outside the prison gawk
the crowds that you will see no more.
A door slams shut behind you. Walk
with turnkeys down a corridor
smelling of lysol, through the gates
to where a drunken sheriff waits.

St. Nicholas who blessed your birth,
whose hands are rich with gifts, will bear
no further gifts to you on earth,
Sacco, whose heart abounds in prayer
neither to Pilate nor a saint
whose earthly sons die innocent.

And you that would not bow your knee
to God, swarthy Bartholomew,
no God will grant you liberty,
nor Virgin intercede for you,
nor bones of yours make sweet the plot
where governors and judges rot.

A doctor sneezes. A chaplain maps
the routes to heaven. You mount the chair.

A jailor buckles tight the straps
like those which aviators wear.
The surgeon makes a signal.
                    Die!
lost symbols of our liberty.

Beyond the chair, beyond the bars
of day and night, your path lies free;
yours is an avenue of stars:
march on, O dago Christs, while we
march on to spread your name abroad
like ashes in the winds of God.

THE HILL ABOVE THE MINE

Nobody comes to the graveyard on the hill,
  lost on the blackened slope above the mine,
where coke-oven fumes drift heavily by day
and creeping fires at night; nobody stirs
here by the crumbling wall, where headstones loom
among the blackberry vines; nobody walks
in the blue starlight under the cedar branches
twisted and black against the moon, nor speaks
except the unquiet company of the dead,

and one who calls the roll:

                    "Ezekiel Cowley?"

Dead.
        "Laban and Uriah Evans?"
                              Dead.

"Jasper McCullough, your three wives, your thirty
children, of whom four bastards?"

                        Dead, all dead.
"Simon Eliot? Sergeant Danny George?
Judge Peter and Sarah Ellen Farbaugh?"

                              Dead,
sleeping under the brambles in the starlight
above the unpainted cabins and the mine.

What have you seen, O dead?

"We saw our woods
butchered, flames curling in the maple tops,
white ashes drifting, a railroad in the valley
bridging the creek, and mines under the hill.
We saw our farms lie fallow and houses grow
all summer in the flowerless meadows. Rats
all winter gnawed the last husks in the barn.
In spring the waters rose, crept through the fields
and stripped them bare of soil, while on the hill
we waited and stood firm."

Wait on, O dead!
The waters still shall rise, the hills fold in,
the tombs open to heaven, and you shall ride
eastward on a rain-wind, spurring the thunder,
your white bones drifting like herons across the moon.

THE LONG VOYAGE

Not that the pines were darker there,
nor mid-May dogwood brighter there,
nor swifts more swift in summer air;
 it was my own country,

having its thunderclap of spring,
its long midsummer ripening,
its corn hoar-stiff at harvesting,
 almost like any country,

yet being mine; its face, its speech,
its hills bent low within my reach,
its river birch and upland beech
 were mine, of my own country.

Now the dark waters at the bow
fold back, like earth against the plow;
foam brightens like the dogwood now
 at home, in my own country.

* K A Y   B O Y L E *

SPIRITUAL FOR NINE VOICES

I WENT last night to a turkey feast (Oh, God, don't fail your
   children now!)
My people were sitting there the way they'll sit in heaven
With their wings spread out and their hearts all singing
Their mouths full of food and the table set with glass
(Oh, God, don't fail your children now!)
There were poor men sitting with their fingers dripping honey.
All the ugly sisters were fair. I saw my brother who never had
      a penny
With a silk shirt on and a pair of golden braces
And gems strewn through his hair.
(Were you looking, Father, when the sheriffs came in?
Was your face turned towards us when they had their say?)

   There was baked sweet potato and fried corn pone
   There was eating galore, there was plenty in the horn.
(Were you there when Victoria Price took the stand?
Did you see the state attorney with her drawers in his hand?
Did you hear him asking for me to burn?)

   There were oysters cooked in amplitude
   There was sauce in every mouth.
   There was ham done slow in spice and clove
   And chicken enough for the young and the old.

(Was it you stilled the waters on horse-swapping day
When the mob came to the jail? Was it you come out in a long
       tail coat
Come dancing high with the word in your mouth?)

    I saw my sister who never had a cent
    Come shaking and shuffling between the seats.
    Her hair was straight and her nails were pointed
    Her breasts were high and her legs double-jointed.

(O, God, don't fail your children now!)

THE LEGION OF IRON

THEY pass through the great iron gates—
Men with eyes gravely discerning,
Skilled to appraise the tonnage of cranes
Or split an inch into thousandths—
Men tempered by fire as the ore is
And planned to resistance
Like steel that has cooled in the trough;
Silent of purpose, inflexible, set to fulfilment—
To conquer, withstand, overthrow. . . .
Men mannered to large undertakings,
Knowing force as a brother
And power as something to play with,
Seeing blood as a slip of the iron,
To be wiped from the tools
Lest they rust.

But what if they stood aside,
Who hold the earth so careless in the crook of their arms?

What of the flamboyant cities
And the lights guttering out like candles in a wind . . .
And the armies halted. . . .
And the train midway on the mountain
And idle men chaffing across the trenches . . .
And the cursing and lamentation

And the clamor for grain shut in the mills of the world?
What if they stayed apart,
Inscrutably smiling,
Leaving the ground encumbered with dead wire
And the sea to row-boats
And the lands marooned—
Till time should like a paralytic sit,
A mildewed hulk above the nations squatting?

(With Rosemary Benét)

Rhymes from A BOOK OF AMERICANS

1

Thomas Jefferson 1743–1825

THOMAS JEFFERSON
What do you say
Under the gravestone
Hidden away?

"I was a giver,
I was a moulder,
I was builder
With a strong shoulder."

Six feet and over,
Large-boned and ruddy,
The eyes grey-hazel
But bright with study.

The big hands clever
With pen and fiddle
And ready, ever,
For any riddle.

From buying empires,
To planting 'taters,
From Declarations
To trick dumb-waiters.

"I liked the people,
The sweat and crowd of them,
Trusted them always
And spoke aloud of them.

"I liked all learning
And wished to share it
Abroad like pollen
For all who merit.

"I liked queer gadgets
And secret shelves,
And helping nations
To rule themselves."

2

John Quincy Adams 1767–1848

When President John Quincy
Set out to take a swim,
He'd hang his Presidential clothes
Upon a hickory limb
And bound in the Potomac
Like a dolphin on the swell.
—He was extremely dignified
But rather plump, as well.
And when Supreme Court Justices
Remarked, from a canoe,
"Our Presidents don't do such things."
He merely said, "I do."

He never asked what people thought
But gave them tit for tat.
The Adamses have always been
Remarkably like that.

3

Daniel Boone 1797–1889

When Daniel Boone goes by at night
The phantom deer arise
And all lost, wild America
Is burning in their eyes.

4

Abraham Lincoln 1809–1865

Lincoln was a long man.
He liked out of doors.
He liked the wind blowing
And the talk in country stores.

He liked telling stories,
He liked telling jokes.
"Abe's quite a character,"
Said quite a lot of folks.

Lots of folks in Springfield
Saw him every day,
Walking down the street
In his gaunt, long way.

Shawl around his shoulders,
Letters in his hat.
"That's Abe Lincoln."
They thought no more than that.

Knew that he was honest,
Guessed that he was odd,
Knew he had a cross wife
Though she was a Todd.

Knew he had three little boys
Who liked to shout and play,
Knew he had a lot of debts
It took him years to pay.

Knew his clothes and knew his house.
"That's his office, here.
Blame good lawyer on the whole,
Though he's sort of queer.

"Sure, he went to Congress, once,
But he didn't stay.
Can't expect us all to be
Smart as Henry Clay.

Need a man for troubled times?
Well, I guess we do.
Wonder who we'll ever find?
Yes—I wonder who."

That is how they met and talked,
Knowing and unknowing.
Lincoln was the green pine.
Lincoln kept on growing.

LITANY FOR DICTATORSHIPS

For all those beaten, for the broken heads,
The fosterless, the simple, the oppressed,
The ghosts in the burning city of our time . . .

For those taken in rapid cars to the house and beaten
By the skilful boys, the boys with the rubber fists,
—Held down and beaten, the table cutting their loins,
Or kicked in the groin and left, with the muscles jerking
Like a headless hen's on the floor of the slaughter-house
While they brought the next man in with his white eyes
    staring.
For those who still said "Red Front!" or "God Save the
    Crown!"
And for those who were not courageous
But were beaten nevertheless.
For those who spit out the bloody stumps of their teeth
Quietly in the hall,
Sleep well on stone or iron, watch for the time
And kill the guard in the privy before they die,
Those with the deep-socketed eyes and the lamp burning.

For those who carry the scars, who walk lame—for those
Whose nameless graves are made in the prison-yard
And the earth smoothed back before morning and the lime
    scattered.
For those slain at once. For those living through months
    and years
Enduring, watching, hoping, going each day
To the work or the queue for meat or the secret club,

Living meanwhile, begetting children, smuggling guns,
And found and killed at the end like rats in a drain.

For those escaping
Incredibly into exile and wandering there.
For those who live in the small rooms of foreign cities
And who yet think of the country, the long green grass,
The childhood voices, the language, the way wind smelt
    then,
The shape of rooms, the coffee drunk at the table,
The talk with friends, the loved city, the waiter's face,
The gravestones, with the name, where they will not lie
Nor in any of that earth. Their children are strangers.
For those who planned and were leaders and were beaten
And for those, humble and stupid, who had no plan
But were denounced, but grew angry, but told a joke,
But could not explain, but were sent away to the camp,
But had their bodies shipped back in the sealed coffins,
"Died of pneumonia." "Died trying to escape."

For those growers of wheat who were shot by their own
    wheat-stacks,
For those growers of bread who were sent to the ice-
    locked wastes,
And their flesh remembers their fields.
For those denounced by their smug, horrible children
For a peppermint-star and the praise of the Perfect State,
For all those strangled or gelded or merely starved
To make perfect states; for the priest hanged in his
    cassock,
The Jew with his chest crushed in and his eyes dying,
The revolutionist lynched by the private guards
To make perfect states, in the names of the perfect states.

For those betrayed by the neighbors they shook hands with
And for the traitors, sitting in the hard chair
With the loose sweat crawling their hair and their fingers
    restless
As they tell the street and the house and the man's name.

And for those sitting at table in the house
With the lamp lit and the plates and the smell of food,
Talking so quietly; when they hear the cars
And the knock at the door, and they look at each other
    quickly
And the woman goes to the door with a stiff face,
Smoothing her dress.
           "We are all good citizens here.
We believe in the Perfect State."

                And that was the last
Time Tony or Karl or Shorty came to the house
And the family was liquidated later.
It was the last time.

         We heard the shots in the night
But nobody knew next day what the trouble was
And a man must go to his work. So I didn't see him
For three days, then, and me near out of my mind
And all the patrols on the streets with their dirty guns
And when he came back, he looked drunk, and the blood
    was on him.
For the women who mourn their dead in the secret night,
For the children taught to keep quiet, the old children,
The children spat-on at school.
           For the wrecked laboratory,
The gutted house, the dunged-picture, the pissed-in well,

The naked corpse of Knowledge flung in the square
And no man lifting a hand and no man speaking.

For the cold of the pistol-butt and the bullet's heat,
For the rope that chokes, the manacles that bind,
The huge voice, metal, that lies from a thousand tubes
And the stuttering machine-gun that answers all.

For the man crucified on the crossed machine-guns
Without name, without resurrection, without stars,
His dark head heavy with death and his flesh long sour
With the smell of his many prisons—John Smith, John
    Doe,
John Nobody—oh, crack your mind for his name!
Faceless as water, naked as the dust,
Dishonored as the earth the gas-shells poison
And barbarous with portent.
                              This is he.
This is the man they ate at the green table
Putting their gloves on ere they touch the meat.
This is the fruit of war, the fruit of peace,
The ripeness of invention, the new lamb,
The answer to the wisdom of the wise.
And still he hangs, and still he will not die,
And still, on the steel city of our years
The light fails and the terrible blood streams down.

We thought we were done with these things but we were
    wrong.
We thought, because we had power, we had wisdom.
We thought the long train would run to the end of Time.
We thought the light would increase.
Now the long train stands derailed and the bandits loot it.

Now the boar and the asp have power in our time.
Now the night rolls back on the West and the night is solid.
Our fathers and ourselves sowed dragon's teeth.
Our children know and suffer the armed men.

* T H O M A S   W O L F E *

THAT SHARP KNIFE

YES,
   And in that month when Proserpine comes back,
And Ceres' dead heart rekindles,
When all the woods
Are a tender smoky blur,
And birds no bigger than a budding leaf
Dart through the singing trees,
And when odorous tar comes spongy in the streets,
And boys roll balls of it upon their tongues,
And they are lumpy with tops and agate marbles;
And there is blasting thunder in the night,
And the soaking million-footed rain,
And one looks out at morning on a stormy sky,
A broken wrack of cloud;
And when the mountain boy brings water
To his kinsmen laying fence,
And as the wind snakes through the grasses
Hears far in the valley below
The long wail of the whistle,
And the faint clangor of a bell;
And the blue great cup of the hills
Seems closer, nearer,
For he has heard an inarticulate promise:
He has been pierced by Spring,
That sharp knife.

And life unscales its rusty weathered pelt
And earth wells out in tender exhaustless strength,
And the cup of a man's heart runs over
With dateless expectancy, tongueless promise,
Indefinable desire.
Something gathers in the throat,
Something blinds him in the eyes,
And faint and valorous horns sound through the earth.

And little girls trot pigtailed
Primly on their dutiful way to school;
But the young gods loiter:
They hear the reed, the oaten-stop,
The running goathoofs in the spongy wood,
Here, there, everywhere;
They dawdle, listen,
Fleetest when they wait,
Go vaguely on to their one fixed home,
Because the earth is full of ancient rumor
And they cannot find the way.

All of the gods have lost the way.

SOMETHING HAS SPOKEN TO ME IN THE NIGHT

SOMETHING has spoken to me in the night,
Burning the tapers of the waning year;
Something has spoken in the night,
And told me I shall die, I know not where.

Saying:
"To lose the earth you know, for greater knowing;
To lose the life you have, for greater life;
To leave the friends you loved, for greater loving;
To find a land more kind than home, more large than
    earth—

"Whereon the pillars of this earth are founded,
Toward which the conscience of the world is tending—
A wind is rising, and the rivers flow."

McSORLEY'S BAR

Mac had a place to drink and talk downtown
Where only men were welcome, or grown boys.
When the grey snow flew, there was the forum stove
Where arguments were slow, and out of noise.
The dust was old as Sumter, and the talking
Had never stopped since Dixie went to war;
And all the men from Grant to Hayes to now
Had lived beside, been buried from that bar.
There, in the evening, the city carpenter
Bumped up a drink with one of Croker's men
And politics and poetry were one
From supper-time until it closed at ten.
The grey-haired men considered from their chairs
How time is emptied like a single ale;
Their china eyes saw tabby woo the fire
As men their recollections, at the rail.
Here, among blackened walls, men's time
Flowed past like peaceful dreams of Chinamen
Who sat in temples thinking of those flowers
That die, and live, and close their blooms again.
Here the day's passions, after dusk,
Would, while the children called beneath the L,
Draw in like coals in pipes to gleam a silence
Between the words that cursed or wished them well.
Privilege, and extortion, and corruption,

Or the wreck of the city, or some newer way to power,
Described the moving lives of living men
In voices where each hero had his hour.
And sorrow that rendezvoused in here
Flowed like a stellar scheme whose dying ions
Cascade toward night, when orders somewhere else
Gather the suns like a summer's dandelions.

THE LABORATORY MIDNIGHT

SCIENCE is what the world is, earth and water.
And what its seasons do. And what space fountained it.
It is forges hidden underground. It is the dawn's slow salvo.
It is in the closed retort. And it is not yet.

It looks up and counts the Perseids in August,
A fire from nowhere like signals overhead
And it looks for portents, as redmen on a hill,
In the white stream where Altair swims with the Andromedid.

Now you who know what to believe, who have God with you
By desk and bed, blue fire in the stove;
Whom the rains from the northeast alter but perfect
Into new powers, and new pities, and new love;

Go look in lava flows for newer elements,
And dismantle the electric shape of matter like a house;
And weigh the mountains in small sensitive scales;
Break buds; and test the senses of a mouse;

And if you are unpanicked, tell me what you find
On how the sun flies and the snow is spent,
What blasts and bessemers we live in, that dissolve
All the loam loaned to spine and ligament.

* BABETTE DEUTSCH *

CARAPACE

NOR tropic suns can smoke
Nor arctic blizzards freeze
The heart that once had broke
At such fine savageries.
Now it is guarded well,
Ribbed with a leathern truss;
Not the mad tiger's fell
But calm rhinoceros'
Obdurate hide affords
Defense against all hurt.
Nothing can shake the cords
Under that armored shirt.
Hang it upon barbed wire
Through which the children stare:
This muscle will not tire,
It will not even tear.
Or send it out to swim
With sailors who go down
At a flaming comber's whim:
This heart will never drown.
Where cities shrivel in
Hot ashes it has learned
How an asbestos skin
Is blackened but not burned.
No wound will make it sore,

So strongly is it knit.
Now grief and rage no more
Can pierce or sicken it.
Beyond the chill of fear,
It beats behind a wall
Too thick for agony
To rock with any call.
It has no eye, no ear.
Then who would hear
If once this heart should cry?

* J O S E P H I N E   W .   J O H N S O N *

FINAL AUTUMN

END will come swiftly in an early autumn,
Forewarned by blooded rising of the moon,
Its great arc swollen like a hill of fire,
And long continuous lightning in the north,
Portent of that unearthly rain whose knives
Shall slash the hard integument of earth
Down to its unknown core.
And man, having ravaged earth's beauty and outlived
        her prime,
Strained from her hands all mystery and dark,
Shall hear
The far wasp-whispering of the flames to come
Over the outworn cities and infertile soil;
Shall know the fierce increasing sound
Of iron cities' great volcanic death,
The roar of oak fire and the straining steel,
The quivering to and fro of towers
Like fiery grass stems in a wind.
And over the broken face of earth shall sear
Iron of the cauterizing flame,
Over the unclean, crying mouths
The clean sound of the flame.

And some men in this hour of death shall know
More heat and glory than had ever come

Into the spare and cautious veins of life,
And cry out with the tardy grief of those who find
Night of a great and unreturning day
In which they had no part.
And some by light of this flame-opened hour
Shall face
The knotted fabric of their lives
—Woven in darkness and unseen till now,
And will be glad to die.

But there shall be no grief so bitter,
Nor any anguish on the earth that can compare
With the intolerable bitterness of those voices that shall
    cry—
Not out of fear of this great tidal flame—
Not for the ashless bodies of the dead,
But out of the knowledge that this burning means
The long ritual of Life brought to a close
In the high horror and red pageantry of Death,
    With still the face of God unseen,
    His great confessional unread.

* R O Y C A M P B E L L *

THE SERF

His naked skin clothed in the torrid mist
    That puffs in smoke around the patient hooves,
The ploughman drives, a slow somnanbulist,
And through the green his crimson furrow grooves.
His heart, more deeply than he wounds the plain,
Long by the rasping share of insult torn,
Red clod, to which the war-cry once was rain
And tribal spears the fatal sheaves of corn,
Lies fallow now. But as the turf divides
I see in the slow progress of his strides
Over the toppled clods and falling flowers,
The timeless, surly patience of the serf
That moves the nearest to the naked earth
And ploughs down palaces, and thrones, and towers.

OUR LADY PEACE

How far is it to peace, the piper sighed,
The solitary, sweating as he paused.
Asphalt the noon; the ravens, terrified,
Fled carrion thunder that percussion caused.

The envelope of earth was powder loud;
The taut wings shivered, driven at the sun.
The piper·put his pipe away and bowed.
Not here, he said. I hunt the love-cool one,

The dancer with the clipped hair. Where is she?
We shook our heads, parting for him to pass.
Our lady was of no such trim degree,
And none of us had seen her face, alas.

She was the very ridges we must scale,
Securing the rough top. And how she smiled
Was how our strength would issue. Not to fail
Was having her, gigantic, undefiled,

For homely goddess, big as the world that burned,
Grandmother and taskmistress, field and town.
We let the stranger go; but when we turned
Our lady lived, fierce in each other's frown.

THE SINGLE HERO

THIS man kept courage when the map of fear
    Was continents, was paleness to the poles,
Was Jupiter milk white, was Venus burning.
The very stones lay liquid with despair,
And the firm earth was bottomless. This man

Could walk upon that water; nay, he stamped
Till the drops gravelled, till a sound returned
Of pillars underheel, of granite growing.
This man, alone on seas, was not afraid.
So continents came back. So color widened:

Bands upon blankness. So the other men,
The millions, lifted feet and let them down;
And the soil held. So courage's cartographer,
Having his globe again, restored each mass,
Each meadow. And the grasshoppers sang to him.

* PAUL ENGLE *

From AMERICA REMEMBERS

HERE by this midland lake, the sand-shored water
  That pulses with no sea-tide heart, where the grain
Of a nation pauses on its golden way
To the world's belly, and the long trains punge . . .

*

                              I remember men, callers
To gods in the gusty rain, to the thunder birds,
Chippers of flint, scratchers of soil thinly
(Now has the earth been torn with the anvil-hammered
Plough deeply for our hunger, and the black shaft sunk).
The trail through the hills was moccasin wide and a stone
Twisted it, the rivers were swum. (What of this
Concrete trampling, the wild arum, the arched bridge?)
The continent lived in its own and eternal way
Dreamless of change.

*

                              And all
The pulses of the earth were stirred by the pounding
Heart of America and poured their blood
Over the great sea arteries, finding
Sometimes a country like their own, the Finns
By the Minnesota lakes, the Germans over
The prairie farms of Iowa, the English
In the Berkshire hills and valleys. The Southern folk

Left the gay dances, the vineyards mellowed with sun-
　　light
On the terraced hills, and as Wop and Dago joined
Polack and Bohunk in the towns of steel
Where the great fires burned their guts out—Bethlehem
(O mockery of the little Christ-found village), Gary,
Youngstown, the hard, trip-hammer-beaten names.
The ancient features of the type were changed
Under a different sun, in a clearer air
That entered the lungs like wine, the swarthy face
Paled, cheek bones lifted and narrowed, hair
Straightened and faded, and the body moved
With a lighter step, the toes springy, the eyes
Eager as a bird's, and every man
Had a coiled spring in his nerves that drove him
In a restless fury of life.

　　　　　　　　　　　　The bloods mingled
Madly, the redflame of the sons of men
Who had rowed Ulysses on the wine-dark sea
Burned in the pale blue eyes of the North, eyes hardened
With centuries of staring from Viking masts
Into the unknown oceans—Leif the Lucky
Once beached their dragon-headed prows on the bare
Coast of this land, the first white man. (Who knows
What strange multi-fathered child will come
Out of the nervous travail of these bloods
To fashion in a new world continent
A newer breed of men?)

From THE RIVER
Soundtrack of the Motion Picture

BLACK spruce and Norway pine,
  Douglas fir and Red cedar,
Scarlet oak and Shagbark hickory.
We built a hundred cities and a thousand towns—
But at what a cost!
We cut the top off the Alleghenies and sent it down the
      river.
We cut the top off Minnesota and sent it down the river,
We cut the top off Wisconsin and sent it down the river.
We left the mountains and the hills slashed and burned,
And moved on.

*

We built a hundred cities and a thousand towns—
But at what a cost!
Poor land makes poor people.
Poor people make poor land.

*

We got the blacks to plant the cotton and they gouged
      the top off the valley.
We got the Swedes to cut the forests, and they sent them
      down the river.
Then we left a hollow-eyed generation to peck at the
      worn-out valley;

And left the Swedes to shiver in their naked North
   country.
1903, 1907, 1913, 1922, 1927, 1936, 1937—
For you can't wall out and dam two-thirds the water in
   the country.
We built dams but the dams filled in.
We built a thousand-mile dyke but it didn't hold;
So we built it higher.
We played with a continent for fifty years.

Flood control? Of the Mississippi?
Control from Denver to Helena;
From Itasca to Paducah;
From Pittsburgh to Cairo—
Control of the wheat, the corn and the cotton land;
Control enough to put back a thousand forests;
Control enough to put the river together again before
   it is too late . . . before it has picked up the heart of a
   continent and shoved it into the Gulf of Mexico.

HOPE IS A TATTERED FLAG

HOPE is a tattered flag and a dream out of time.
    Hope is a heartspun word, the rainbow, the shadblow in
    white,
The evening star inviolable over the coal mines,
The shimmer of northern lights across a bitter winter night,
The blue hills beyond the smoke of the steel works,
The birds who go on singing to their mates in peace, war,
        peace,
The ten-cent crocus bulb blooming in a used-car salesroom,
The horseshoe over the door, the luckpiece in the pocket,
The kiss and the comforting laugh and resolve—
Hope is an echo, hope ties itself yonder, yonder.

The spring grass showing itself where least expected,
The rolling fluff of white clouds on a changeable sky,
The broadcast of strings from Japan, bells from Moscow,
Of the voice of the prime minister of Sweden carried
Across the sea in behalf of a world family of nations
And children singing chorals of the Christ child
And Bach being broadcast from Bethlehem, Pennsylvania
And tall skyscrapers practically empty of tenants
And the hands of strong men groping for handholds
And the Salvation Army singing God loves us. . . .

THE PEOPLE, YES, THE PEOPLE

THE people, yes, the people,
Until the people are taken care of one way or another,
Until the people are solved somehow for the day and hour,
Until then one hears "Yes but the people what about the
people?"
Sometimes as though the people is a child to be pleased or
fed
Or again a hoodlum you have to be tough with
And seldom as though the people is a caldron and a res-
ervoir
Of the human reserves that shape history,
The river of welcome wherein the broken First Families
fade,
The great pool wherein wornout breeds and clans drop
for restorative silence.

Fire, chaos, shadows,
Events trickling from a thin line of flame
On into cries and combustions never expected!
The people have the element of surprise.
Where are the kings today?
What has become of their solid and fastened thrones?
Who are the temporary puppets holding sway while any-
thing,
"God only knows that," waits around a corner, sits in
the shadows and holds an ax, waiting for the ap-
pointed hour?

"The czar has eight million men with guns and
bayonets.

"Nothing can happen to the czar.
"The czar is the voice of God and shall live forever.
"Turn and look at the forest of steel and cannon
"Where the czar is guarded by eight million soldiers.
"Nothing can happen to the czar."

They said that for years and in the summer of 1914
In the Year of Our Lord Nineteen Hundred and Four-
       teen
As a portent and an assurance they said with owl faces:
    "Nothing can happen to the czar."
Yet the czar and his bodyguard of eight million vanished
And the czar stood in the cellar before a little firing squad
And the command of fire was given
And the czar stepped into regions of mist and ice
The czar travelled into an ethereal uncharted siberia
While two kaisers also vanished from thrones
Ancient and established in blood and iron—
Two kaisers backed by ten million bayonets
Had their crowns in a gutter, their palaces mobbed.
    In fire, chaos, shadows,
In hurricanes beyond foretelling of probabilities,
In the shove and whirl of unforseen combustions
    The people, yes, the people,
Move eternally in the elements of surprise,
Changing from hammer to bayonet and back to hammer,
The hallelujah chorus forever shifting its star soloists.

SLEEP IS A SUSPENSION

SLEEP is a suspension midway
and a conundrum of shadows
lost in the meadows of the moon.
    The people sleep.
    Ai! ai! the people sleep.
Yet the sleepers toss in sleep
and an end comes of sleep
and the sleepers wake.
    Ai! ai! the sleepers wake!

THE PEOPLE WILL LIVE ON

THE people will live on.
   The learning and blundering people will live on.
   They will be tricked and sold and again sold
And go back to the nourishing earth for rootholds,

   The people so peculiar in renewal and comeback,
   You can't laugh off their capacity to take it.
The mammoth rests between his cyclonic dramas.

The people so often sleepy, weary, enigmatic,
is a vast huddle with many units saying:
   "I earn my living.
   I make enough to get by
   and it takes all my time.
   If I had more time
   I could do more for myself
   and maybe for others.
   I could read and study
   and talk things over
   and find out about things.
   It takes time.
   I wish I had the time."

The people is a tragic and comic two-face:
hero and hoodlum: phantom and gorilla twisting to moan with a gargoyle mouth: "They
buy me and sell me . . . it's a game . . .
sometime I'll break loose . . ."
         Once having marched
      Over the margins of animal necessity,

Over the grim line of sheer subsistence
    Then man came
To the deeper rituals of his bones,
To the lights lighter than any bones,
To the time for thinking things over,
To the dance, the song, the story,
Or the hours given over to dreaming,
    Once having so marched.

Between the finite limitations of the five senses
and the endless yearnings of man for the beyond
the people hold to the humdrum bidding of work and
        food
while reaching out when it comes their way
for lights beyond the prison of the five senses,
for keepsakes lasting beyond any hunger or death.
    This reaching is alive.
The panderers and liars have violated and smutted it.
    Yet this reaching is alive yet
    for lights and keepsakes.

    The people know the salt of the sea
    and the strength of the winds
    lashing the corners of the earth.
    The people take the earth
    as a tomb of rest and a cradle of hope.
    Who else speaks for the Family of Man?
    They are in tune and step
    with constellations of universal law.

    The people is a polychrome,
    a spectrum and a prism
    held in a moving monolith,

a console organ of changing themes,
a clavilux of color poems
wherein the sea offers fog
and the fog moves off in rain
and the labrador sunset shortens
to a nocturne of clear stars
serene over the shot spray
of northern lights.

The steel mill sky is alive.
The fire breaks white and zigzag
shot on a gun-metal gloaming.
Man is a long time coming.
Man will yet win.
Brother may yet line up with brother:

This old anvil laughs at many broken hammers.
There are men who can't be bought.
The fireborn are at home in fire.
The stars make no noise.
You can't hinder the wind from blowing.
Time is a great teacher.
Who can live without hope?
In the darkness with a great bundle of grief
the people march.
In the night, and overhead a shovel of stars for
keeps, the people march:
"Where to? What next?"

* PART THREE *

A poem should be palpable and mute
As a globed fruit

Dumb
As old medallions to the thumb

Silent as the sleeve-worn stone
Of casement ledges where the moss has grown—

A poem should be wordless
As the flight of birds

*

A poem should be motionless in time
As the moon climbs

Leaving, as the moon releases
Twig by twig the night-entangled trees,

Leaving, as the moon behind the winter leaves,
Memory by memory the mind—

A poem should be motionless in time
As the moon climbs

*

A poem should be equal to:
Not true

For all the history of grief
An empty doorway and a maple leaf

For love
The leaning grasses and two lights above the sea—

A poem should not mean
But be

ARCHIBALD MACLEISH

LITTLE IVORY FIGURES PULLED WITH STRING

Is it the tinkling of mandolins which disturbs you?
Or the dropping of bitter-orange petals among the coffee-
cups?
Or the slow creeping of the moonlight between the olive-
trees?
Drop! drop! the rain
Upon the thin plates of my heart.

String your blood to chord with this music,
Stir your heels upon the cobbles to the rhythm of a dance-
tune.
They have slim thighs and arms of silver;
The moon washes away their garments;
They make a pattern of fleeing feet in the branch shadows,
And the green grapes knotted about them
Burst as they press against one another.
The rain knocks upon the plates of my heart,
They are crumpled with its beating.

Would you drink only from your brains, Old Man?
See, the moonlight has reached your knees,
It falls upon your head in an accolade of silver.
Rise up on the music,
Fling against the moon-drifts in a whorl of young light
bodies:

[*153*]

Leaping grape-clusters,
Vine leaves tearing from a grey wall.
You shall run, laughing, in a braid of women,
And weave flowers with the frosty spines of thorns.
Why do you gaze into your glass,
And jar the spoons with your finger-tapping?
    The rain is rigid on the plates of my heart.
    The murmur of it is loud—loud.

* EZRA POUND *

THE RETURN

SEE, they return; ah, see the tentative
Movements, and the slow feet,
The trouble in the pace and the uncertain
Wavering!

See, they return, one, and by one,
With fear, as half-awakened;
As if the snow should hesitate
And murmur in the wind,
        and half turn back;
These were the "Wing'd-with-Awe,"
        Inviolable.

Gods of the wingéd shoe!
With them the silver hounds,
        sniffing the trace of air!

Haie! Haie!
        These were the swift to harry;
These the keen-scented;
These were the souls of blood.

Slow on the leash,
        pallid the leash-men!

THE RIVER-MERCHANT'S WIFE: A LETTER

WHILE my hair was still cut straight across my forehead
I played about the front gate, pulling flowers.
You came by on bamboo stilts, playing horse,
You walked about my seat, playing with blue plums.
And we went on living in the village of Chokan:
Two small people, without dislike or suspicion.

At fourteen I married My Lord you.
I never laughed, being bashful.
Lowering my head, I looked at the wall.
Called to, a thousand times, I never looked back.

At fifteen I stopped scowling,
I desired my dust to be mingled with yours,
Forever and forever and forever.
Why should I climb the look out?

At sixteen you departed,
You went into far Ku-to-yen, by the river of swirling eddies,
And you have been gone five months.
The monkeys make sorrowful noise overhead.

You dragged your feet when you went out.
By the gate now, the moss is grown, the different mosses,
Too deep to clear them away!
The leaves fall early this autumn, in wind.
The paired butterflies are already yellow with August
Over the grass in the West garden;
They hurt me. I grow older.

If you are coming down through the narrows of the river
    Kiang,
Please let me know beforehand,
And I will come out to meet you
        As far as Cho-fu-Sa.

From the Chinese of Rihaku.

CANTO XVII

So THAT the vines burst from my fingers
And the bees weighted with pollen
Move heavily in the vine-shoots:
    chirr-chirr-chir-rikk—a purring sound,
And the birds sleepily in the branches.
    ZAGREUS! IO ZAGREUS!
With the first pale-clear of the heaven
And the cities set in their hills,
And the goddess of the fair knees
Moving there, with the oak-woods behind her,
The green slope, with white hounds
    leaping about her;
And thence down to the creek's mouth, until evening,
Flat water before me,
    and the trees growing in water,
Marble trunks out of stillness,
On past the palazzi,
        in the stillness,
The light now, not of the sun.
        Chrysophrase,
And the water green clear, and blue clear;
On, to the great cliffs of amber.
          Between them,
Cave of Nerea,
    she like a great shell curved,
And the boat drawn without sound,
Without odour of ship-work,
Nor bird-cry, nor any noise of wave moving,
Nor splash of porpoise, nor any noise of wave moving,

Within her cave, Nerea,

                      she like a great shell curved

In the suavity of the rock,

                         cliff green-gray in the far,

In the near, the gate-cliffs of amber,

And the wave

                green clear, and blue clear,

And the cave salt-white, and glare-purple,

        cool, porphyry smooth,

        the rock sea-worn.

No gull-cry, no sound of porpoise,

Sand as of malachite, and no cold there,

      the light not of the sun.

Zagreus, feeding his panthers,

      the turf clear as on hills under light.

And under the almond-trees, gods,

      with them, *choros nympharum*. Gods,

Hermes and Athene,

                As shaft of compass,

Between them, trembled—

To the left is the place of fauns,

          sylva nympharum;

The low wood, moor-scrub,

      the doe, the young spotted deer,

      leap up through the broom-plants,

        as dry leaf amid yellow.

And by one cut of the hills,

      the great alley of Memnons.

Beyond sea, crests seen over dune

Night sea churning shingle,

To the left, the alley of cypress.

                    A boat came,

One man holding her sail,
Guiding her with oar caught over gunwale, saying:
" There, in the forest of marble,
" the stone trees—out of water—
" the arbours of stone—
" marble leaf, over leaf,
" silver, steel over steel,
" silver beaks rising and crossing,
" prow set against prow,
" stone, ply over ply,
" the gilt beams flare of an evening"
Borso, Carmagnola, the men of craft, *i vitrei*,
Thither at one time, time after time,
And the waters richer than glass,
Bronze gold, the blaze over the silver,
Dye-pots in the torch-light,
The flash of wave under prows,
And the silver beaks rising and crossing.
        Stone trees, white and rose-white in the darkness,
Cypress there by the towers,
        Drift under hulls in the night.
            "In the gloom the gold
Gathers the light about it. . . ."

Now supine in burrow, half over-arched bramble,
One eye for the sea, through that peek-hole,
Gray light, with Athene.
Zothar and her elephants, the gold loin-cloth,
The sistrum, shaken, shaken,
            the cohorts of her dancers.
And Aletha, by bend of the shore,
            with her eyes seaward,
            and in her hands sea-wrack

Salt-bright with the foam.
Koré through the bright meadow,
             with green-gray dust in the grass:
"For this hour, brother of Circe."
Arm laid over my shoulder,
Saw the sun for three days, the sun fulvid,
As a lion lift over sand-plain;
                             and that day,
And for three days, and none after,
Splendour, as the splendour of Hermes,
And shipped thence
                     to the stone place,
Pale white, over water,
                     known water,
And the white forest of marble, bent bough over bough,
The pleached arbour of stone,
Thither Borso, when they shot the barbed arrow at him,
And Carmagnola, between the two columns,
Sigismundo, after that wreck in Dalmatia.
     Sunset like the grasshopper flying.

E. P. ODE POUR L'ELECTION DE SON SEPULCHRE

For three years, out of key with his time,
He strove to resuscitate the dead art
Of poetry; to maintain 'the sublime'
In the old sense. Wrong from the start—

No, hardly, but seeing he had been born
In a half-savage country, out of date;
Bent resolutely on wringing lilies from the acorn;
Capaneus; trout for factitious bait;

Ἴδμεν γάρ τοι πάνθ', ὅσ' ἐνί Τροίῃ
Caught in the unstopped ear;
Giving the rocks small lee-way
The chopped seas held him, therefore, that year.

His true Penelope was Flaubert,
He fished by obstinate isles;
Observed the elegance of Circe's hair
Rather than the mottoes on sundials.

Unaffected by 'the march of events,'
He passed from men's memory in *l'an trentiesme,
De son eage;* the case presents
No adjunct to the Muses' diadem.

II

The age demanded an image
Of its accelerated grimace,
Something for the modern stage,
Not, at any rate, an Attic grace;

Not, not certainly, the obscure reveries
Of the inward gaze;
Better mendacities
Than the classics in paraphrase!

The 'age demanded' chiefly a mould in plaster,
Made with no loss of time,
A prose kinema, not, not assuredly, alabaster
Or the 'sculpture' of rhyme.

III

The tea-rose tea-gown, etc.
Supplants the mousseline of Cos,
The pianola 'replaces'
Sappho's barbitos.

Christ follows Dionysus,
Phallic and ambrosial
Made for macerations;
Caliban casts out Ariel.

All things are a flowing,
Sage Heracleitus says;
But a tawdry cheapness
Shall outlast our days.

Even the Christian beauty
Defects—after Samothrace;
We see τὸ καλὸν
Decreed in the market-place.

Faun's flesh is not to us,
Nor the saint's vision.
We have the Press for wafer;
Franchise for circumcision.

All men, in law, are equals.
Free of Pisistratus,
We choose a knave or an eunuch
To rule over us.

O bright Apollo,
τίν άνορα, τίν'ήρωα, τίνα θεòν,
What god, man, or hero
Shall I place a tin wreath upon!

IV

These fought in any case,
and some believing,
     pro domo, in any case . . .

Some quick to arm,
some for adventure,
some from fear of weakness,
some from fear of censure,
some for love of slaughter, in imagination,
learning later . . .
some in fear, learning love of slaughter;

Died some, pro patria,
     non 'dulce' non 'et decor' . . .
walked eye-deep in hell
believing in old men's lies, then unbelieving
came home, home to a lie,
home to many deceits,
home to old lies and new infamy;
usury age-old and age-thick
and liars in public places.

Daring as never before, wastage as never before.
Young blood and high blood,
fair cheeks, and fine bodies;

fortitude as never before

frankness as never before,
disillusions as never told in the old days,
hysterias, trench confessions,
laughter out of dead bellies.

V

There died a myriad,
And of the best, among them,
For an old bitch gone in the teeth,
For a botched civilization,

Charm, smiling at the good mouth,
Quick eyes gone under earth's lid,

For two gross of broken statues,
For a few thousand battered books.

* WILLIAM CARLOS WILLIAMS *

THE YACHTS

CONTEND in a sea which the land partly encloses
shielding them from the too heavy blows
of an ungoverned ocean which when it chooses

tortures the biggest hulls, the best man knows
to pit against its beating, and sinks them pitilessly.
Mothlike in mists, scintillant in the minute

brilliance of cloudless days, with broad bellying sails
they glide to the wind tossing green water
from their sharp prows while over them the crew crawls

ant-like, solicitously grooming them, releasing,
making fast as they turn, lean far over and having
caught the wind again, side by side, head for the mark.

In a well guarded arena of open water surrounded by
lesser and greater craft which, sycophant, lumbering
and flittering follow them, they appear youthful, rare

as the light of a happy eye, live with the grace
of all that in the mind is feckless, free and
naturally to be desired. Now the sea which holds them

is moody, lapping their glossy sides, as if feeling
for some slightest flaw but fails completely.
Today no race. Then the wind comes again. The yachts

move, jockeying for a start, the signal is set and they
are off. Now the waves strike at them but they are too
well made, they slip through, though they take in canvas

Arms with hands grasping seek to clutch at the prows.
Bodies thrown recklessly in the way are cut aside.
It is a sea of faces about them in agony, in despair

until the horror of the race dawns staggering the mind,
the whole sea become an entanglement of watery bodies
lost to the world bearing what they cannot hold. Broken,

beaten, desolate, reaching from the dead to be taken up
they cry out, failing, failing! their cries rising
in waves still as the skillful yachts pass over.

* E . E . C U M M I N G S *

MY SWEET OLD ETCETERA

MY sweet old etcetera
aunt lucy during the recent

war could and what
is more did tell you just
what everybody was fighting

for,
my sister

isabel created hundreds
(and
hundreds) of socks not to
mention shirts fleaproof earwarmers

etcetera wristers etcetera, my
mother hoped that

i would die etcetera
bravely of course my father used
to become hoarse talking about how it was
a privilege and if only he
could meanwhile my

self etcetera lay quietly
in the deep mud et

cetera
(dreaming,
et
  cetera, of
Your smile
eyes knees and of your Etcetera)

PARIS; THIS APRIL SUNSET COMPLETELY UTTERS

Paris; this April sunset completely utters
utters serenely silently a cathedral

before whose upward lean magnificent face
the streets turn young with rain,

spiral acres of bloated rose
coiled within cobalt miles of sky
yield to and heed
the mauve
        of twilight(who slenderly descends,
daintily carrying in her eyes the dangerous first stars)
people move love hurry in a gently

arriving gloom and
see!(the new moon
fills abruptly with sudden silver
these torn pockets of lame and begging colour)while
there and here the lithe indolent prostitute
Night,argues

with certain houses

IMPOSSIBLY, MOTIVATED BY MIDNIGHT

IMPOSSIBLY
 motivated by midnight
the flyspecked abdominous female
indubitably tellurian
strolls
          emitting minute grins

each an intaglio.
Nothing
has also carved upon her much

too white forehead a pair of
eyes which mutter thickly (as one merely
terriculous American an instant doubts
the authenticity

of these antiquities—relaxing
                              hurries

elsewhere;to blow

incredible wampum

IF I HAVE MADE, MY LADY, INTRICATE

IF i have made, my lady,intricate
imperfect various things chiefly which wrong
your eyes(frailer than most deep dreams are frail)
songs less firm than your body's whitest song
upon my mind—if I have failed to snare
the glance too shy—if through my singing slips
the very skillful strangeness of your smile
the keen primeval silence of your hair

—let the world say "his most wise music stole
nothing from death"—
                 you only will create
(who are so perfectly alive)my shame:
lady through whose profound and fragile lips
the sweet small clumsy feet of April came

into the ragged meadow of my soul.

MY FATHER MOVED THROUGH DOOMS OF LOVE

Mʏ father moved through dooms of love
   through sames of am through haves of give,
singing each morning out of each night
my father moved through depths of height

this motionless forgetful where
turned at his glance to shining here;
that if(so timid air is firm)
under his eyes would stir and squirm

newly as from unburied which
floats the first who,his april touch
drove sleeping selves to swarm their fates
woke dreamers to their ghostly roots

and should some why completely weep
my father's fingers brought her sleep:
vainly no smallest voice might cry
for he could feel the mountains grow.

Lifting the valleys of the sea
my father moved through griefs of joy;
praising a forehead called the moon
singing desire into begin

joy was his song and joy so pure
a heart of star by him could steer
and pure so now and now so yes
the wrists of twilight would rejoice

keen as midsummer's keen beyond
conceiving mind of sun will stand,
so strictly(over utmost him
so hugely)stood my father's dream

his flesh was flesh his blood was blood:
no hungry man but wished him food;
no cripple wouldn't creep one mile
uphill to only see him smile.

Scorning the pomp of must and shall
my father moved through dooms of feel;
his anger was as right as rain
his pity was as green as grain

septembering arms of year extend
less humbly wealth to foe and friend
than he to foolish and to wise
offered immeasurable is

proudly and(by octobering flame
beckoned)as earth will downward climb,
so naked for immortal work
his shoulders marched against the dark

his sorrow was as true as bread:
no liar looked him in the head;
if every friend became his foe
he'd laugh and build a world with snow.

My father moved through theys of we,
singing each new leaf out of each tree
(and every child was sure that spring
danced when she heard my father sing)

then let men kill which cannot share,
let blood and flesh be mud and mire,
scheming imagine, passion willed,
freedom a drug that's bought and sold

giving to steal and cruel kind,
a heart to fear, to doubt a mind,
to differ a disease of same,
conform the pinnacle of am

though dull were all we taste as bright,
bitter all utterly things sweet,
maggoty minus and dumb death
all we inherit, all bequeath

and nothing quite so least as truth
—i say though hate were why men breathe—
because my father lived his soul
love is the whole and more than all

* T . S . E L I O T *

THE HIPPOPOTAMUS

And when this epistle is read among you, cause
that it be read also in the church of the Laodiceans.

THE broad-backed hippopotamus
    Rests on his belly in the mud;
Although he seems so firm to us
He is merely flesh and blood.

Flesh-and-blood is weak and frail,
Susceptible to nervous shock;
While the True Church can never fail
For it is based upon a rock.

The hippo's feeble steps may err
In compassing material ends,
While the True Church need never stir
To gather in its dividends.

The 'potamus can never reach
The mango on the mango-tree;
But fruits of pomegranate and peach
Refresh the Church from over sea.

At mating time the hippo's voice
Betrays inflexions hoarse and odd,
But every week we hear rejoice
The Church, at being one with God.

The hippopotamus's day
Is passed in sleep; at night he hunts;
God works in a mysterious way—
The Church can sleep and feed at once

I saw the 'potamus take wing
Ascending from the damp savannas,
And quiring angels round him sing
The praise of God, in loud hosannas.

Blood of the lamb shall wash him clean
And him shall heavenly arms enfold,
Among the saints he shall be seen
Performing on a harp of gold.

He shall be washed as white as snow,
By all the martyr'd virgins kist,
While the True Church remains below
Wrapt in the old miasmal mist.

GERONTION

*Thou hast nor youth nor age
But as it were an after dinner sleep
Dreaming of both.*

HERE I am, an old man in a dry month,
Being read to by a boy, waiting for rain.
I was neither at the hot gates
Nor fought in the warm rain
Nor knee deep in the salt marsh, heaving a cutlass,
Bitten by flies, fought.
My house is a decayed house,
And the Jew squats on the window sill, the owner,
Spawned in some estaminet of Antwerp,
Blistered in Brussels, patched and peeled in London,
The goat coughs at night in the field overhead;
Rocks, moss, stonecrop, iron, merds.
The woman keeps the kitchen, makes tea,
Sneezes at evening, poking the peevish gutter.

I an old man,
A dull head among windy spaces.

Signs are taken for wonders. "We would see a sign!"
The word within a word, unable to speak a word,
Swaddled with darkness. In the juvescence of the year
Came Christ the tiger.
In depraved May, dogwood and chestnut, flowering judas,
To be eaten, to be divided, to be drunk
Among whispers; by Mr. Silvero

With caressing hands, at Limoges
Who walked all night in the next room;

By Hakagawa, bowing among the Titians;
By Madame de Tornquist, in the dark room
Shifting the candles; Fraulein von Kulp
Who turned in the hall, one hand on the door. Vacant
    shuttles
Weave the wind. I have no ghosts,
An old man in a draughty house
Under a windy knob.

After such knowledge, what forgiveness? Think now
History has many cunning passages, contrived corridors
And issues, deceives with whispering ambitions,
Guides us by vanities. Think now
She gives when our attention is distracted
And what she gives, gives with such supple confusions
That the giving famishes the craving. Gives too late
What's not believed in, or if still believed,
In memory only, reconsidered passion. Gives too soon
Into weak hands, what's thought can be dispensed with
Till the refusal propagates a fear. Think
Neither fear nor courage saves us. Unnatural vices
Are fathered by our heroism. Virtues
Are forced upon us by our impudent crimes.
These tears are shaken from the wrath-bearing tree.

The tiger springs in the new year. Us he devours. Think
    at last
We have not reached conclusion, when I
Stiffen in a rented house. Think at last
I have not made this show purposelessly

And it is not by any concitation
Of the backward devils.
I would meet you upon this honestly.
I that was near your heart was removed therefrom
To lose beauty in terror, terror in inquisition.
I have lost my passion: why should I need to keep it
Since what is kept must be adulterated?
I have lost my sight, smell, hearing, taste and touch:
How should I use them for your closer contact?

These with a thousand small deliberations
Protract the profit, of their chilled delirium,
Excite the membrane, when the sense has cooled,
With pungent sauces, multiply variety
In a wilderness of mirrors. What will the spider do,
Suspend its operations, will the weevil
Delay? De Bailhache, Fresca, Mrs. Cammell, whirled
Beyond the circuit of the shuddering Bear
In fractured atoms. Gull against the wind, in the windy
    straits
Of Belle Isle, or running on the Horn,
White feathers in the snow, the Gulf claims,
And an old man driven by the Trades
To a sleepy corner.
                Tenants of the house,
Thoughts of a dry brain in a dry season.

THE HOLLOW MEN

A penny for the Old Guy

I

WE ARE the hollow men
We are the stuffed men
Leaning together
Headpiece filled with straw. Alas!
Our dried voices, when
We whisper together
Are quiet and meaningless
As wind in dry grass
Or rats' feet over broken glass
In our dry cellar

Shape without form, shade without colour,
Paralyzed force, gesture without motion;

Those who have crossed
With direct eyes, to death's other Kingdom
Remember us—if at all—not as lost
Violent souls, but only
As the hollow men
The stuffed men.

II

Eyes I dare not meet in dreams
In death's dream kingdom
These do not appear:
There, the eyes are
Sunlight on a broken column

There, is a tree swinging
And voices are
In the wind's singing
More distant and more solemn
Than a fading star.

Let me be no nearer
In death's dream kingdom
Let me also wear
Such deliberate disguises
Rat's coat, crowskin, crossed staves
In a field
Behaving as the wind behaves
No nearer—

Not that final meeting
In the twilight kingdom

III

This is the dead land
This is cactus land
Here the stone images
Are raised, here they receive
The supplication of a dead man's hand
Under the twinkle of a fading star.

Is it like this
In death's other kingdom
Waking alone
At the hour when we are
Trembling with tenderness
Lips that would kiss
Form prayers to broken stone.

IV

The eyes are not here
There are no eyes here
In this valley of dying stars
In this hollow valley
This broken jaw of our lost kingdoms

In this last of meeting places
We grope together
And avoid speech
Gathered on this beach of the tumid **river**

Sightless, unless
The eyes reappear
As the perpetual star
Multifoliate rose
Of death's twilight kingdom
The hope only
Of empty men.

V

Here we go round the prickly pear
Prickly pear prickly pear
Here we go round the prickly pear
At five o'clock in the morning.

Between the idea
And the reality
Between the motion
And the act
Falls the Shadow
                    For Thine is the Kingdom

Between the conception
And the creation
Between the emotion
And the response
Falls the Shadow
Life is very long

Between the desire
And the spasm
Between the potency
And the existence
Between the essence
And the descent
Falls the Shadow
For Thine is the Kingdom

For Thine is
Life is
For Thine is the

This is the way the world ends
This is the way the world ends
This is the way the world ends
Not with a bang but a whimper.

From THE ROCK

THE Eagle soars in the summit of Heaven,
The Hunter with his dogs pursues his circuit,
O perpetual revolution of configured stars,
O perpetual recurrence of determined seasons,
O world of spring and autumn, birth and dying!
The endless cycle of idea and action,
Endless invention, endless experiment,
Brings knowledge of motion, but not of stillness;
Knowledge of speech, but not of silence;
Knowledge of words, and ignorance of the Word.
All our knowledge brings us nearer to our ignorance,
All our ignorance brings us nearer to death,
But nearness to death no nearer to God.
Where is the Life we have lost in living?
Where is the wisdom we have lost in knowledge?
Where is the knowledge we have lost in information?
The cycles of Heaven in twenty centuries
Bring us farther from God and nearer to the Dust.
I journey to London, to the timekept City,
Where the River flows, with foreign flotations.
There I was told: we have too many churches,
And too few chop-houses. There I was told
Let the vicars retire. Men do not need the Church
In the place where they work, but where they spend
      their Sundays.
In the City, we need no bells:
Let them waken the suburbs.
I journeyed to the suburbs, and there I was told:
We toil for six days, on the seventh we must motor

To Hindhead, or Maidenhead.
If the weather is foul we stay at home and read the
    papers,
In industrial districts, there I was told
Of economic laws.
In the pleasant countryside, there it seemed
That the country now is only fit for picnics.
And the church does not seem to be wanted
In country or in suburb; and in the town
Only for important weddings.

Section II of BURNT NORTON

G ARLIC and sapphires in the mud
   Clot the bedded axle-tree.
The trilling wire in the blood
Sings below inveterate scars
And reconciles forgotten wars.
The dance along the artery
The circulation of the lymph
Are figured in the drift of stars
Ascend to summer in the tree
We move above the moving tree
In light upon the figured leaf
And hear upon the sodden floor
Below, the boarhound and the boar
Pursue their pattern as before
But reconciled among the stars.

At the still point of the turning world. Neither flesh nor fleshless
Neither from nor towards; at the still point, there the dance is,
But neither arrest nor movement. And do not call it fixity,
Where past and future are gathered. Neither movement from nor
        towards,
Neither ascent nor decline. Except for the point, the still point,
There would be no dance, and there is only the dance.
I can only say, *there* we have been: but I cannot say where.
And I cannot say, how long, for that is to place it in time.

The inner freedom from the practical desire,
The release from action and suffering, release from the inner
And the outer compulsion, yet surrounded

By a grace of sense, a white light still and moving,
Erhebung without motion, concentration
Without elimination, both a new world
And the old made explicit, understood
In the completion of its partial ecstasy,
The resolution of its partial horror.
Yet the enchainment of past and future
Woven in the weakness of the changing body,
Protects mankind from heaven and damnation
Which flesh cannot endure.
                          Time past and time future
Allow but a little consciousness.
To be conscious is not to be in time
But only in time can the moment in the rose-garden,
The moment in the arbour where the rain beat,
The moment in the draughty church at smokefall
Be remembered; involved with past and future.
Only through time time is conquered.

IN TIME LIKE GLASS

IN TIME like glass the stars are set,
And seeming-fluttering butterflies
Are fixéd fast in Time's glass net
With mountains and with maids' bright eyes.

Above the cold Cordilleras hung
The wingéd eagle and the Moon:
The gold, snow-throated orchid sprung
From gloom where peers the dark baboon:

The Himalayas' white, rapt brows;
The jewel-eyed bear that threads their caves;
The lush plains' lowing herds of cows;
That Shadow entering human graves:

All these like stars in Time are set,
They vanish but can never pass;
The Sun that with them fades is yet
Fast-fixed as they in Time like glass.

* E D I T H   S I T W E L L *

SAID KING POMPEY

SAID King Pompey, the Emperor's ape,
Shuddering black in his temporal cape
Of dust: "The dust is everything—
The heart to love and the voice to sing,
Indianapolis,
And the Acropolis,
Also the hairy sky that we
Take for a coverlet comfortably." . . .
Said the Bishop
Eating his ketchup—
"There still remains Eternity
(Swelling the diocese)—
That elephantiasis,
The flunkeyed and trumpeting Sea!"

STILL FALLS THE RAIN

(The Raids, 1940. Night and Dawn)

STILL falls the Rain—
Dark as the world of man, black as our loss—
Blind as the nineteen hundred and forty nails
Upon the Cross.

Still falls the Rain
With a sound like the pulse of the heart that is changed
$\qquad\qquad\qquad\qquad$ to the hammer-beat
In the Potter's Field, and the sound of the impious feet

On the Tomb:
$\qquad\qquad$ Still falls the Rain
In the Field of Blood where the small hopes breed and
$\qquad\qquad\qquad\qquad\qquad$ the human brain
Nurtures its greed, that worm with the brow of Cain.

Still falls the Rain
At the feet of the Starved Man hung upon the Cross.
Christ that each day, each night, nails there,
$\qquad\qquad\qquad\qquad\qquad$ have mercy on us—
On Dives and on Lazarus:
Under the Rain the sore and the gold are as one.

Still falls the Rain—
Still falls the blood from the Starved Man's wounded Side:
He bears in His Heart all wounds,—those of the light
$\qquad\qquad\qquad\qquad\qquad$ that died,
That last faint spark
In the self-murdered heart, the wounds of the sad
$\qquad\qquad\qquad\qquad\qquad$ uncomprehending dark,

The wounds of the baited bear,—
The blind and weeping bear whom the keepers beat
On his helpless flesh . . . the tears of the hunted hare.

Still falls the Rain—
Then—O Ile leape up to my God: who pulles me doune—
See, see where Christ's blood streames in the firmament:
It flows from the Brow we nailed upon the tree
Deep to the dying, to the thirsting heart
That holds the fires of the world,—dark-smirched with pain
As Caesar's laurel crown.

Then sounds the voice of One who like the heart of man
Was once a child who among beasts has lain—
"Still do I love, still shed my innocent light, my Blood,
                                        for thee."

AN OLD WOMAN

I, AN old woman in the light of the sun,
Wait for my Wanderer, and my upturned face
Has all the glory of the remembering Day
The hallowed grandeur of the primeval clay
That knew the Flood, and suffered all the dryness
Of the uncaring heaven, the sun its lover.

For the sun is the first lover of the world,
Blessing all humble creatures, all life-giving,
Blessing the end of life and the work done,
The clean and the unclean, ores in earth, and splendours
Within the heart of man, that second sun.

For when the first founts and deep waterways
Of the young light flow down and lie like peace
Upon the upturned faces of the blind
From life, it comes to bless
Eternity in its poor mortal dress,—
Shining upon young lovers and old lechers
Rising from their beds, and laying gold
Alike in the unhopeful path of beggars
And in the darkness of the miser's heart.
The crookéd has a shadow light made straight,
The shallow places gain their strength again,—
And desert hearts, waste heavens, the barren height
Forget that they are cold.
The man-made chasms between man and man
Of creeds and tongues are fill'd, the guiltless light
Remakes all men and things in holiness.

And he who blessed the fox with a golden fleece
And covered earth with ears of corn like the planets
Bearded with thick ripe gold,
For the holy bread of mankind, blessed my clay:
For the sun cares not that I am a simple woman,
To him, laughing, the veins in my arms and the wrinkles
From work on my nursing hands are sacred as branches
And furrows of harvest . . . to him, the heat of the earth
And beat of the heart are one,—
Born from the energy of the world, the love
That keeps the Golden Ones in their place above,
And hearts and blood of beasts even in motion,—
Without which comets, sun, plants, and all living beings
And warmth in the inward parts of the earth would freeze.
And the sun does not care if I live in holiness,
To him, my mortal dress
Is sacred, part of the earth, a lump of the world
With my splendours, ores, impurities, and harvest,
Over which shines my heart, that ripening sun.

Though the dust, the shining racer, overtake me,
I too was a golden woman like those that walk
In the fields of the heavens:—but am now grown old
And must sit by the fire and watch the fire grow cold,
—A country Fate whose spool is the household task.
Yet still I am loved by the sun, and still am part
Of earth. In the evenings bringing home the workers,
Bringing the wanderer home and the dead child,
The child unborn and never to be conceived,
Home to the mother's breast, I sit by the fire
Where the seed of gold drops dead and the kettle simmers
With a sweet sound like that of a hive of bees,
And I wait for my Wanderer to come home to rest—

Covered with earth as if he had been working
Among the happy gardens, the holy fields
Where the bread of mankind ripens in the stillness.
Unchanged to me by death, I shall hold to my breast
My little child in his sleep, I shall seem the consoling
Earth, the mother of corn, muse of the unreturning.

Wise is the earth, consoling grief and glory,
The golden heroes proud as pomp of waves,—
Great is the earth embracing them, their graves,
And great is the earth's story.
For though the soundless wrinkles fall like snow
On many a golden cheek, and creeds grow old
And change,—man's heart, that sun,
Outlives all terrors shaking the old night:
The world's huge fevers burn and shine, turn cold,
Yet the heavenly bodies and young lovers burn and shine,
The golden lovers walk in the holy fields
Where the Abraham-bearded sun, the father of all things
Is shouting of ripeness, and the whole world of dews and
                                        splendours are singing

To the cradles of earth, of men, beasts, harvests, swinging
In the peace of God's heart. And I, the primeval clay
That has known earth's grief and harvest's happiness,
Seeing mankind's dark seed-time, come to bless,—
Forgive and bless all men like the holy light.

* JEAN GARRIGUE *

FROM VENICE WAS THAT AFTERNOON

FROM Venice was that afternoon
Though it was our land's canal we viewed.
Where willows cleaved the bluish heat
By drooping leaf or two, gold green,
And every tuft of hill beyond
Stood bright, distinct, as if preserved
By glass that sealed out light but not
Its gold or influence.
And floated on the speckled stream
A child of brilliant innocence
Where on the docks of green we stood
Naming it love for its perfection.
This seemed to be . . .
But the current carried the leaves ·swiftly,
So flowed that child away from us,
So stared we sternly at the water's empty face.
Ah, in the greenhouse of that hour
Waited in the tare and sorrel
The mouth of fleshliness that stopped;
The leaves that dappled on that breast
The five-sensed image of our pleasance
Have now destroyed its lineaments.
For the waters of that afternoon
Flowed through Negation's glassy land,
Where in this civil, gate-closed hour

The verges of those waters now
Drown that joy that was our power.
What tyranny imposed this pride
That caused love's gift to be denied
And our destroying features to
Cast perpetually on its brow
The glass accepting no leaves now?
In rages of the intellect
We gave to heaven abstinence
Who said our love must issue from
No cisterns of the ruddy sun
But like the artifice of fountains
Leap from cold, infertile sources.
And our destroying features thus
Cast from that land its beingness
And strewed upon the green fleshed hills
Sands of our darkening great ills.

* WALLACE STEVENS *

PETER QUINCE AT THE CLAVIER

I

JUST as my fingers on these keys
Make music, so the self-same sounds
On my spirit make a music too.

Music is feeling then, not sound;
And thus it is that what I feel,
Here in this room, desiring you,

Thinking of your blue-shadowed silk,
Is music. It is like the strain
Waked in the elders by Susanna:

Of a green evening, clear and warm,
She bathed in her still garden, while
The red-eyed elders, watching, felt

The basses of their being throb
In witching chords, and their thin blood
Pulse pizzicati of Hosanna.

II

In the green evening, clear and warm,
Susanna lay.
She searched
The touch of springs,

And found
Concealed imaginings.
She sighed
For so much melody.

Upon the bank she stood
In the cool
Of spent emotions.
She felt, among the leaves,
The dew
Of old devotions.

She walked upon the grass,
Still quavering.
The winds were like her maids,
On timid feet,
Fetching her woven scarves,
Yet wavering.

A breath upon her hand
Muted the night.
She turned—
A cymbal clashed,
And roaring horns.

III

Soon, with a noise like tambourines,
Came her attendant Byzantines.

They wondered why Susanna cried
Against the elders by her side:

And as they whispered, the refrain
Was like a willow swept by rain.

Anon their lamps' uplifted flame
Revealed Susanna and her shame.

And then the simpering Byzantines,
Fled, with a noise like tambourines.

IV

Beauty is momentary in the mind—
The fitful tracing of a portal;
But in the flesh it is immortal.

The body dies; the body's beauty lives.
So evenings die, in their green going,
A wave, interminably flowing.

So gardens die, their meek breath scenting
The cowl of Winter, done repenting.
So maidens die to the auroral
Celebration of a maiden's choral.

Susanna's music touched the bawdy strings
Of those white elders; but, escaping,
Left only Death's ironic scraping.
Now in its immortality, it plays
On the clear viol of her memory,
And makes a constant sacrament of praise.

THE MECHANICAL OPTIMIST

A LADY dying of diabetes
   Listened to the radio,
Catching the lesser dithyrambs.
So heaven collects its bleating lambs.

Her useless bracelets fondly fluttered,
Paddling the melodic swirls,
The idea of god no longer sputtered
At the roots of her indifferent curls.

The idea of the Alps grew large,
Not yet, however, a thing to die in.
It seemed serener just to die,
To float off on the floweriest barge.

Accompanied by the exegesis
Of familiar things in a cheerful voice,
Like the night before Christmas and all the carols.
Dying lady, rejoice, rejoice!

* H A R T   C R A N E *

SUNDAY MORNING APPLES

To William Sommer, Painter

THE leaves will fall again sometime and fill
The fleece of nature with those purposes
That are your rich and faithful strength of line.

But now there are challenges to spring
In that ripe nude with head
                              reared

Into a realm of swords, her purple shadow
Bursting on the winter of the world
From whiteness that cries defiance to the snow.

A boy runs with a dog before the sun, straddling
Spontaneities that form their independent orbits,
Their own perennials of light
In the valley where you live
                              (called Brandywine).

I have seen the apples there that toss you secrets,—
Beloved apples of seasonable madness
That feed your inquiries with aerial wine.

Put them again beside a pitcher with a knife,
And poise them full and ready for explosion—
The apples, Bill, the apples!

EMBLEMS OF CONDUCT

BY A peninsula the wanderer sat and sketched
 The uneven valley graves. While the apostle gave
Alms to the meek the volcano burst
With sulphur and aureate rocks . . .
For joy rides in stupendous coverings
Luring the living into spiritual gates.

Orators follow the universe
And radio the complete laws to the people.
The apostle conveys thought through discipline.
Bowls and cups fill historians with adorations,—
Dull lips commemorating spiritual gates.

The wanderer later chose this spot of rest
Where marble clouds support the sea
And where was finally borne a chosen hero.
By that time summer and smoke were past.
Dolphins still played, arching the horizons,
But only to build memories of spiritual gates.

VOYAGES II

And yet this great wink of eternity,
  Of rimless floods, unfettered leewardings,
Samite sheeted and processioned where
Her undinal vast belly moonward bends,
Laughing the wrapt inflections of our love;

Take this Sea, whose diapason knells
On scrolls of silver snowy sentences,
The sceptred terror of whose sessions rends
As her demeanors motion well or ill,
All but the pieties of lovers' hands.

And onward, as bells off San Salvador
Salute the crocus lustres of the stars,
In these poinsettia meadows of her tides,—
Adagios of islands, O my Prodigal,
Complete the dark confessions her veins spell.

Mark how her turning shoulders wind the hours,
And hasten while her penniless rich palms
Pass superscription of bent foam and wave,—
Hasten, while they are true,—sleep, death, desire,
Close round one instant in one floating flower.

Bind us in time, O Seasons clear, and awe.
O minstrel galleons of Carib fire,
Bequeath us to no earthly shore until
Is answered in the vortex of our grave
The seal's wide spindrift gaze toward paradise.

From THE BRIDGE

The River

> *. . . and past*
> *the din and slogans*
> *of the year—*

Stick your patent name on a signboard
  brother—all over—going west—young man
Tintex—Japalac—Certain-teed Overalls ads
and lands sakes! under the new playbill ripped
in the guaranteed corner—see Bert Williams what?
Minstrels when you steal a chicken just
save me the wing for if it isn't
Erie it ain't for miles around a
Mazda—and the telegraphic night coming on Thomas

a Ediford—and whistling down the tracks
a headlight rushing with the sound—can you
imagine—while an EXpress makes time like
SCIENCE—COMMERCE and the HOLYGHOST
RADIO ROARS IN EVERY HOME WE HAVE THE
    NORTHPOLE
WALLSTREET AND VIRGINBIRTH WITHOUT
    STONES OR
WIRES OR EVEN RUNning brooks connecting ears
and no more sermons windows flashing roar
breathtaking—as you like it . . . eh?

          So the 20th Century—so
whizzed the Limited—roared by and left
three men, still hungry on the tracks, ploddingly

watching the tail lights wizen and converge, slip-
ping gimleted and neatly out of sight.

*

*to those
whose addresses
are never near*

The last bear, shot drinking in the Dakotas
Loped under wires that span the mountain stream.
Keen instruments, strung to a vast precision
Bind town to town and dream to ticking dream.
But some men take their liquor slow—and count
—Though they'll confess no rosary nor clue—
The river's minute by the far brook's year.
Under a world of whistles, wires and steam
Caboose-like they go ruminating through
Ohio, Indiana—blind baggage—
To Cheyenne tagging . . . Maybe Kalamazoo.

Time's rendings, time's blendings they construe
As final reckonings of fire and snow;
Strange bird-wit, like the elemental gist
Of unwalled winds they offer, singing low
My Old Kentucky Home and *Casey Jones,*
Some Sunny Day. I heard a road-gang chanting so.
And afterwards, who had a colt's eyes—one said,
"Jesus! Oh I remember watermelon days!" And sped
High in a cloud of merriment, recalled
"—And when my Aunt Sally Simpson smiled," he
        drawled—
"It was almost Louisiana, long ago."
"There's no place like Booneville though, Buddy,"
One said, excising a last burr from his vest,
"—For early trouting." Then peering in the can,

"—But I kept on the tracks." Possessed, resigned,
He trod the fire down pensively and grinned,
Spreading dry shingles of a beard. . . .

                               Behind
My father's cannery works I used to see
Rail-squatters ranged in nomad raillery,
The ancient men—wifeless or runaway
Hobo-trekkers that forever search
An empire wilderness of freight and rails.
Each seemed a child, like me, on a loose perch,
Holding to childhood like some termless play.
John, Jake or Charley, hopping the slow freight
—Memphis to Tallahassee—riding the rods,
Blind fists of nothing, humpty-dumpty clods.

                               but who have
                          touched her, knowing
                          her without name

Yet they touch something like a key perhaps.
From pole to pole across the hills, the states
—They know a body under the wide rain;
Youngsters with eyes like fjords, old reprobates
With racetrack jargon,—dotting immensity
They lurk across her, knowing her yonder breast
Snow-silvered, sumac-stained or smoky blue—
Is past the valley-sleepers, south or west.
—As I have trod the rumorous midnights, too,

And past the circuit of the lamp's thin flame
(O Nights that brought me to her body bare!)
Have dreamed beyond the print that bound her name.
Trains sounding the long blizzards out—I heard
Wail into distances I knew were hers.
Papooses crying on the wind's long mane

Screamed redskin dynasties that fled the brain,
—Dead echoes! But I knew her body there,
Time like a serpent down her shoulder, dark,
And space, an eaglet's wing, laid on her hair.

> *nor the myths*
> *of her fathers . . .*

Under the Ozarks, domed by Iron Mountain,
The old gods of the rain lie wrapped in pools
Where eyeless fish curvet a sunken fountain
And re-descend with corn from querulous crows.
Such pilferings make up their timeless eatage,
Propitiate them for their timber torn
By iron, iron—always the iron dealt cleavage!
They doze now, below axe and powder horn.

And Pullman breakfasters glide glistening steel
From tunnel into field—iron strides the dew—
Straddles the hill, a dance of wheel on wheel.
You have a half-hour's wait at Siskiyou,
Or stay the night and take the next train through.
Southward, near Cairo passing, you can see
The Ohio merging,—borne down Tennessee;
And if it's summer and the sun's in dusk
Maybe the breeze will lift the River's musk
—As though the waters breathed that you might know
Memphis Johnny, Steamboat Bill, Missouri Joe.
Oh, lean from the window, if the train slows down,
As though you touched hands with some ancient clown,
—A little while gaze absently below
And hum *Deep River* with them while they go.

Yes, turn again and sniff once more—look see,
O Sheriff, Brakeman and Authority—

Hitch up your pants and crunch another quid,
For you, too, feed the River timelessly.
And few evade full measure of their fate;
Always they smile out eerily what they seem.
I could believe he joked at heaven's gate—
Dan Midland—jolted from the cold brake-beam.

Down, down—born pioneers in time's despite,
Grimed tributaries to an ancient flow—
They win no frontier by their wayward plight,
But drift in stillness, as from Jordan's brow.

You will not hear it as the sea; even stone
Is not more hushed by gravity . . . But slow,
As loth to take more tribute—sliding prone
Like one whose eyes were buried long ago

The River, spreading, flows—and spends your dream.
What are you, lost within this tideless spell?
You are your father's father, and the stream—
A liquid theme that floating niggers swell.

Damp tonnage and alluvial march of days—
Nights turbid, vascular with silted shale
And roots surrendered down of moraine clays:
The Mississippi drinks the farthest dale.

O quarrying passion, undertowed sunlight!
The basalt surface drags a jungle grace
Ochreous and lynx-barred in lengthening might;
Patience! and you shall reach the biding place!

Over De Soto's bones the freighted floors
Throb past the City storied of three thrones.

Down two more turns the Mississippi pours
(Anon tall ironsides up from salt lagoons)

And flows within itself, heaps itself free.
All fades but one thin skyline 'round . . . Ahead
No embrace opens but the stinging sea;
The River lifts itself from its long bed,

Poised wholly on its dream, a mustard glow
Tortured with history, its one will—flow!
—The Passion spreads in wide tongues, choked and slow,
Meeting the Gulf, hosannas silently below.

PURGATORIO

MY COUNTRY, O my land, my friends—
Am I apart—here from you in a land
Where all your gas lights—faces—sputum gleam
Like something left, forsaken—here am I—
And are these stars—the high plateau—the scents
Of Eden and the dangerous tree—are these
The landscape of confession—and if confession
So absolution? Wake pines—but pines wake here.
I dream the too-keen cider—the too-soft snow.
Where are the bayonets that the scorpion may not grow?
Here quakes of earth make houses fall—
And all my countrymen I see rush toward one stall;
Exile is thus purgatory—not such as Dante built,

But rather like a blanket than a quilt,
And I have no decision—is it green or brown
That I prefer to country or to town?
I am unraveled, umbilical anew,
As ring the church bells here in Mexico—
(They ring too obdurately here to heed my call)
And what hours they forget to chime I'll know,
As one whose altitude at one time, was not so.

* JOHN CROWE RANSOM *

HERE LIES A LADY

HERE lies a lady of beauty and high degree.
  Of chills and fever she died, of fever and chills,
The delight of her husband, her aunts, an infant of
    three,
And of medicos marvelling sweetly on her ills.

For either she burned, and her confident eyes would
    blaze,
And her fingers fly in a manner to puzzle their heads—
What was she making? Why, nothing; she sat in a maze
Of old scraps of laces, snipped into curious shreds—

Or this would pass, and the light of her fire decline
Till she lay discouraged and cold as a thin stalk white
    and blown,
And would not open her eyes, to kisses, to wine;
The sixth of these states was her last; the cold settled
    down.

Sweet ladies, long may ye bloom, and toughly I hope ye
    may thole,
But was she not lucky? In flowers and lace and mourning,
In love and great honour we bade God rest her soul
After six little spaces of chill, and six of burning.

PRELUDE LVI

RIMBAUD and Verlaine, precious pair of poets,
Genius in both (but what is genius?) playing
Chess on a marble table at an inn
With chestnut blossom falling in blond beer
And on their hair and between knight and bishop—
Sunlight squared between them on the chess-board
Cirrus in heaven, and a squeal of music
Blown from the leathern door of Ste. Sulpice—

Discussing, between moves, iamb and spondee
Anacoluthon and the open vowel
God the great peacock with his angel peacocks
And his dependent peacocks the bright stars:
Disputing too of fate as Plato loved it,
Or Sophocles, who hated and admired,
Or Socrates, who loved and was amused:

Verlaine puts down his pawn upon a leaf
And closes his long eyes, which are dishonest,
And says 'Rimbaud, there is one thing to do:
We must take rhetoric, and wring its neck! . . .'
Rimbaud considers gravely, moves his Queen;
And then removes himself to Timbuctoo.

And Verlaine dead,—with all his jades and mauves;
And Rimbaud dead in Marseilles with a vision,

His leg cut off, as once before his heart;
And all reported by a later lackey,
Whose virtue is his tardiness in time.

Let us describe the evening as it is:—
The stars disposed in heaven as they are:
Verlaine and Shakespeare rotting, where they rot,
Rimbaud remembered, and too soon forgot;

Order in all things, logic in the dark;
Arrangement in the atom and the spark;
Time in the heart and sequence in the brain—

Such as destroyed Rimbaud and fooled Verlaine
And let us then take godhead by the neck—
And strangle it, and with it, rhetoric.

IDIOT

THE idiot greens the meadows with his eyes,
The meadow creeps implacable and still;
A dog barks, the hammock swings, he lies.
One two three the cows bulge on the hill.

Motion which is not time erects snowdrifts
While sister's hand sieves waterfalls of lace.
With a palm fan closer than death he lifts
The Ozarks and tilted seas across his face.

In the long sunset where impatient sound
Strips niggers to a multiple of backs
Flies yield their heat, magnolias drench the ground
With Appomattox! The shadows lie in stacks.

The julep glass weaves echoes in Jim's kinks
While ashy Jim puts murmurs in the day:
Now in the idiot's heart a chamber stinks
Of dead asters, as the potter's field of May.

All evening the marsh is a slick pool
Where dream wild hares, witch hazel, pretty girls.
"Up from the important picnic of a fool
Those rotted asters!" Eddy on eddy swirls

The innocent mansion of a panther's heart!
It crumbles, tick-tick time drags it in
And now his arteries lag and now they start
Reverence with the frigid gusts of sin—

The stillness pelts the eye, assaults the hair;
A beech sticks out a branch to warm the stars,
A lightning-bug jerks angles in the air,
Diving. "I am the captain of new wars!"

The dusk runs down the lane driven like hail;
Far off a precise whistle is escheat
To the dark; and then the towering weak and pale
Covers his eyes with memory like a sheet.

THE MILITARY HARPIST

STRANGELY assorted, the shape of song and the bloody man.

Under the harp's gilt shoulder and rainlike strings,
Prawn-eyed, with prawnlike bristle, well-waxed moustache,
With long tight cavalry legs, and the spurred boot
Ready upon the swell, the Old Sweat waits.

Now dies, and dies hard, the stupid, well-relished fortissimo,
Wood-wind alone inviting the liquid tone,
The voice of the holy and uncontending, the harp.

Ceasing to ruminate interracial fornications,
He raises his hands, and his wicked old mug is David's,
Pastoral, rapt, the king and the poet in innocence,
Singing Saul in himself asleep, and the ancient Devil
Clean out of countenance, as with an army of angels.

He is now where his bunion has no existence,
Breathing an atmosphere free of pipeclay and swearing,
He wears the starched nightshirt of the hereafter, his halo
Is plain manly brass with a permanent polish,
Requiring no oily rag and no Soldier's Friend.

His place is with the beloved poet of Israel,
With the wandering minnesinger and the loves of Provence,

With Blondel footsore and heartsore, the voice in the darkness
Crying like beauty bereaved beneath many a donjon,
O Richard! O king! where is the lion of England!
With Howell, Llewellyn, and far in the feral north
With the savage fame of the hero in glen and in ben,
At the morning discourse of saints in the island Eire,
And at nameless doings in the stone-circle, the dreadful grove.

Thus far into the dark do I delve for his likeness:
He harps at the Druid sacrifice, where the golden string
Sings to the golden knife and the victim's shriek.

Strangely assorted, the shape of song and the bloody man.

From THE DESTROYERS

Speech of the First Sentry

Now all things melt and shift in the moon's light.
The walls before you alter. The landscape
Alters. Familiar things
Take unfamiliar shape.
The building you knew at noon of such a height
Will shrink by dusk. The very street
That led you to your house begins to change,
And as you walk the thing within your mind
Takes form before the echo of your feet.
And there, behind the door you knew you locked yourself
Twist the key and find
A dead man in his winding sheet.

The knowledge you had at morning by the night
Will cope with nothing. The measured mile
Between two landmarks stretches and contracts.
Time no longer fixed
To the actuated shadow on a dial
Will break and waver like your image
In wind-blown water.
                                All laws have broken
According to some law you sense, but worse
Than none because you cannot understand,

Seeing it only as unappeasable curse
Making you stranger to your own hand.
All problems crossed—no sum
You learned at school will quite work out;
Nothing constant but the power
To prove upon the world your every doubt.
It is the moment of the whirlpool, moment
Of that abyss where all things stream.
O you who sleep tonight within this city!
Think now of order, for in what's to come
You'll learn how 'be' and 'seem'
May interchange along with 'plan' and 'chance'
And hear above your heads destruction dance
On the curved roof of the universe as a drum.

From IN TIME OF FOREIGN WAR

ALL summer long I felt it in the air
As if those armies on another continent
Shifting into position to prepare
Demolition of an age—the tent
Pitched in the public park by antiaircraft,
The guns unlimbered, the tanks set, the brief
Flights of reconnaissance, the fortress shaft
Mined and occupied—set here the leaf
Fluttering on a windless day, the dawn
To come on me working with a whispered
"Wait!"
A blurring of all previous lines drawn,
An inability to concentrate,
So strained the ear with listening; in the lap
Of heat waves on horizon the dull hour
Unfolded like a flower, like a trap
Whose center was a cone prolonged in space.
Unconscious expectancy of some one word—
An inattention marked on every face
As if someone had spoken and they half-heard.

✳

The age descends: dictator, president,
Premier, priest, or vacant formal king
Pass now like masks as hollow, arrogant,
Another voice takes over, mastering
Distraction. Do you believe in the sequence
Guided by phrases, the sentences
Falling from the lips of the men in power?
Attribute anarchy? Forget; the deeper sense is
Constrained by the forces let loose in this hour.

A time that harped on mass and weight, that dreamed
Its revolutions in a million bellies,
A time that clung in shipwreck to what seemed
And sank on instabilities, its eyes
Ravished by the meaningless appearance,
That edited its ideals by one use—
Its popular faith, art and thought by chance
Compacted and all together an abuse
Of the soul's truth—now when
It most needs just and integrated men
Self-mastering, self-aware, finds it has run
Bewilderingly barren in the stock,
And has, instead, such effigies as on
The platform of a medieval clock
Creak and revolve: the jerky, leaden shells
Traverse the hours to the sound of bells.

A time, now, like a globe, where underground
Or overhead whispers reverberate
And footfalls from the dead past sound
Upon the future with the ring of plate;
Where premonition sees in field of strife
Tomorrow's pattern like a fixture of stars
Where tortured fatalism forgets that life
Is not restrained by any system's bars
Nor any formulation of the mind,
That living is continual overflow—
That only what is dead can be defined.

Therefore—before the gongs let go—
Remember now that the most precious ward
Of every individual, his right
To his own evolution, here you guard
That neither mob nor tyrant may command.

And this a promise, only by your hand
A process: a progression of fulfillments.

Remember here where whispers dislocate
Among our cities still-far-off events
And everywhere, decision is so great,
An inner silence into which we sense
Other figures enter—a measured tread
Re-echoes. Under hearing, out of sight,
We are surrounded by the honored dead;
Their forms patrol the arches of the night.

*

SPIRIT: A SPIRAL: A SPIRE

S PIRIT: a spiral: a spire:
   The immanent Lotus blooming from the mire.
What has the downpour of our guts and blood
And two milleniums of western thought
Raging on act and object ever brought
But suffocation in the intellectual mud?

From fifty motionless cedars in the light
Of darkness lifting up the curved midnight
Depend the pin-point, plate-shaped galaxies
Like cones: a contemplation: a Here and Now
Obliterates the individual bough,
Whose roots embrace all seasons and all seas.

The playground empties science has defiled:
Let that murderous, alienated child
Urinating ruin, be put to bed.
The Patriarch resolved all questioning
By silence when a bird began to sing.
Has anyone spoken? Has anything been said?

TOMBSTONE WITH CHERUBIM

NO NOTICE in the papers,
only a voice over the telephone
Saying she was dead, casually,
remarkably definite.
                         Somebody whispered syphilis—
a sentimental lie.
                    Somebody spoke of her
(rococo) a Florentine olive tree
that should have twined (O unmistakably!)
around the person of a football-captain stock-broker
     asleep
Upon Miami sands.
                   She shrieked at poverty.
divorced from silks, furs, and patented nickel-plated
     limousines.
                  She loved relaxed security,
sleeping with men occasionally
as it were exotic dreams
                         and rich meaningless words
draping the tender portions of her body:
                                         Hello, Marie
you should have gone out like a row of mazda lamps
smashed with a crowbar.
                        Even this epitaph,
true enough for a beautiful girl

[225]

pacing with unforgettable ease
down Michigan Boulevard one April morning,
does not contain the facts.
                    The facts were these:
She died in Lesbian serenity
                    neither hot nor cold
until the chaste limbs stiffened.
                    Disconnect the telephone;

cut the wires.

SALVOS FOR RANDOLPH BOURNE

O BITTERNESS never spoken, the death mask etched in
   silver,
the dark limbs rolled in lead where the shallow grave
     conceals
despair: the image of a large head, forward, devouring
the collarbone. No general in brass over it and no
conquering angel kneels.

II

This was the end:
          There were no firing squads
No City Hall Nathan Hale with a bronze cord at his
     throat
Speaking of lives and his country where a hundred mil-
     lion lives
rose, wavered, shattered like an invisible sea coiling
against a rock (no longer there) but sunken
into a shore line of weeds and sand.

Only a small room and a million words to be written
     before midnight
against poverty and idiot death like the gray face of
     Emerson
fading in New England winter twilight; the hard face
     vanishing
in snow, the passionately soft words issuing from the
     mouth—
O listen to the rock, the oracle no longer there!

III

To be the last American, an embryo coiled in a test tube,
To be a fixed and paralytic smile cocked upward to the
    clouds,
To see friends and enemies depart (around the corner)
Their sticks and smart fedoras bright in sunlight,
To be or not to be Hamlet, the Prince of Wales,
or last week's *New Republic;*
to be death delicately walking between chimney pots on
    Eighth Street,
possibly this is best to be
                or not to be.

THE BURNING WHEEL

THEY followed the course of heaven as before
Trojan in smoky armor westward fled
Disastrous walls and on his shoulder bore
A dotard recollection had made mad,

Depraved by years, Anchises: on the strong
Tall bronze upborne, small sack of impotence;
Yet still he wore the look of one who young
Had closed with love in cloudy radiance.

So the discoverers when they wading came
From shallow ships and climbed the wooded shores:
They saw the west, a sky of falling flame,
And by the stream savage ambassadors.

O happy, brave and vast adventure! Where
Each day the sun beat rivers of new gold;
The wild grape ripened, springs reflected fear;
The wild deer fled; the bright snake danger coiled.

They, too, the stalwart conquerors of space,
Each on his shoulders wore a wise delirium
Of memory and age: ghostly embrace
Of fathers slanted toward a western tomb.

A hundred and a hundred years they stayed
Aloft, until they were as light as autumn
Shells of locusts. Where then were they laid?
And in what wilderness oblivion?

THIS DIM AND PTOLEMAIC MAN

For forty years, for forty-one,
Sparing the profits of the sun,
This farmer piled his meagre hoard
To buy at last a rattly Ford.

Now crouched on a scared smile he feels
Motion spurt beneath his heels,
Rheumatically intent shifts gears,
Unloosing joints of rustic years.

Morning light obscures the stars,
He swerves avoiding other cars,
Wheels with the road, does not discern
He eastward goes at every turn,

Nor how his aged limbs are hurled
Through all the motions of the world,
How wild past farms, past ricks, past trees,
He perishes toward Hercules.

* E. B. WHITE *

I PAINT WHAT I SEE
A Ballad of Artistic Integrity

WHAT do you paint, when you paint a wall?"
    Said John D.'s grandson Nelson.
"Do you paint just anything there at all?
"Will there be any doves, or a tree in fall?
"Or a hunting scene, like an English hall?"

   "I paint what I see," said Rivera.

"What are the colors you use when you paint?"
    Said John D.'s grandson Nelson.
"Do you use any red in the beard of a saint?
"If you do, is it terribly red, or faint?
"Do you use any blue? Is it Prussian?"

   "I paint what I paint," said Rivera.

"Whose is that head that I see on my wall?"
    Said John D.'s grandson Nelson.
"Is it anyone's head whom we know, at all?
"A Rensselaer, or a Saltonstall?
"Is it Franklin D.? Is it Mordaunt Hall?
"Or is it the head of a Russian?"

   "I paint what I think," said Rivera

"I paint what I paint, I paint what I see,
    "I paint what I think," said Rivera,
"And the thing that is dearest in life to me
"In a bourgeois hall is Integrity;
    "However . . .
"I'll take out a couple of people drinkin'
"And put in a picture of Abraham Lincoln,
"I could even give you McCormick's reaper
"And still not make my art much cheaper.
"But the head of Lenin has got to stay
"Or my friends will give me the bird today
    "The bird, the bird, forever."

"It's not good taste in a man like me,"
    Said John D.'s grandson Nelson,
"To question an artist's integrity
"Or mention a practical thing like a fee,
"But I know what I like to a large degree
    "Though art I hate to hamper;
"For twenty-one thousand conservative bucks
"You painted a radical. I say shucks,
    "I never could rent the offices—
    "The capitalistic offices.
"For this, as you know, is a public hall
"And people want doves, or a tree in fall,
"And though your art I dislike to hamper,
"I owe a *little* to God and Gramper,
    "And after all,
    "It's *my* wall . . ."

    "We'll see if it is," said Rivera.

✳ F R E D E R I C   P R O K O S C H ✳

THE CONSPIRATORS

A ND if the dead, and the dead
Of spirit now join, and in their horrifying ritual
Proceed till at last with oriental grace
End their concluding dance with the candles guttering,
The cymbals sobbing, the wind harassing the curtains,
The chill from the flood embracing the golden stairway.
The scent devoured and the bowls blown clean of
    incense:

Ah then, farewell, sweet northern music;
No longer the flight of the mind across the continents,
The dazzling flight of our words across the tempestuous
Black, or the firelit recital of a distant battle.

No. All that we loved is lost, if the intricate
Languor of recollected centuries
Descends in its terrible sweetness on our limbs.
No shot will echo; no fire; no agonizing
Cry will resound in the city's thickets: only,
The ivy falling gently across the bridges,
The larches piercing the roofs, the reclining steeples,
The cellars rich with the agony of the reptiles,
The contemplative worms, the victorious rodents,
And at last, the climax entrancingly serene,
The inconclusive note drowned on the ascendant:

Our lovely shapes in marble still shine through the
    greenery,
Our exquisite silver bones still glide with the glaciers
That split our familiar hills, still fall with the avalanche
And weaving their vast wing's thunder over the Indies
The birds, the birds, sob for the time of man.

* ARCHIBALD MACLEISH *

THE TOO-LATE BORN

WE TOO, we too, descending once again
   The hills of our own land, we too have heard
Far off—Ah, que ce cor a longue haleine—
The horn of Roland in the passages of Spain,
The first, the second blast, the failing third,
And with the third turned back and climbed once more
The steep road southward, and heard faint the sound
Of swords, of horses, the disastrous war,
And crossed the dark defile at last, and found
At Roncevaux upon the darkening plain
The dead against the dead and on the silent ground
The silent slain—

INVOCATION TO THE SOCIAL MUSE

Señora it is true the Greeks are dead:

It is true also that we here are Americans:
That we use the machines: that a sight of the god is
　　unusual:
That more people have more thoughts: that there are

Progress and science and tractors and revolutions and
Marx and the wars more antiseptic and murderous
And music in every home: there is also Hoover:

Does the lady suggest we should write it out in The
　　Word?
Does Madame recall our responsibilities? We are
Whores Fraulein: poets Fraulein are persons of

Known vocation following troops: they must sleep with
Stragglers from either prince and of both views:
The rules permit them to further the business of neither:

It is also strictly forbidden to mix in maneuvers:
Those that infringe are inflated with praise on the
　　plazas—
Their bones are resultantly afterwards found under
　　newspapers:

Preferring life with the sons to death with the fathers
We also doubt on the record whether the sons
Will still be shouting around with the same huzzas—

For we hope Lady to live to lie with the youngest:
There are only a handful of things a man likes
Generation to generation hungry or

Well fed: the earth's one: life's
One: Mister Morgan is not one:

There is nothing worse for our trade than to be in style:

He that goes naked goes farther at last than another:
Wrap the bard in a flag or a school and they'll jimmy his
Door down and be thick in his bed—for a month:

(Who recalls the address now of the Imagists?)
But the naked man has always his own nakedness:
People remember forever his live limbs:

They may drive him out of the camps but one will take
     him:
They may stop his tongue on his teeth with a rope's
     argument—
He will lie in a house and be warm when they are
     shaking:

Besides Tovarishch how to embrace an army?
How to take to one's chamber a million souls?
How to conceive in the name of a column of marchers?

The things of the poet are done to a man alone
As the things of love are done—or of death when he
     hears the
Step withdraw on the stair and the clock tick only:

Neither his class nor his kind nor his trade may come
    near him
There where he lies on his left arm and will die:
Nor his class nor his kind nor his trade when the blood
    is jeering

And his knee's in the soft of the bed where his love lies:

I remind you Barinya the life of the poet is hard—
A hardy life with a boot as quick as a fiver:

Is it just to demand of us also to bear arms?

OIL PAINTING OF THE ARTIST AS THE ARTIST

THE plump Mr. Pl'f is washing his hands of America:
The plump Mr. Pl'f is in ochre with such hair:

America is in blue-black-grey-green-sandcolor:
America is a continent—many lands:

The plump Mr. Pl'f is washing his hands of America:
He is pictured at Pau on the place and his eyes glaring:

He thinks of himself as an exile from all this:
As an émigré from his own time into history—

(History being an empty house without owners
A practical man may get in by the privy stones—

The dead are excellent hosts: they have no objections—
And once in he can nail the knob on the next one

Living the life of a classic in bad air with
Himself for the Past and his face in the glass for Posterity)

The Cinquecento is nothing at all like Nome
Or Natchez or Wounded Knee or the Shenandoah:

Your vulgarity Tennessee: your violence Texas:
The rocks under your fields Ohio Connecticut:

Your clay Missouri your clay: you have driven him out:
You have shadowed his life Appalachians purple mountains:

There is much too much of your flowing Mississippi:
He prefers a tidier stream with a terrace for trippers and

Cypresses mentioned in Horace or Henry James:
He prefers a country where everything carries the name
    of a

Countess or real king or an actual palace or
Something in Prose and the stock prices all in Italian:

There is more shade for an artist under a fig
Than under the whole damn range (he finds) of the
    Big Horns

POLE STAR FOR THIS YEAR

WHERE the wheel of light is turned:
Where the axle of the night is
Turned: is motionless: where holds
And has held ancient sureness always:

Where of faring men the eyes
At oar bench at the rising bow
Have seen—torn shrouds between—the Wain
And that star's changelessness: not changing:

There upon that intent star:
Trust of wandering men: of truth
The most reminding witness: we
Fix our eyes also: waylost: the wanderers:

We too turn now to that star:
We too in whose trustless hearts
All truth alters and the lights
Of earth are out now turn to that star:

Liberty of man and mind
That once was mind's necessity
And made the West blaze up has burned
To bloody embers and the lamp's out:

Hope that was a noble flame
Has fanned to violence and feeds
On cities and the flesh of men
And chokes where unclean smoke defiles it:

Even the small spark of pride
That taught the tyrant once is dark
Where gunfire rules the starving street
And justice cheats the dead of honor:

Liberty and pride and hope
And every guide-mark of the mind
That led our blindness once has vanished.
This star will not. Love's star will not.

Love that has beheld the face
A man has with a man's eyes in it
Bloody from the slugger's blows
Or heard the cold child cry for hunger—

Love that listens where the good:
The virtuous: the men of faith:
Proclaim the paradise on earth
And murder starve and burn to make it—

Love that cannot either sleep
Or keep rich music in the ear
Or lose itself for the wild beat
The anger in the blood makes raging—

Love that hardens into hate—
Love like hatred and as bright—
Love is that one waking light
That leads now when all others darken.

✽ PART FOUR ✽

THESE are the live,
  Not silhouettes or dead men.
  That dull murmur is their tread on the street:
  Those brass quavers are their shouts.
Here is the wind blowing through the crowded square.
  Here is the violence and secret change.
  And these are figures of life beneath the sea.
These are the lovely women
  And the exhilarations that die.
  Here is a stone lying on the sidewalk
  In the shadow of the wall.
Hey? What saith the noble poet now,
  Drawing his hand across his brow?
  Claude, is the divine afflatus upon you?
  Hey? Hey Claude?
Here are a million taxi drivers, social prophets,
  The costume for an attitude,
  A back-stage shriek,
  The heat and speed of the earth.

Here is a statue of Burns.
There is the modern moon.
That song is the latest dance.
Hey? Of what doth the noble poet brood
In a tragic mood?

KENNETH FEARING

* WILFRED OWEN *

THE SHOW

We have fallen in the dreams the ever-living
Breathe on the tarnished mirror of the world,
And then smooth out with ivory hands and sigh

W. B. YEATS

MY SOUL looked down from a vague height with Death,
As unremembering how I rose or why,
And saw a sad land, weak with sweats of dearth,
Gray, cratered like the moon with hollow woe,
And pitted with great pocks and scabs of plagues.

Across its beard, that horror of harsh wire,
There moved thin caterpillars, slowly uncoiled.
It seemed they pushed themselves to be as plugs
Of ditches, where they writhed and shrivelled, killed.

By them had slimy paths been trailed and scraped
Round myriad warts that might be little hills.

From gloom's last dregs these long-strung creatures crept,
And vanished out of dawn down hidden holes.

(And smell came up from those foul openings
As out of mouths, or deep wounds deepening.)

On dithering feet upgathered, more and more,
Brown strings, towards strings of gray, with bristling
    spines,
All migrants from green fields, intent on mire.

Those that were gray, of more abundant spawns,
Ramped on the rest and ate them and were eaten.

I saw their bitten backs curve, loop, and straighten,
I watched those agonies curl, lift, and flatten.

Whereat, in terror what that sight might mean,
I reeled and shivered earthward like a feather.

And Death fell with me, like a deepening moan.
And He, picking a manner of worm, which half had hid
Its bruises in the earth, but crawled no further,
Showed me its feet, the feet of many men,
And the fresh-severed head of it, my head.

ARMS AND THE BOY

L ET the boy try along this bayonet-blade
How cold steel is, and keen with hunger of blood;
Blue with all malice, like a madman's flash;
And thinly drawn with famishing for flesh.

Lend him to stroke these blind, blunt bullet-heads
Which long to nuzzle in the hearts of lads,
Or give him cartridges of fine zinc teeth,
Sharp with the sharpness of grief and death.

For his teeth seem for laughing round an apple.
There lurk no claws behind his fingers supple;
And god will grow no talons at his heels,
Nor antlers through the thickness of his curls.

STRANGE MEETING

IT SEEMED that out of battle I escaped
Down some profound dull tunnel, long since scooped
Through granites which titanic wars had groined.
Yet also there encumbered sleepers groaned,
Too fast in thought or death to be bestirred.
Then, as I probed them, one sprang up, and stared
With piteous recognition in fixed eyes,
Lifting distressful hands as if to bless.
And by his smile, I knew that sullen hall,
By his dead smile I knew we stood in Hell.
With a thousand pains that vision's face was grained;
Yet no blood reached there from the upper ground,
And no guns thumped, or down the flues made moan.
"Strange friend," I said, "here is no cause to mourn."
"None," said the other, "save the undone years,
The hopelessness. Whatever hope is yours,
Was my life also; I went hunting wild
After the wildest beauty in the world,
Which lies not calm in eyes, or braided hair,
But mocks the steady running of the hour,
And if it grieves, grieves richlier than here.
For by my glee might many men have laughed,
And of my weeping something had been left,
Which must die now. I mean the truth untold,
The pity of war, the pity war distilled.
Now men will go content with what we spoiled.
Or discontent, boil bloody, and be spilled.
They will be swift with swiftness of the tigress,
None will break ranks, though nations trek from progress.

Courage was mine, and I had mystery,
Wisdom was mine and I had mastery;
To miss the march of this retreating world
Into vain citadels that are not walled.
Then, when much blood had clogged their chariot-
      wheels
I would go up and wash them from sweet wells,
Even with truths that lie too deep for taint.
I would have poured my spirit without stint
But not through wounds; not on the cess of war.
Foreheads of men have bled where no wounds were.
I am the enemy you killed, my friend.
I knew you in this dark; for so you frowned
Yesterday through me as you jabbed and killed.
I parried; but my hands were loath and cold.
Let us sleep now. . . ."

GREATER LOVE

R ED lips are not so red
   As the stained stones kissed by the English dead.
Kindness of wooed and wooer
Seems shame to their love pure.
O Love, your eyes lose lure
    When I behold eyes blinded in my stead!

Your slender attitude
    Trembles not exquisite like limbs knife-skewed,
Rolling and rolling there
Where God seems not to care;
Till the fierce Love they bear
    Cramps them in death's extreme decrepitude.

Your voice sings not so soft,—
    Though even as wind murmuring through raftered
       loft,—
Your dear voice is not dear,
Gentle, and evening clear,
As theirs whom none now hear,
    Now earth has stopped their piteous mouths that
       coughed.

Heart, you were never hot,
    Nor large, nor full like hearts made great with shot;
And though your hand be pale,
Paler are all which trail
Your cross through flame and hail:
    Weep, you may weep, for you may touch them not.

SONG OF SONGS

Sing me at morn but only with your laugh;
Even as Spring that laugheth into leaf;
Even as Love that laugheth after Life.

Sing me but only with your speech all day,
As voluble leaflets do; let viols die;
The least word of your lips is melody!

Sing me at eve but only with your sigh!
Like lifting seas it solaceth; breathe so,
Slowly and low, the sense that no songs say.

Sing me at midnight with your mumurous heart!
Let youth's immortal-moaning chords be heard
Throbbing through you, and sobbing, unsubdued.

* K E N N E T H   F E A R I N G *

DIRGE

1–2–3 was the number he played but today the number
      came 3–2–1;
    bought his Carbide at 30 and it went to 29; had the
      favorite at Bowie but the track was slow—

O, executive type, would you like to drive a floating
      power, knee-action, silk-upholstered six? Wed a
      Hollywood star? Shoot the course in 58? Draw to
      the ace, king, jack?
    O, fellow with a will who won't take no, watch out
      for three cigarettes on the same, single match; O,
      democratic voter born in August under Mars, be-
      ware of liquidated rails—

Denouement to denouement, he took a personal pride in
      the certain, certain way he lived his own, private
      life,
    but nevertheless, they shut off his gas; nevertheless,
      the bank foreclosed; nevertheless, the landlord
      called; nevertheless, the radio broke,

And twelve o'clock arrived just once too often,
    just the same he wore one grey tweed suit, bought one
      straw hat, drank one straight Scotch, walked one

short step, took one long look, drew one deep
breath,
just one too many,

And wow he died as wow he lived,
going whop to the office and blooie home to sleep and
biff got married and bam had children and oof got
fired,
zowie did he live and zowie did he die,

With who the hell are you at the corner of his casket,
and where the hell we going on the right hand
silver knob, and who the hell cares walking second
from the end with an American Beauty wreath
from why the hell not,

Very much missed by the circulation staff of the New
York Evening Post; deeply, deeply mourned by the
B.M.T.,

Wham, Mr. Roosevelt; pow, Sears Roebuck; awk, big
dipper; bop, summer rain;
bong, Mr., bong, Mr., bong, Mr., bong.

* E D M U N D   W I L S O N *

THE OMELET OF A. MACLEISH

I

AND the mist: and the rain on West Rock: and the
wind steady:

There were elms in that place: and graven inflexible
laws:

Men of Yale: and the shudder of Tap Day: the need for
a man to make headway

Winning a way through the door in the windowless
walls:

And the poems that came easy and sweet with a blurring
of Masefield

(The same that I later denied): a young man smooth
but raw

*Mac-
Leish
breaks
an egg
for his
omelet.*

Eliot alarmed me at first: but my later abasement:

And the clean sun of France: and the freakish but
beautiful fashion:

Striped bathhouses bright on the sand: *Anabase* and *The
Waste Land:*

These and the *Cantos* of Pound: O how they came pat!

Nimble at other men's arts how I picked up the trick
of it:

Rode it reposed on it drifted away on it: passing

*He puts
plovers'
eggs and
truffles
into his
omelet.*

Shores that lay dim in clear air: and the cries of
    affliction
Suave in somniferous rhythms: there was rain there and
    moons:
Leaves falling: and all of a flawless and hollow felicity:

In that land there were summer and autumn and   *He slips*
    nighttime and noon   *in a few*
But all seemed alike: and the new-polished planets by   *prizes*
    Einstein: *for*
                                                philos-
And a wind out of Valéry's graveyard but it never   *ophers.*
    blew anything loose:

And the questions and questions
                       questioning
                                   What am I? O
What shall I remember?
                      O my people
                               a pensive dismay
What have I left unsaid?
                    Till the hearer cried:

"If only MacLeish could remember if only could say   *The*
    it!" . . .   *omelet*
                                                  becomes
And young girls came out: they were innocent strong   *a na-*
    in the tendons   *tional*
Hungry for all that was new: and hearing their eyelids   *institu-*
    were hazy with   *tion and*
                                                  gets into
                                                  Fanny
Tears and delight: and the campuses brown in Novem-   *Farmer.*
    ber:
Ha but white shirt fronts pink faces: the prizes won:
The celluloid tower with bold intonations defended:

And the mean tang of Cummings turned saltless and
sleek on the tongue:
And a Dante gone limp: and a shimmer and musical
sound
That gleamed in the void and evoked approbation and
wonder

*He ex-
periments
with a
new kind
of pepper-
corn.*

That the poet need not be a madman or even a bounder.

II

And at last I drew close to a land dark with fortifica-
tions:
Men shrieking outlandish reproaches till all my blood
tingled:
It was ragged and harsh there: they hated: heart hor-
ribly quaked in me:

*He seems
likely to
lose his
invest-
ment in
his
omelet.*

Then I thought "I have staved off the pricking of many
a sting:
These perchance I may placate too": I put in at that
place:
I met them with scorn and good-natured agreement
mingled:

Their fierce cries of "Aesthete!" and "Fascist!": and
like them I railed at the
Bankers and builders of railroads: I said "Social
Credit":
(He's a tough lad under the verse mister all the same!):

And the Polacks and Dagoes and Hunkies undoubtedly
dead:
And behold these savage and sybarite-baiting strangers
Had many among them like me well-mannered well-fed

*He is
obliged to
reopen
his ome-
let and*

Bubbling over with schoolboy heroics: their line had
    been changing:

And long in that plentiful land I dwelt honored in peace:

And then schoolboys from Britain came over us flying
    like angels:

*put a
little
garlic in.*

Them too I courted: I labored to roughen the sweet

To stiffen the wilt of a style that seemed lax in that
    land:

A starch of Greek tragedy: stark Anglo-Saxon the beat
    of it:

*He is
doomed
to go on
doctoring
his
omelet.*

Stock-market talk: still my numbers as mawkishly ran:

(Señora, I could go on like this forever:

It is a strange thing to be an American):

I was wired for sound as I started again down the river:

And my colons went out on the air to the clang of a
    gong:

O when shall I ring with the perilous pain and the fever?

A clean and clever lad
          who is doing
              his best
                  to get on. . . .

1938

* R O B E R T   P E N N   W A R R E N *

PONDY WOODS

THE buzzards over Pondy Woods
Achieve the blue tense altitudes,
Black figments that the woods release,
Obscenity in form and grace,
Drifting high through the pure sunshine
Till the sun in gold decline.

Big Jim Todd was a slick black buck
Laying low in the mud and muck
Of Pondy Woods when the sun went down
In gold, and the buzzards tilted down
A windless vortex to the black-gum trees
To sit along the quiet boughs,
Devout and swollen, at their ease.

By the buzzard roost Big Jim Todd
Listened for hoofs on the corduroy road
Or for the foul and sucking sound
A man's foot makes on the marshy ground.
Past midnight, when the moccasin
Slipped from the log and, trailing in
Its obscured water, broke
The dark algae, one lean bird spoke.

"Nigger, you went this afternoon
For your Saturday spree at the Blue Goose saloon,

So you've got on your Sunday clothes,
On your big splay feet got patent-leather shoes.
But a buzzard can smell the thing you've done;
The posse will get you—run, nigger, run—
There's a fellow behind you with a big shot-gun.
Nigger, nigger, you'll sweat cold sweat
In your patent-leather shoes and Sunday clothes
When down your track the steeljacket goes
Mean and whimpering over the wheat.

"Nigger, your breed ain't metaphysical."
The buzzard coughed. His words fell
In the darkness, mystic and ambrosial.
"But we maintain our ancient rite,
Eat the gods by day and prophesy by night.
We swing against the sky and wait;
You seize the hour, more passionate
Than strong, and strive with time to die—
With Time, the beaked tribe's astute ally.

"The Jew-boy died. The Syrian vulture swung
Remotely above the cross whereon he hung
From dinner-time to supper-time, and all
The people gathered there watched him until
The lean brown chest no longer stirred,
Then idly watched the slow majestic bird
That in the last sun above the twilit hill
Gleamed for a moment at the height and slid
Down the hot wind and in the darkness hid.
Nigger, regard the circumstance of breath:
Non omnis moriar, the poet saith."

Pedantic, the bird clacked its grey beak,
With a Tennessee accent to the classic phrase;

Jim understood, and was about to speak,
But the buzzard drooped one wing and filmed the eyes.

At dawn unto the Sabbath wheat he came,
That gave to the dew its faithless yellow flame
From kindly loam in recollection of
The fires that in the brutal rock once strove.
To the ripe wheat fields he came at dawn.
Northward the printed smoke stood quiet above
The distant cabins of Squiggtown.
A train's far whistle blew and drifted away
Coldly; lucid and thin the morning lay
Along the farms, and here no sound
Touched the sweet earth miraculously stilled.
Then down the damp and sudden wood there belled
The musical white-throated hound.

In Pondy Woods in the August drouth
Lurk fever and the cottonmouth.
And buzzards over Pondy Woods
Achieve the blue tense altitudes,
Drifting high in the pure sunshine
Till the sun in gold decline;
Then golden and hieratic through
The night their eyes burn two by two.

MUSEUMS

MUSEUMS offer us, running from among the 'buses,
  A centrally heated refuge, parquet floors and sarcopha-
    guses,
Into whose tall fake porches we hurry without a sound
Like a beetle under a brick that lies, useless on the ground.
Warmed and cajoled by the silence, the cowed cipher revives,
Mirrors himself in the cases of pots, paces himself by marble
    lives,
Makes believe it was he that was the glory that was Rome,
Soft on his cheek the nimbus of other people's martyrdom,
And then returns to the street, his mind an arena where
    sprawls
Any number of consumptive Keatses and dying Gauls.

THEIR LAST WILL AND TESTAMENT

(With W. H. Auden)

WE, WYSTAN HUGH AUDEN and Louis MacNeice,
  Brought up to speak and write the English tongue
Being led in the eighteenth year of the Western Peace

To the duck-shaped mountainous island with the Danish
    King,
At Melgraseyri in Isafjördardjup
Under the eaves of a glacier, considering

The autumns, personal and public, which already creep
Through city-crowded Europe, and those in want
Who soon must look up at the winter sky and weep.

Do set down this, our will and testament:
Believing man responsible for what he does,
Sole author of his terror and his content.

∗

We leave to Stanley Baldwin, our beloved P.M.,
The false front of Lincoln Cathedral, and a school
Of Empire poets. As for his Cabinet, to them

We leave their National character and strength of will.
To Winston Churchill Ballinrobe's dry harbour
And Randolph, un bel pezzo, in a codicil.

To Sir Maurice Hankey for his secretarial labour
The Vicar of Bray's discretion; and to Lord Lloyd
We leave a flag-day and a cavalry sabre.

To Vickers the Gran Chaco (for agents must be paid),
The Balkan Conscience and the sleepless night we think
The inevitable diseases of their dangerous trade.

*

Item, to I. A. Richards who like a mouse
Nibbles linguistics with the cerebral tooth
We leave a quiet evening in a boarding-house

Where he may study the facts of birth and death
In their inexplicable oddity
And put a shilling in the slot for brains and breath.

And Julian Huxley we leave an ant, a bee,
An axolotl and Aldous; item, to Bert-
rand Russell we leave belief in God (D.V.)

Item, we leave a bottle of invalid port
To Lady Astor; item, the Parthenon
On the Calton Hill to Basil de Selincourt.

Item, we leave the phases of the moon
To Mr. Yeats to rock his bardic sleep;
And to Dr. Cyril Norwood a new spittoon;

And Tubby Clayton can have some gingerpop;
And General O'Duffy can take the Harp That Once
Started and somehow was never able to stop.

We leave a mens sana qui mal y pense
To the Public Schools of England, plus Ian Hay
That the sons of gents may have La Plus Bonne Chance.

*

[265]

And to Sir Oswald (please forgive the stench
Which taints our parchment from that purulent name)
We leave a rather unpleasant word in French.

✳

As for the parts of our bodies in this will

We allot them here as follows: to the Home
For Lost Dogs and Cats our livers and lights,
And our behinds to the Birmingham Hippodrome.

And our four eyes which cannot see for nuts
We leave to all big-game hunters and to all
Apprentices to murder at the butts;

Our feet to hikers when their own feet fail;
To all escapists our Islands of Langerhans;
And to Imperial Chemicals a pail

Of what in us would otherwise join the drains:
The Watch Committee can have our noses and
The British Association can have our brains:

Item, our ears, apt for the slightest sound,
We leave those Statesmen who happen to be debarred
From hearing how the wheels of State run round. . . .

✳

To all the dictators who look so bold and fresh
The midnight hours, the soft wind from the sweeping
     wing
Of madness, and the intolerable tightening of the mesh

[266]

Of history. We leave their marvellous native tongue
To Englishmen, and for our intelligent island pray
That to her virtuous beauties by all poets sung

She add at last an honest foreign policy.
For her oppressed, injured, insulted, and weak
The logic and the passion proper for victory.

We leave our age the quite considerable spark
Of private love and goodness which never leaves
An age, however awful, in the utter dark.

We leave the unconceived and unborn lives
A closer approximation to real happiness
Than has been reached by us, our neighbours or their
      wives.

To those who by office or from inclination use
Authority, a knowledge of their own misdeed
And all the hate that coercion must produce.

For the lost who from self-hatred cannot hide,
Such temporary refuge or engines of escape
From pain as Chance and Mercy can provide

And to the good who know how wide the gulf, how deep
Between Ideal and Real, who being good have felt
The final temptation to withdraw, sit down and weep,

We pray the power to take upon themselves the guilt
Of human action, though still as ready to confess
The imperfection of what can and must be built,
The wish and power to act, forgive, and bless.

PRAYER BEFORE BIRTH

I AM not yet born; O hear me.
    Let not the bloodsucking bat or the rat or the stoat or the
    club-footed ghoul come near me.

I am not yet born, console me.
I fear that the human race may with tall walls wall me,
    with strong drugs dope me, with wise lies lure me,
        on black racks rack me, in blood-baths roll me.

I am not yet born; provide me
With water to dandle me, grass to grow for me, trees to talk
    to me, sky to sing to me, birds and a white light
        in the back of my mind to guide me.

I am not yet born; forgive me
For the sins that in me the world shall commit, my words
    when they speak me, my thoughts when they think me,
        my treason engendered by traitors beyond me,
            my life when they murder by means of my
            hands, my death when they live me.

I am not yet born; rehearse me
In the parts I must play and the cues I must take when
    old men lecture me, bureaucrats hector me, mountains
        frown at me, lovers laugh at me, the white
            waves call me to folly and the desert calls
              me to doom and the beggar refuses
                my gift and my children curse me.

I am not yet born; O hear me,
Let not the man who is beast or who thinks he is God
    come near me.

I am not yet born; O fill me
With strength against those who would freeze my
    humanity, would dragoon me into a lethal automaton,
      would make me a cog in a machine, a thing with
        one face, a thing, and against all those
          who would dissipate my entirety, would
            blow me like thistledown hither and
              thither or hither and thither
                like water held in the
                  hands would spill me.

Let them not make me a stone and let them not spill me.
Otherwise kill me.

* C. DAY LEWIS *

TEMPT ME NO MORE; FOR I

TEMPT me no more; for I
Have known the lightning's **hour,**
The poet's inward pride,
The certainty of power.

Bayonets are closing round.
I shrink; yet I must wring
A living from despair
And out of steel a song.

Though song, though breath be **short,**
I'll share not the disgrace
Of those that ran away
Or never left the base.

Comrades, my tongue can **speak**
No comfortable words,
Calls to a forlorn hope,
Gives work and not rewards.

Oh keep the sickle sharp
And follow still the plough:
Others may reap, though **some**
See not the winter through.

Father, who endest all,
Pity our broken sleep;
For we lie down with tears
And waken but to weep.

And if our blood alone
Will melt this iron earth,
Take it. It is well spent
Easing a saviour's birth.

* J A M E S   A G E E *

RAPID TRANSIT

SQUEALING under city stone
The millions on the millions run,
Every one a life alone,
Every one a soul undone:

There all the poisons of the heart
Branch and abound like whirling brooks
And there through every useless art
Like spoiled meats on a butcher's hooks

Pour forth upon their frightful kind
The faces of each ruined child:
The wrecked demeanors of the mind
That now is tamed, and once was wild.

SUNDAY: OUTSKIRTS OF KNOXVILLE, TENN.

T HERE, in the earliest and chary spring, the dogwood flowers.

Unharnessed in the friendly sunday air
By the red brambles, on the river bluffs,
Clerks and their choices pair.

Thrive by, not near, washed all away by shrub and juniper,
The ford v eight, racing the chevrolet.

They cannot trouble her:

Her breasts, helped open from the afforded lace,
Lie like a peaceful lake;
And on his mouth she breaks her gentleness:

Oh, wave them awake!

They are not of the birds. Such innocence
Brings us to break us only.
Theirs are not happy words.
We that are human cannot hope.
Our tenderest joys oblige us most.
No chain so cuts the bone; and sweetest silk most shrewdly
     strangles.

How this must end, that now please love were ended,
In kitchens, bedfights, silences, women's-pages,
Sickness of heart before goldlettered doors,
Stale flesh, hard collars, agony in antiseptic corridors,
Spankings, remonstrances, fishing trips, orange juice,

Policies, incapacities, a chevrolet,
Scorn of their children, kind contempt exchanged,
Shouted corrections of missed syllables,
Hot water bags, gallstones, falls down stairs,
Old fashioned christmases, suspicions of theft,
Arrangements with morticians taken care of by sons in law,
Small rooms beneath the gables of brick bungalows,
The tumbler smashed, the glance between daughter and husband,
The empty body in the lonely bed
And, in the empty concrete porch, blown ash
Grandchildren wandering the betraying sun

Now, on the winsome crumbling shelves of the horror
God show, God blind these children.

MILLIONS ARE LEARNING HOW

From now on kill America out of your mind.
America is dead these hundred years.
You've better work to do, and things to find:
   Waste neither time nor tears.

See, rather, all the millions and all the land
Mutually shapen as a child of love.
As individual as a hand
   And to be thought highly of.

The wrinkling mountains stay: the master stream
Still soils the Gulf a hundred amber miles:
A people as a creature in a dream
   Not yet awakened, smiles.

Those poisons which were low along the air
Like mists, like mists are lifting. Even now,
Thousands are breathing health in, here and there:
   Millions are learning how.

* O G D E N   N A S H *

Three Rhymes from HARD LINES

1. LINES IN DISPRAISE OF DISPRAISE

I HEREBY bequeath to the Bide-a-Wee Home all people
   who have statistics to prove that a human
Is nothing but a combination of iron and water and
     potash and albumen.
That may very well be the truth
But it's just like saying that a cocktail is nothing
     but ice and gin and vermouth.
People who go around analyzing
Are indeed very tanalizing.
They always want to get at the bottom
Of everything from spring to ottom.
They can't just look at a Rembrandt or a Bartolozzi
And say, Boy! that's pretty hozzi-tozzi!
No, they have to break it up into its component parts
And reconstruct it with blueprints and charts.
My idea is that while after looking around me and even
     at me
     I may not be proud of being a human
I object to having attention called to my iron and water
     and potash and albumen.
In the first place, it's undignified,
And in the second place, nothing by it is signified.
Because it isn't potash etcetera that makes people
     Republicans or Democrats or Ghibellines or Guelphs,

It's the natural perversity of the people themselfs.

No, no, you old analysts, away with the whole kit and
kaboodle of you.

I wouldn't even make mincemeat to give to a poodle of
you.

2. SONG OF THE OPEN ROAD

I think that I shall never see
A billboard lovely as a tree.
Perhaps, unless the billboards fall,
I'll never see a tree at all.

3. AUTRES BÊTES, AUTRES MOEURS

(i)

The fish, when he's exposed to air
Can show no trace of savoir faire
But in the sea regains his balance
And exploits all his manly talents;
The chastest of the vertebrates,
He never even sees his mates,
But when they've finished, he appears
And O.K.'s all their bright ideas.

(ii)

The turtle lives 'twixt plated decks
Which practically conceal its sex.
I think it clever of the turtle
In such a fix to be so fertile.

* S T E P H E N   S P E N D E R *

THE EXPRESS

AFTER the first powerful plain manifesto
The black statement of pistons, without **more fuss**
But gliding like a queen, she leaves the station.
Without bowing and with restrained unconcern
She passes the houses which humbly crowd **outside,**
The gasworks and at last the heavy page
Of death, printed by gravestones in the **cemetery.**
Beyond the town there lies the open country
Where, gathering speed, she acquires mystery,
The luminous self-possession of ships on **ocean.**
It is now she begins to sing—at first quite **low**
Then loud, and at last with a jazzy madness—
The song of her whistle screaming at curves,
Of deafening tunnels, brakes, innumerable bolts.
And always light, aerial, underneath
Goes the elate metre of her wheels.
Steaming through metal landscape on **her lines**
She plunges new eras of wild happiness
Where speed throws up strange shapes, broad **curves**
And parallels clean like the steel of guns.
At last, further than Edinburgh or Rome,
Beyond the crest of the world she reaches **night**
Where only a low streamline brightness

Of phosphorus on the tossing hills is white.
Ah, like a comet through flame she moves entranced
Wrapt in her music no bird song, no, nor bough
Breaking with honey buds, shall ever equal.

I THINK CONTINUALLY OF THOSE WHO
WERE TRULY GREAT

I THINK continually of those who were truly great.
Who, from the womb, remembered the soul's history
Through corridors of light where the hours are suns
Endless and singing. Whose lovely ambition
Was that their lips, still touched with fire,
Should tell of the Spirit clothed from head to foot in
    song.
And who hoarded from the Spring branches
The desires falling across their bodies like blossoms.

What is precious is never to forget
The essential delight of the blood drawn from ageless
    springs
Breaking through rocks in worlds before our earth.
Never to deny its pleasure in the morning simple light
Nor its grave evening demand for love.
Never to allow gradually the traffic to smother
With noise and fog the flowering of the spirit.

Near the snow, near the sun, in the highest fields
See how these names are fêted by the waving grass
And by the streamers of white cloud
And whispers of wind in the listening sky.
The names of those who in their lives fought for life
Who wore at their hearts the fire's centre.
Born of the sun they travelled a short while towards the
    sun,
And left the vivid air signed with their honour.

THE FUNERAL

DEATH is another milestone on their way.
 With laughter on their lips and with winds blowing
 round them
They record simply
How this one excelled all others in making driving belts.

This is festivity, it is the time of statistics
When they record what one unit contributed:
They are glad as they lay him back in the earth
And thank him for what he gave them.

They walk home remembering the straining red flags,
And with pennons of song still fluttering through their
 blood
They speak of the world state
With its towns like brain-centres and its pulsing arteries.

They think how one life hums, revolves and toils,
One cog in a golden and singing hive:
Like spark from fire, its task happily achieved,
It falls away quietly.

No more are they haunted by the individual grief
Nor the crocodile tears of European genius,
The decline of culture
Mourned by scholars who dream of the ghosts of Greek
 boys.

OH YOUNG MEN OH YOUNG COMRADES

OH YOUNG men oh young comrades
it is too late now to stay in those houses
your fathers built where they built you to build to breed
money on money it is too late
to make or even to count what has been made
Count rather those fabulous possessions
which begin with your body and your fiery soul:—
the hairs on your head the muscles extending
in ranges with their lakes across your limbs
Count your eyes as jewels and your valued sex
then count the sun and the innumerable coined light
sparkling on waves and spangled under trees
It is too late to stay in great houses where the ghosts are
 prisoned
—those ladies like flies perfect in amber
those financiers like fossils of bones in coal.
Oh comrades, step beautifully from the solid wall
advance to rebuild and sleep with friend on hill
advance to rebel and remember what you have
no ghost ever had, immured in his hall.

SPIRITUAL EXERCISES
To Cecil Day Lewis

We fly through a night of stars
Whose remote frozen tongues speak
A language of mirrors, mineral Greek
Glittering across space, each to each—
O dream of Venus and Mars,
In a hollow dome of extinct life, far far far from our wars.

I

UNDER their nakedness, they are naked still.
    Within the mind, myths, and the stars, expose
The frailty of their skulls. A new dawn blows
Away the external structure of their will.
    The Universe, by inches, minutes, fills
Their tongues and eyes, where name and image show,
With words and pictures. The days overflow
Minds in which world is conscious. And Time kills.
        Voyaging through their universal fate,
All of these pulsing knots of thought and breath
Join in one thought, though all are separate.
Through aeons and through cities, underneath
Distraction of sword and temple, they await
The lonely naked drama of their death.

II

You were born, must die; were loved, must love.
Born naked; were clothed; yet naked walk
Under your naked dress; naked thoughts move
Hollow, hollow, within clock-talk, star-talk.
    Time and space shall on you feed;

Upon your purple eyes, their distance;
Upon your heart, their clawing need;
Upon your death, lost, lost significance.
There is one fate beneath those ignorances
Into whose separate knots of flesh you're split,
Homunculus of skin and thought and breath;
Chalk-white, gay, pranking skeleton, it
Strums on your gut such songs and merry dances
Amor, o solitude, o seldom death.

III

Since we are what we are, what shall we be
But what we are? We are, we have,
Six feet and seventy years, to see
The light, and then release it for the grave.
We are not worlds, no, nor infinity,
We have no claims on stones, except to prove
In the invention of the human city
Our selves, our breath, our death, our love.
The tower we build soars like an arrow
From the earth's rim into the sky's,
Upwards and downwards in that blazing pond
Climbing and diving from our life, to narrow
The gap between the world shut in the eyes
And the receding space of light beyond.

IV

That which divides, joins again in belief.
We see the invisible knots which bind
The ends of life, where sight at last is blind
And the eye becomes the leaden color of grief.
Each circular life gnaws at its little leaf
Of here and now. Each is bound into one kind.

Only, nature outside, within the mind,
Tempts with its tree each one to be a thief.
      Mortals are not aeons, they are not space,
Not empires, not maps; they have only
Bodies and graves. Yet all the past, the race,
Knowledge and memory, are unfurled
Within each separate head, grown lonely
With time, growing, shedding, the world.

V

The immortal spirit is that single ghost
Of all the time, incarnate in our time,
Which through our breathing skeletons must climb
Within our supple skin to be engrossed.
      Without that ghost within, our lives are lost
Fragments, haunting the earth's rim.
Unless we will it live, that ghost pines, dim,
Lost in our lives; its death, our death, the cost.
      One being, of past, present, futurity,
Seeks within these many-headed wills
To uncage the flame-winged dove in the stone city.
Shut in ourselves, each blind beaked subject kills
His neighbor and himself, and shuts out pity
For that one soaring spirit which fulfills.

VI

I am that witness through whom the whole
Knows it exists. Within my coils of blood,
Whispering under sleep, unfurls the flood
Of stars, battles, the dark and distant pole.
      All that I am I am not. The cold stone
Unfolds an angel for me. On my dreams ride
The timeless legends. The stars outside

[285]

Glitter under my ribs. Being all, I am alone.
      I who say I call that word I
Which is the mirror in which things see
Nothing except themselves. I die.
The things, and the word, still will be.
Upon this word reflections of stars lie,
And that which passes, passes away, is I.

VII

Outside, the external star-tall mountains gleam
Where changeless changing past and future lock
Their fusing streams into an age of rock
Against whose day my days but shadows seem.
      Within my shut skull, flows a historied stream
Of myths, fears, crimes, that chiselling stock
Which hews my limbs out of the daylight block
And makes my lives the slaves of their dead dream.
      The Universe, the dead, humanity, fill
Each world-wide generation with the sigh
That breathes the pattern of their will.
Their sensitive perceiving witness, I,
See mirrored in my consciousness, the ill
Chameleon-colored fool of words, who'll die.

VIII

Transparent light,
Piercing through eyes, through mind, through windows,
Of the body, the will, the house: Your knife
Gleams over interlocked stones, where power's
Fused barriers enclose
Ruinous malicious life
Of internecine, fratricidal strife.
Your fate, bright

With lightning stamped from the dark hours,
Will strike down, unlock, expose
The entrails, fouled will, piteous heart
Of the leaders, the populace, those
Shut in their mind's own night,
Lost and lolling among the shadows.

To the unborn lend your healing powers
To the son returning from the sword-bright wars
Restore his winged steed.
Assist him to rise, demonstrate what towers,
What aeroplanes, what roads, your fluent grace needs.
Tell him he does inherit
The vague past focussed clearly in the present,
Life-stream he must guide through the city
Forward to futurity.
Tell him he does inhabit
His body your body, his spirit your spirit,
And let your purposes his purposes
Unfold through buds of him their flowers;
Through walls he builds and towers
O be your will transparent,
Make his hands shine with your burning roses.

* EUNICE CLARK *

THE PEOPLE HAS NO OBITUARY

DEATH cannot surprise us who are driven
　Century after century through seas of men.
No drought of life is here, no person
Too rare to lose, who cannot be found again.

Partings are not final. No self is past changing
And replacing. Grains from a deep bin,
Male and female we are broadcast. Without ritual
Seed is severed from flower, kith from kin.

Death does not frighten us who read the notices
Of thousands dying. We have won
Only a number by our borning, and another
Long number when the sand has run.

Death is a word the rich love, keening
Over the precise career of a lost one.
We are the seed spent lavishly in cities:
We wander, mourning all but naming none.

Men, women in cities, multitudes, millions,
Receding, increasing without annual plan,
The people is the jungle-soil of heroes, flourishing
When death dries out the special planted man.

* ALFRED HAYES *

THE DEATH OF THE CRANEMAN

HAPPENED like this: it was hot as hell
    That afternoon, sand, stone dust, the sun,
We were in the mountains.
Drinking-water was by the gasoline drum
We were all drinking like fish that day.
He must have come down from the crane
For a drink I guess, a cigarette
Might have done it, blew it bang up, that drum,
Like dynamite been dropped in it.
We came running down from the mountains.
The blacksmith got to him first: gasoline
Had made a bonfire of him, and we shouted
Craneman! Craneman! with the wops talking
Their language, and nobody knowing his name.
Standing there you could see him, a flame
Lighter and yellower than the sunlight,
And burning, hands and feet, his hair on fire,
Getting up from the ground, standing there,
Yelling out of the fire, flame shooting white
In the sunlight: Lemme alone! Lemme alone!
I'm all right!

Well, we get him here and here he dies.
And that's where we buried him out there,
In the goldenrod beyond them pines,

It's a Potter's Field and nobody'd care.
We dug the grave with our drills and hands.
You got to bury a guy somewhere.
Funny I thought as I looked at him
Blackened, with a pair of holes for eyes,
You bury a stiff and there he lies,
And Christ only knows where he come from
And whether there's kids somewhere or a dame,
We buried him like he came in this world,
A stiff, naked, without a name.

From THE AIRMEN

1. LEONARDO'S DREAM

THE Bird flies westward.
Its shadow lengthens
To the shape of a man
Asking a question.
The man turns to stone
And the earth grows hard.

The stalk's sap dries
And the parchment shrivels.
The stones are loosened.
The earth begins to crack.
Though Fall is everywhere
The Bird still flies.

Then the Bird's flight ceases.
The tombs are built
While the dying live
In the shadow of Winter;
Man is gone,
But the crowd increases.

Then comes the Word
Of the Absent Lover:

The candle in the crypt.
The slant-eyed face,
The promise and the curse:
The worship of the Bird.

But the Bird flies on.
As the ritual congeals
And the vaulted stonework
Writhes in boredom,
And the worshippers envy
His aimless freedom,

Comes the birth of Spring.
Born of that fury
In the love of Beauty,
The saint assumes the flesh,
The prince his ermine,
And the scholars sing.

To the cradle of the boy
The Great Bird comes
On a summer morning:
Covering the sky,
The Mother and the Lover,
To make and to destroy.

Wed to art, made half
By terror and by love,
The child's divided soul
Exceeds the well man's wholeness.
But to justify the Bird
He must sacrifice himself.

2. THE BATTLE OF ANGHIARI

Around a blot of ink
Tinctured with chrome and pink,
A jaw begins to sink,
 A face to grow;
Wide as the mouth of Hell,
Bright as a bursting shell,
Horror assumes a yell
 The shape of O.

Tangled in anger's grip
Cleaver and saber rip
At ankle, neck and hip,
 While on the ground
One who has lost his hand
Struggles in vain to stand
Kicking at comrade, and
 Dog licking wound.

Caught in that froth of fright
Steeds and their riders bite,
The very steel hold tight
 In splintering teeth.
Yet, tender, almost gay,
Over the whole scene play
Shadows in green and gray
 And the wind's breath.

There, where the battle's run,
Mother bends over son,
All that she gave him gone,
 And seems to smile:

Expression that sufficed
Lisa, the Virgin, Christ,
Serene in secret tryst,
    —Not love, not guile!

But something so compact
Of every mortal act,
Attackers and attacked,
    One understands
Peace that is more than joy;
Love that cannot destroy;
Smile not of maid or boy
    But Everyman's.

3. TRIAL BY FLIGHT

> *"From the mountain that bears its
> name, the famous Bird will make its
> flight, filling the whole world with
> amazement, all records with its fame,
> and bringing eternal glory to its
> birthplace . . ."*
>
>   —LEONARDO

Poised for that glory on the peak,
The Will is strong, the Flesh is weak;
The breastbone narrow; secular brain
Inexpert in the hurricane;
Not any length of arm or thigh
Sure refuge in the wind-wide sky;
Nor any armor proof for shock
Of body's plunge on upthrust rock.
He stands alone. Though outward-gazing
The fire of his two eyes, blazing,
Smolders within. He has forgot

Mind's precepts: "Do this . . ." "That do not . . ."
Item: "Substance exerts the pressure
Of air against that substance." "Measure
The footstep of a springing man."
"Construct a circular, bladed fan."
Item: "No strip of spring-steel wound
To drum will lift man off the ground."—
But in the heat of his defiance,
Abandoning the old reliance
On tested truth and measured fact
And calculation—vows to act.

Bitterly, lest to human eyes
The secret of his project rise,
Provide a target for their laughing,
Or, worse than that, a common plaything,
He carries nightly, bit by bit,
The wings, the seat where he will sit,
The wired pedals and the fuselage,
A glass-balled inclination gauge,
A parachute with roof of silk,
And last (why not?) a jar of milk
Under his seat, and on his lap
A European landing map.

He who had written: "Man will fly
Securely as he soars most high";
He who had warned that hills with trees
And valleys swept by cross-draughts, ease
The hardiest herons from their course—
With silk for membranes, arms for oars,

And fiercely at his back the breeze,
Exchanges for Experience, Force.

But wait! Suddenly as he kneels
To slip the blocks that hold the wheels,
Behind a cloudbank overhead
The moon slides out, all round and red;
"Only the sun's great light conceals,"
He thinks, "the fact that it is dead;
And what if we deny such light
As mind vouchsafes, before the night
Covers us up? My body found
Crushed in the framework on the ground
—That is no great catastrophe,
For men must die, and I must die.
But should men say: 'He had less love
Than pride, less skill than spite; here's proof
That man was never meant to fly
And science is but vanity'?"

Knowing his safety will insure
No search of that forgotten spur
Under the cliff's head; that below
Only the curious bird will know
The secret that each Spring lays bare
Age after age in melted snow:
Abandoned manhood, lost renown,
The wings in which he might have flown—
With blinding tears upon his eyes,
And clutching at his throat, despair,
He kicks the blocks.
                    It falls . . . It flies!
Twice circling in the tenuous air

And vanishes. But at that crash
Of crumbling tail-work, splintering ash,
Lifting his head, he wildly cries.
For in the wreckage settling there
The passion that pursued him dies.

* O S C A R   W I L L I A M S *

THE SUBWAY

UNDER the church's lawn, in the land of electric clocks,
    The subway train is plunging into the lungs of the rocks:
And as the bald Negro with the glasses reads his *True Story*
And the old woman is quivering behind her morning glory
The inconceivable girl with the timetable, feather and leer,
A mammoth dumpling of sex, is ensconced on the atmosphere.

Beneath the tons of complacence the subway deftly delves
With people sitting satisfied with their incomparable selves:
A child across the way is dangling out of a fairy tale book
Dipping in the advertisements the divining rod of her look:
The dismal fans are languidly stroking the beard of the wind:
Behind the newspaper fronts the sins of thought are sinned.

This is the skin of death and every pore is a face
Pulsating against tomorrow, the vacuum thighs of space:
This is life the story teller, telling endless tales
To keep himself alive as the iron eyelid falls:
This is the explosion chamber, the secret room of the spark
Where the populations whirl with the poured breath of the dark.

A jungle of prongs is scraping the tough hide of the present:
The huge centipede of station leaps at the vein imprisoned:
The subway's galvanized throat is torn into craters of speed:
The sullen meantime is bulging with the ingots of greed:
And what is true is in conspiracy with the thing that seems
And steel continues to scream, so long as man screams.

REFLECTIONS IN AN IRON WORKS

WOULD you resembled the metal you work with,
  Would the iron entered into your souls,
Would you became like steel on your own behalf!
You are still only putty that tyranny rolls
Between its fingers! You makers of bayonets and guns
For your own destruction! No wonder that those
Weapons you make turn on you and mangle and
    murder—
You fools who equip your otherwise helpless foes!

AT THE CENOTAPH

ARE the living so much use
That we need to mourn the dead?
Or would it yield better results
To reverse their roles instead?
The millions slain in the War—
Untimely, the best of our seed?—
Would the world be any the better
If they were still living indeed?
The achievements of such as are
To the notion lend no support;
The whole history of life and death
Yields no scrap of evidence for't.—
Keep going to your wars, you fools, as of yore;
I'm the civilization you're fighting for.

FOR ONE WHO WOULD NOT TAKE HIS LIFE IN HIS
HANDS

ATHLETE, virtuoso,
Training for happiness,
Bend arm and knee, and seek
The body's sharp distress;
For pain is pleasure's cost,
Denial is the route
To speech before the millions
Or personal with the flute.

The ape and great Achilles,
Heavy with their fate,
Batter doors down, strike
Small children at the gate;
Driven by love to this,
As knock-kneed Hegel said,
To seek with a sword for peace
That the child may be lifted from
The recent dead.

"Ladies and Gentlemen," said
The curious Socrates,
"I have asked: What is this life
But a childermass,
As Abraham recognized,

A working with the knife
At animal, maid, and stone
Until we have cut down
All but the soul alone:
Through hate we come to love,
No other means is known."

IN THE NAKED BED, IN PLATO'S CAVE

IN THE naked bed, in Plato's cave,
Reflected headlights slowly slid the wall,
Carpenters hammered under the shaded window,
Wind troubled the window curtains all night long,
A fleet of trucks strained uphill, grinding,
Their freights covered, as usual.
The ceiling lightened again, the slanting diagram
Slid slowly forth.
                          Hearing the milkman's chop,
His striving up the stair, the bottle's chink,
I rose from bed, lit a cigarette,
And walked to the window. The stony street
Displayed the stillness in which buildings stand,
The street-lamp's vigil and the horse's patience.
The winter sky's pure capital
Turned me back to bed with exhausted eyes.

Strangeness grew in the motionless air. The loose
Film grayed. Shaking wagons, hooves' waterfalls,
Sounded far off, increasing, louder and nearer.
A car coughed, starting. Morning, softly
Melting the air, lifted the half-covered chair
From underseas, kindled the looking-glass,
Distinguished the dresser and the white wall.
The bird called tentatively, whistled, called,
Bubbled and whistled, so! Perplexed, still wet
With sleep, affectionate, hungry and cold. So, so,
A son of man, the ignorant night, the travail
Of early morning, the mystery of beginning
Again and again,
                          while History is unforgiven.

* M U R I E L R U K E Y S E R *

CITY OF MONUMENTS

Washington, 1934

BE PROUD you people of these graves
these chiseled words this precedent
From these blind ruins shines our monument.

Dead navies of the brain will sail
stone celebrate its final choice
when the air shakes, a single voice
a strong voice able to prevail:

Entrust no hope to stone although the stone
shelter the root: see too-great burdens placed
with nothing certain but the risk
set on the infirm column of
the high memorial obelisk

erect in accusation sprung against
a barren sky taut over Anacostia:

give over, Gettysburg! a word will shake your glory:
blood of the starved fell thin upon this plain,
this battle is not buried with its slain.

Gravestone and battlefield retire
the whole green South is shadowed dark,

the slick white domes are cast in night.
But uneclipsed above the park

the veteran of the Civil War
sees havoc in the tended graves
the midnight bugles blown to free
still unemancipated slaves

Blinded by chromium or transfiguration
we watch, as through a miscroscope, decay:
down the broad streets the limousines
advance in passions of display.

Air glints with diamonds, and these clavicles
emerge through orchids by whose trailing spoor
the sensitive cannot mistake
the implicit anguish of the poor.

The throats incline, the marble men rejoice
careless of torrents of despair.

Split by a tendril of revolt
stone cedes to blossom everywhere.

BOY WITH HIS HAIR CUT SHORT

SUNDAY shuts down on this twentieth-century evening.
The L passes. Twilight and bulb define
the brown room, the overstuffed plum sofa,
the boy, and the girl's thin hands above his head.
A neighbor's radio sings stocks, news, serenade.

He sits at the table, head down, the young clear neck exposed,
watching the drugstore sign from the tail of his eye;
tattoo, neon, until the eye blears, while his
solicitous tall sister, simple in blue, bending
behind him, cuts his hair with her cheap shears.

The arrow's electric red always reaches its mark,
successful neon! He coughs, impressed by that precision.
His child's forehead, forever protected by his cap,
is bleached against the lamplight as he turns head
and steadies to let the snippets drop.

Erasing the failure of weeks with level fingers,
she sleeks the fine hair, combing: "You'll look fine tomorrow!
You'll surely find something, they can't keep turning you down;
the finest gentleman's not so trim as you!" Smiling, he raises
the adolescent forehead wrinkling ironic now.

He sees his decent suit laid out, new-pressed,
his carfare on the shelf. He lets his head fall, meeting

her earnest hopeless look, seeing the sharp blades split-
    ting,
the darkened room, the impersonal sign, her motion,
the blue vein, bright on her temple, pitifully beating.

CITATION FOR HORACE GREGORY

THESE are our brave, these with their hands in on the
  work,
hammering out beauty upon the painful stone
turning their grave heads passionately finding
truth and alone and each day subtly slain
and each day born.
           Revolves
a measured system, world upon world, stemmed fires
and regulated galaxies behind the flattened head,
behind the immortal skull, ticking eternity
in blood and the symbols of living.

The brass voice speaks in the street
                      STRIKE STRIKE
    the nervous fingers continue elaborately
      drawing consciousness, examining, doing.
Rise to a billboard world of Chesterfield,
Mae West hip-wriggles, Tarzan prowess, the little
nibbling and despicable minds.
                  Here, gentlemen,
here is our gallery of poets:
                Jeffers,
a long and tragic drum-roll beating anger,
sick of a catapulting nightmare world,
Eliot, who lead us to the precipice
subtly and perfectly; there striking an attitude
rigid and ageing on the penultimate step,
the thoughtful man MacLeish who bent his head
feeling the weight of the living; bent, and turned
the grave important face round to the dead.

And on your left, ladies and gentlemen: poets.

Young poets and makers, solve your anguish, see
the brave unmedalled, who dares to shape his mind,
printed with dignity, to the machines of change.
A procession of poets adds one footbeat to the
implacable metric line: the great and unbetrayed
    after the sunlight and the failing yellow,
    after the lips bitten with passion and
    gentle, after the deaths, below
    dance-floors of celebration we turn we turn
these braveries are permanent. These gifts
flare on our lives, clarifying, revealed.

We are too young to see our funerals
in pantomime nightly before uneasy beds,
too near beginnings for this hesitation
obliterated in death or carnival.
Deep into time extend the impersonal stairs,
    established barricades will stand,
before they die the brave have set their hand
on rich particular beauty for their heirs.

* W . H . A U D E N *

IT IS TIME FOR THE DESTRUCTION OF ERROR

IT IS time for the destruction of error.
The chairs are being brought in from the garden,
The summer talk stopped on that savage coast
Before the storms, after the guests and birds:
In sanatoriums they laugh less and less,
Less certain of cure; and the loud madman
Sinks now into a more terrible calm.

The falling leaves know it, the children,
At play on the fuming alkali-tip
Or by the flooded football ground, know it—
This is the dragon's day, the devourer's:
Orders are given to the enemy for a time
With underground proliferation of mould,
With constant whisper and the casual question,
To haunt the poisoned in his shunned house,
To destroy the efflorescence of the flesh,
The intricate play of the mind, to enforce
Conformity with the orthodox bone,
With organized fear, the articulated skeleton.

You whom I gladly walk with, touch,
Or wait for as one certain of good,
We know it, we know that love
Needs more than the admiring excitement of union,

More than the abrupt self-confident farewell,
The heel on the finishing blade of grass,
The self-confidence of the falling root,
Needs death, death of the grain, our death,
Death of the old gang; would leave them
In sullen valley where is made no friend,
The old gang to be forgotten in the spring,
The hard bitch and the riding-master,
Stiff underground; deep in clear lake
The lolling bridegroom, beautiful, there.

LOOK, STRANGER

Look, stranger. at this island now
The leaping light for your delight discovers,
Stand stable here
And silent be,
That through the channels of the ear
May wander like a river
The swaying sound of the sea.

Here at the small field's ending pause
Where the chalk wall falls to the foam, and its tall ledges
Oppose the pluck
And knock of the tide,
And the shingle scrambles after the suck-
ing surf, and the gull lodges
A moment on its sheer side.

Far off like floating seeds the ships
Diverge on urgent voluntary errands;
And the full view
Indeed may enter
And move in memory as now these clouds do,
That pass the harbour mirror
And all the summer through the water saunter.

PROLOGUE

O LOVE, the interest itself in thoughtless Heaven,
  Make simpler daily the beating of man's heart; within,
There in the ring where name and image meet,

Inspire them with such a longing as will make his thought
Alive like patterns a murmuration of starlings
Rising in joy over wolds unwittingly weave;

Here too on our little reef display your power,
This fortress perched on the edge of the Atlantic scarp,
The mole between all Europe and the exile-crowded sea;

And make us as Newton was, who in his garden watching
The apple falling toward England, became aware
Between himself and her of an eternal tie.

For now that dream which so long has contented our will,
I mean, of uniting the dead into a splendid empire,
Under whose fertilising flood the Lancashire moss

Sprouted up chimneys, and Glamorgan hid a life
Grim as a tidal rock-pool's in its glove-shaped valleys,
Is already retreating into her maternal shadow;

Leaving the furnaces gasping in the impossible air,
The flotsam at which Dumbarton gapes and hungers;
While upon wind-loved Rowley no hammer shakes

The cluster of mounds like a midget golf course, graves
Of some who created these intelligible dangerous marvels;
Affectionate people, but crude their sense of glory.

Far-sighted as falcons, they looked down another future;
For the seed in their loins were hostile, though afraid
    of their pride,
And, tall with a shadow now, inertly wait.

In bar, in netted chicken-farm, in lighthouse,
Standing on these impoverished constricting acres,
The ladies and gentlemen apart, too much alone,

Consider years of the measured world begun,
The barren spiritual marriage of stone and water.
Yet, O, at this very moment of our hopeless sigh

When inland they are thinking their thoughts but are
    watching these islands,
As children in Chester look to Moel Fammau to decide
On picnics by the clearness or withdrawl of her tree-
    less crown,

Some possible dream, long coiled in the ammonite's
    slumber
Is uncurling, prepared to lay on our talk and kindness
Its military silence, its surgeon's idea of pain;

And out of the Future, into actual History,
As when Merlin, tamer of horses, and his lords to whom
Stonehenge was still a thought, the Pillars passed

And into the undared ocean swung north their prow,
Drives through the night and star-concealing dawn
For the virgin roadsteads of our hearts an unwavering
    keel.

MUSÉE DES BEAUX ARTS

About suffering they were never wrong,
The Old Masters: how well they understood
Its human position; how it takes place
While someone else is eating or opening a window or just
    walking dully along;
How, when the aged are reverently, passionately waiting
For the miraculous birth, there always must be
Children who did not specially want it to happen, skating
On a pond at the edge of the wood:
They never forgot
That even the dreadful martyrdom must run its course
Anyhow in a corner, some untidy spot
Where the dogs go on with their doggy life and the tor-
    turer's horse
Scratches its innocent behind on a tree.

In Breughel's *Icarus*, for instance: how everything turns
    away
Quite leisurely from the disaster; the ploughman may
Have heard the splash, the forsaken cry,
But for him it was not an important failure; the sun shone
As it had to on the white legs disappearing into the green
Water; and the expensive delicate ship that must have seen
Something amazing, a boy falling out of the sky,
Had somewhere to get to and sailed calmly on.

From FOR THE TIME BEING

1. NARRATOR

IF, ON account of the political situation,
There are quite a number of homes without roofs, and men
Lying about in the countryside neither drunk nor asleep,
If all sailings have been cancelled till further notice,
If it's unwise now to say much in letters, and if,
Under the subnormal temperatures prevailing,
The two sexes are at present the weak and the strong,
That is not at all unusual for the time of the year.
If that were all we should know how to manage. Flood, fire,
The dessication of grasslands, restraint of princes,
Piracy on the high seas, physical pain and fiscal grief,
These after all are our familiar tribulations,
And we have been through them before, many, many times,
As events which belong to the natural world where
The occupation of space is the real and final fact
And time turns round itself in an obedient circle,
They occur again and again but only to pass
Again and again into their formal opposites,
From sword to ploughshare, coffin to cradle, war to work,
So that, taking the bad with the good, the pattern composed
By the ten thousand odd things that can possibly happen
Is permanent in a general sort of way.

Till lately we knew of no other, and between us we seemed
To have what it took—the adrenal courage of the tiger,
The chameleon's discretion, the modesty of the doe,
Or the fern's devotion to spatial necessity:
To practice one's peculiar civic virtue was not

So impossible after all; to cut our losses
And bury our dead was really quite easy: That was **why**
We were always able to say: "We are children of God,
And our Father has never forsaken His people."

But then we were children: That was a moment ago,
Before an outrageous novelty had been introduced
Into our lives. Why were we never warned? Perhaps **we were**
Perhaps that mysterious noise at the back of the brain
We noticed on certain occasions—sitting alone
In the waiting room of the country junction, looking
Up at the toilet window—was not indigestion
But this Horror starting already to scratch Its way in?
Just how, just when It succeeded we shall never know:
We can only say that now It is there and that nothing
We learnt before It was there is now of the slightest use,
For nothing like It has happened before. It's as if
We had left our house for five minutes to mail a letter,
And during that time the living room had changed places
With the room behind the mirror over the fireplace;
It's as if, waking up with a start, we discovered
Ourselves stretched out flat on the floor, watching our
        shadow
Sleepily stretching itself at the window. I mean
That the world of space where events reoccur is still there,
Only now it's no longer real; the real one is nowhere
Where time never moves and nothing can ever happen:
I mean that although there's a person we know all about
Still bearing our name and loving himself as before,
That person has become a fiction; our true existence
Is decided by no one and has no importance to love.

That is why we despair; that is why we should **welcome**
The nursery bogey or the winecellar ghost, why even

The violent howling of winter and war has become
Like a juke-box tune that we dare not stop. We are afraid
Of pain but more afraid of silence; for no nightmare
Of hostile objects could be as terrible as this Void.
This is the Abomination. This is the wrath of God.

2. CHORUS

O where is that immortal and nameless Center from which
          our points of
     definition and death are all equi-distant? Where
The well of our wish to wander, the everlasting fountain
     Of the waters of joy that our sorrow uses for tears?
O where is the garden of Being that is only known in Existence
     As the command to be never there, the sentence by which
Alephs of throbbing fact have been banished into position,
     The clock that dismisses the moment into the turbine of time?

O would I could mourn over Fate like the others, the resolute
          creatures,
     By seizing my chance to regret. The Stone is content
With formal anger and falls and falls; the plants are indignant
     With one dimension only and can only doubt
Whether light or darkness lies in the worse direction; and
          the subtler
     Exiles who try every path are satisfied
With proving that none have a goal: why must Man also
          acknowledge
     It is not enough to bear witness, for even protest is wrong?

Earth is cooled and fire is quenched by his unique excitement
     All answers expire in the clench of his questioning hand,
His singular emphasis frustrates all possible order:
     Alas, his genius is wholly for envy; alas,

The vegetative sadness of lakes, the locomotive beauty
    Of choleric beasts of prey, are nearer than he
To the dreams that deprive him of sleep, the powers that
        compel him to idle,
    To his amorous nymphs and his sanguine athletic gods.

How can his knowledge protect his desire for truth from illu-
        sion?
    How can he wait without idols to worship, without
Their overwhelming persuasion that somewhere, over the high
        hill,
    Under the roots of the oak, in the depths of the sea,
Is a womb or a tomb wherein he may halt to express some
        attainment?
    How can he hope and not dream that his solitude
Shall disclose a vibrating flame at last and entrust him forever
    With its magic secret of how to extemporize life?

* PART FIVE *

        . . . and we have paid
For poetry with living blood. What age
But ours can boast this terrifying truth?
Nor can we minister the antidote
To art, to science or to society
Through more and more and more analysis.
We must not now embroider the confusion;
Toward language we must show the piety
Of simple craftsmen for their wood. I wish
I might agree with Yeats in his opinion
That in our forty years we have produced
More poets of worth than any generation
From 1630 on! Were we so good
These vices of our rime would not be loosed
So carelessly upon us. We would find
More art, more love, more poetry of the kind
That Yeats bequeathed, and less verse of the mind.

KARL SHAPIRO

* RICHARD EBERHART *

NOW IS THE AIR MADE OF CHIMING BALLS

Now is the air made of chiming balls.
The stormcloud, wizened, has rolled its rind away.
Now is the eye with hill and valley laved
And the seeds, assuaged, peep from the nested spray.
The bluebird drops from a bough. The speckled meadow lark
Springs in his lithe array. Fresh air
Blesses the vanished tear; the bunched anguish.
The laughing balls their joyful pleasure tear.
Renewed is the whole world and the sun
Begins to dress with warmth again every thing.
The lettuce in pale burn; the burdock tightening;
And naked necks of craning fledglings.

I WALKED OUT TO THE GRAVEYARD TO SEE THE DEAD

I WALKED out to the graveyard to see the dead
The iron gates were locked, I couldn't get in,
A golden pheasant on the dark fir boughs
Looked with fearful method at the sunset,

Said I, Sir bird, wink no more at me
I have had enough of my dark eye-smarting,
I cannot adore you, nor do I praise you,
But assign you to the rafters of Montaigne.

Who talks with the Absolute salutes a Shadow,
Who seeks himself shall lose himself;
And the golden pheasants are no help
And action must be learned from love of man.

IF I COULD ONLY LIVE AT THE PITCH THAT IS NEAR MADNESS

IF I could only live at the pitch that is near madness
When everything is as it was in my childhood
Violent, vivid, and of infinite possibility:
That the sun and the moon broke over my head.

Then I cast time out of the trees and fields,
Then I stood immaculate in the Ego;
Then I eyed the world with all delight,
Reality was the perfection of my sight.

And time has big handles on the hands,
Fields and trees a way of being themselves.
I saw battalions of the race of mankind
Standing stolid, demanding a moral answer.

I gave the moral answer and I died
And into a realm of complexity came
Where nothing is possible but necessity
And the truth wailing there like a red babe.

THE HUMANIST

HUNTING for the truly human
I looked for the true man
And saw an ape at the fair
With the circle still to square. Learning
Breeds its own ignorance. Fame and power
Demand a rush and pounding.
Those who rush through rush through, and who
Are they but those who rush through?
Yet truth resides in contemplation
And comprehension of contemplation
Not necessarily of Plato. Action explains
A field full of folk and golden football flexions,
Action for actors. Truth through contemplation
Resurrects the truly human,
Makes known the true man
Whom these lines can scan:
But miss his secret final point.
The world is too much in joint. No use
Setting that right, that squaring, that harrying: **for**
The true man lives in mystery
Of God; God his agile soul will see
But he will not see God's majesty,
And that is what makes you and me
Whether man or woman
Neither true nor free
But truly human.

* JOHN WHEELWRIGHT *

FATHER

A<small>N</small> E<small>AST</small> W<small>IND</small> asperges Boston with Lynn's sulphurous brine.
Under the bridge of turrets my father built,—from
    turning sign
of CHEVROLET, out-topping our gilt State House Dome
to burning sign of CARTER'S INK,—drip multitudes
of checker-board shadows. Inverted turreted reflections
sleeping over axle-grease billows, through all directions
cross-cut parliamentary gulls, who toss like gourds.

  Speak. Speak to me again, as fresh as saddle leather
  (Speak; talk again) to a hunter smells of heather.
  Come home. Wire a wire of warning without words.
  Come home and talk to me again, my first friend. Father,
  come home, dead man, who made your mind my home.

* R . P . B L A C K M U R *

ALL THINGS ARE A FLOWING

FLOWERS do better here than peas and beans,
Here nothing men may save can save its mark;
Reason a glitter flowing blues to greens
Beyond the offshore shoals gains ocean dark,
> The poor within us climb the cliff and stare
> Through second eyes and are sea-beggared there.

Sun warms the flesh, but in the marrow, wind;
The seagulls over head and neater tern
Scream woodthrush in the birches out of mind.
How warm a marrow cold enough to burn!
> There is no shelter here, no self-warm lair,
> When every lung eddies the ocean air.

All's weather here and sure, visible change;
It is the permutation of the stone,
The inner crumbling of the mountain range,
Breathes in our air sea râle and moan,
> And this the steadied heart, our own, must bear,
> Suncalm and stormcalm, both in breathless air.

Here men wear natural colours, mostly blue,
Colour of fusion, shade of unison,
Colour of nothingness seen twice, come true,
Colour the gods must be that come undone:
> Colour of succour and mirage, O snare
> And reservoir, death ravens in arrear.

OCTOBER FROST

THE comfortable noise long reading makes
  brimming within the inward ear,
at midnight stopped like a sharp cough,
like a warm garment taken off.
I heard the kitchen slowly creak,
unsettling all its ancient gear,
and saw beyond the lamplight loom
the further darkness of the room.
Life was a draining out, until,
need and custom joining will,
I went outside into the night
where in the moon the frost was bright.

Cold in the temples, cold
lifting the rooted hair,
it is the new cold
quickening the richened air.

Across the mudflats of Flat Bay
the tide was moonwards making way,
and on the water's rising edge
among the eelgrass and salt sedge
the endless rustle and soft clucks
of a thousand feeding ducks
made a warm noise about my ears.
Quiet, I crept between the tiers
of young white birch. But a stick cracked
under my foot and a duck quacked

loudly in the comfortable night.
Like wind breaking, their thousand-flight
soared up. Transfixed on the bright ground
I filled with the full frost of sound.

NOW, ON THIS DAY OF THE FIRST HUNDRED FLOWERS

Now, on this day of the first hundred flowers,
  Fate pauses for us in imagination,
As it shall not ever in reality—
As these swifts that link endless parabolas
Change guard unseen in their secret crevices.
Other anniversaries that we have walked
Along this hillcrest through the black fir forest,
Past the abandoned farm, have been just the same—
Even the fog necklaces on the fencewires
Seem to have gained or lost hardly a jewel;
The annual and diurnal patterns hold.
Even the attrition of the cypress grove
Is slow and orderly, each year one more tree
Breaks ranks and lies down, decrepit in the wind.
Each year, on summer's first luminous morning,
The swallows come back, whispering and weaving
Figure eights around the sharp curves of the swifts,
Plaiting together the summer air all day,
That the bats and owls unravel in the nights.
And we come back, the signs of time upon us,
In the pause of fate, the threading of the year.

HERE I SIT, READING THE STOIC

HERE I sit, reading the Stoic
Latin of Tacitus.
Tiberius sinks in senile
Gloom as Aeneas sank
In the smoky throat of Hades;
And the prose glitters like
A tray of dental instruments.
The toss head president,
Deep in his private catacomb,
Is preparing to pull
The trigger. His secretaries
Make speeches. In ten years
The art of communication
Will be more limited.
The wheel, the lever, the incline,
May survive, and perhaps,
The alphabet. At the moment
The intellectual
Advance guard is agitated
Over the relation
Between the Accumulation
Of Capital and the
Systematic Derangement of
The Senses, and the Right
To Homosexuality.

REMEMBER THAT BREAKFAST ONE NOVEMBER

REMEMBER that breakfast one November—
  Cold black grapes smelling faintly
Of the cork they were packed in,
Hard rolls with hot, white flesh
And thick, honey sweetened chocolate?
And the parties at night; the gin and the tangos?
The torn hair nets, the lost cuff links?
Where have they all gone to,
The beautiful girls, the abandoned hours?
They said we were lost, mad and immoral,
And interfered with the plans of the management.
And today, millions and millions, shut alive
In the coffins of circumstance,
Beat on the buried lids,
Huddle in the cellars of ruins, and quarrel
Over their own fragmented flesh.

ADONIS IN SUMMER

THE Lotophagi with their silly hands
 Haunt me in sleep, plucking at my sleeve;
Their gibbering laughter and blank eyes
Hide on the edge of the mind's vision
In dusty subways and crowded streets.
Late in August, asleep, Adonis
Appeared to me, frenzied and bleeding
And showed me, clutched in his hand, the plow
That broke the dream of Persephone.
The next day, regarding the scorched grass
In the wilting park, I became aware
That beneath me, beneath the gravel
And the hurrying ants, and the loam
And the subsoil, lay the glacial drift,
The Miocene jungles, the reptiles
Of the Jurassic, the cuttlefish
Of the Devonian, Cambrian
Worms, and the mysteries of the gneiss;
Their histories folded, docketed
In darkness; and deeper still the hot
Black core of iron, and once again
The inscrutable archaic rocks,
And the long geologic ladder,
And the living soil and the strange trees,
And the tangled bodies of lovers
Under the strange stars.
 And beside me,
A mad old man, plucking at my sleeve.

* WILLIAM EMPSON *

IGNORANCE OF DEATH

THEN there is this civilizing love of death, by which
Even music and painting tell you what else to love.
Buddhists and Christians contrive to agree about death

Making death their ideal basis for different ideals.
The communists however disapprove of death
Except when practical. The people who dig up

Corpses and rape them are I understand not reported.
The Freudians regard the death-wish as fundamental,
Though the 'clamour of life' proceeds from its rival 'Eros'.

Whether you are to admire a given case for making less clamour
Is not their story. Liberal hopefulness
Regards death as a mere border to an improving picture.

Because we have neither hereditary nor direct knowledge of death
It is the trigger of the literary man's biggest gun
And we are happy to equate it to any conceived calm.

Heaven me, when a man is ready to die about something
Other than himself, and is in fact ready because of that,
Not because of himself, that is something clear about himself.

Otherwise I feel very blank upon this topic,
And think that though important, and proper for anyone to bring
    up,
It is one that most people should be prepared to be blank upon.

* JOSE GARCIA VILLA *

BE BEAUTIFUL, NOBLE, LIKE THE ANTIQUE ANT

BE BEAUTIFUL, noble, like the antique ant,
Who bore the storms as he bore the sun,
Wearing neither gown nor helmet,
Though he was archbishop and soldier:
Wore only his own flesh.

Salute characters with gracious dignity:
Though what these are is left to
Your own terms. Exact: the universe is
Not so small but these will be found
Somewhere. Exact: they will be found.

Speak with great moderation: but think
With great fierceness, burning passion:
Though what the ant thought
No annals reveal, nor his descendants
Break the seal.

Trace the tracelessness of the ant,
Every ant has reached this perfection.
As he comes, so he goes,
Flowing as water flows,
Essential but secret like a rose.

HORAE

I

IT PALES. As if a look
Invisible, came in the east.
In some far vale a rooster
Expels his cry of life.

Now dark but not formless
On the grey meads the trees
Lean and are looming soft.

In those towers of night
Ruffling things awake
Their declaration and chuckle.

Starpoint fades from the dew.

To every mile that sleeps
The cock's barbaric cry
And the wind comes cool.

Shiver of day break.

II

Now air, gentle pillager
In the citadels of summer,
Lifts a leaf here and there.

Some holds the cornfield still
In his dream of the real.

From a wavering of bees
One droning steers away,
Elated in his golden car.
A cow stumbles and streams,
Reaching the meadow.

Tiny brutality in the grass
Manipulates the foe
Sawing and champing. Oh, soundless.

What burning contemplation
Rests in these distances?
What is seen by the leaves
Mirrored as in fair water
Millionfold?—as the eye of man
Finds itself in myriads.

III

The limber shadow is longer.
Air moves now breathing
In the plumes of corn.

Gnats on their elastics
Are busy with evening.
Heavy with night the owl
Floats through the forest.

Shadow takes all the grass.

Beyond indigo mountains
Golden sheaves are fastened

Lightly on the infinite
West. What joy or feast
Has these for ornament?
What reclining host?

They sink away in peace.

MEMENTOES

THE inland cities on the rivers
  Stream into the clear morning.
Rust and slag, junk in the marshes,
Where the wind shivers the tall weeds.
From the gliding Pullman see
Steamy light on the weather vanes,
Golden crosses on distant steeples
Risen above the smoke and dew.
A child in a dirty shift watches
From a tumbledown garden or threadbare
Screen door; wide-eyed pickaninnies
Curl their toes in the sweet air.
Slower with swaying jerks and turning
A long curve between factory windows,
Blackened fences, cindery yards,
Enter the early hustle of men:
The grey drayhorses smiting, backing,
On Market Street; moustachioed
Entrepreneurs with golden fobs
Brisk on the cobbles; rumble and yell.

The lumber schooners pass on the lake
And the slow barges from the north
Pass in the offshore bite of whitecaps:
Superior, Erie, Michigan,
Loaded with ore from the wilderness
For the furnaces of Pennsylvania,
Loaded with grain from the cool prairies,
Passing the evergreen shores and the beaches.

The wind out of the south blows over
The stony mansions in the sunlight,
A browner haze, bringing the odor
Of blood and offal. The long and short-horns
Crowd from the West, from the lone corrals
Of Kansas, Texas, high Wyoming.
There the sun makes the land shimmer,
Tawny and pale, the vast rangeland;
There the smoke from a locomotive
Worms up slowly all morning long.

Trainmen and rangeriders: remember
The water tanks, the peeling clapboards,
The silent noon of desert towns;
Remember the hot nights and whiskey
And silver dollars on the tables;
Remember the women and the badman
Out of the badlands, wiping his mouth;
Goodbye, you fast thumbs on the sixgun,
Knee-ers and rabbit-punchers, dusty
Bastards in from the plains with pay;
Goodbye Belle and Jenny and Mister
LaPorte from St. Louis with yellow vests;
Goodbye to buckboards and Winchesters,
To the hobbled ponies, the trading post.
Cody, pray for us; Wister, bless us;
So long, strangers, so long.

II

Patent leathers and white kid gloves:
Lovely, humiliated or gay,
Arrogant or dreaming with the dance,
They move in grace between the mirrors,

In candle light. The cool odor,
"Cologne," breathes above "bodices,"
And the ever-so-silken, continual
Draping, re-draping of skirts. Hushabye.
Smiles of trust or invitation
Whirl away on lustrous lapels
Laughing under the fiddles. Comely
Shoulders, powdery backs, warm
Flanks under ruffles, smooth elbows,
All are turning in the courteous
Viennese music, end of the century.
Newport, Narragansett, Richmond,
Boston, New York and Baltimore,
Far into morning. Sheering the snow,
The cutters at a good clip jingle
Uphill running into starlight,
Bundled and singing. Stilly night.

Goodbye to all your tears, sweethearts,
And your stern gentlemen at home;
Goodbye to the shy lieutenant, the gigglers,
The convents and the musical studies,
The crushes and the exclamations;
Goodbye to the box at the theatre
And the slow fanning in the gaslight;
To summers at Sheepshead Bay, to muslins,
To bare forearms and serenaders,
Ribbons and billets-doux, goodbye.

Milly and Daisy and Henrietta
And Isabel, beauties, pray for us
In your fresh heaven, on those lawns
By Thames under the copper beeches,

Behind the iron gates in ducal
Shadow: ambassadors! At Venice
Where the old and weary and splendid
Spiders of the world devoured you,
Who were not ever in anything
Quite so correct as they. Sisters,
Mothers later corrupted, maidens
Living like men into bewilderment
With a stiff upper lip: you masks
At operas and marriages,
Matriarchs with knobby canes,
Goodbye, goodbye gentlewomen.

* KENNETH PATCHEN *

HE THOUGHT OF MAD ELLEN'S RAVINGS AND OF THE WRETCHED SKELETON ON THE ROCK

IT's more than a hundred years now . . .
That yellow hair, the white throat, the witching thighs
Gone! Left to rot in the wind and blue-assed water.
Tell me about your cities, your flame-footed ships,
Your proud maps and monkey-dung; tell me of conquest,
Tell me how the blacks tugged your fat around
I don't want to hear it. I want to see her face again
I want to tell her not to be afraid. God! I don't want this
I want to hear her voice. I want to take her into my arms
I don't want to fight their wars. I don't want to kill anyone
And I don't want anyone to kill me. I don't want people
To come smelling round me like dogs with their damn tricks.

There's a huge house on the sand
And every day the gardener should water
The munition maker who lives there

Fires burn in a few places . . .
Ellen's wanton beauty . . . lost in the black water

Have you heard the mad fiddles?
Jig it, Death; slap it round, God
I love the wikgirl, the sly moodus,
The stinking honker; make mine

You, O grinning angel, my gregbird,
Luklove, higbard, no holes barred babe.
Turtle in the bough and waterhawk hello.

Here rixnag, hi piphog, riding the bubsea,
Reeling like a soplad after this dohgal,
Hark my hundipper, pimpgetter whole.
Smear it up, Death; knock it down, Godie-Boy.

Tell me about the legend that can never die.
Were there proud songs? was there singing?
Christ! I don't want this. I want to hear her voice
I want her arms to go round me and the sea howling at another
    coast—
With all the lost dreams of men watching us and not crying

Flames hollow the face of our humble song

THE CHARACTER OF LOVE SEEN AS A SEARCH FOR THE LOST

You, the woman; I, the man; this, the world:
And each is the work of all.

There is the muffled step in the snow; the stranger;
The crippled wren; the nun; the dancer; the Jesus-wing
Over the walkers in the village; and there are
Many beautiful arms about us and the things we know.

See how those stars tramp over heaven on their sticks
Of ancient light: with what simplicity that blue
Takes eternity into the quiet cave of God, where Caesar
And Socrates, like primitive paintings on a wall,
Look, with idiot eyes, on the world where we two are.

You, the sought for; I, the seeker; this, the search:
And each is the mission of all.

For greatness is only the drayhorse that coaxes
The built cart out; and where we go is reason.
But genius is an enormous littleness, a trickling
Of heart that covers alike the hare and the hunter.

How smoothly, like the sleep of a flower, love,
The grassy wind moves over night's tense meadow:
See how the great wooden eyes of the forest
Stare upon the architecture of our innocence.

You, the village; I, the stranger; this, the road:
And each is the work of all.

Then, not that man do more, or stop pity; but that he be
Wider in living; that all his cities fly a clean flag . . .
We have been alone too long, love; it is terribly late
For the pierced feet on the water and we must not die now.

Have you wondered why all the windows in heaven were broken?
Have you seen the homeless in the open grave of God's hand?
Do you want to acquaint the larks with the fatuous music of war?

There is the muffled step in the snow; the stranger;
The crippled wren; the nun; the dancer; the Jesus-wing
Over the walkers in the village; and there are
Many desperate arms about us and the things we know.

THE GRAND PALACE OF VERSAILLES

A N ELEPHANT made of cotton . . .
Towers of lace under which satin-heeled
Gentlemen sit, playing with the bustles
Of slightly desiccated Grandes Damns.
Good morning, Louis; it's a fine day
In the mirror.

A chaise longue carved
Out of the living body of a white leopard . . .
Spools of silk placed in buckets
Of gilt milk . . . A three-headed dancer
Prancing to the music of a little bell
Languidly swung by a Negro with a hairlip.
Two visiting kings having their canes reheaded,
While a painter to the court tints their eyebrows
With the juice of mildly sickening berries.
What does Salvador Ernst Matta, Louis?
It's a fine day in the mirror.

It must be amusing to be poor, n'est-ce pas?

WHAT IS THE BEAUTIFUL?

THE narrowing line.
Walking on the burning ground.
The ledges of stone.
Owlfish wading near the horizon.
Unrest in the outer districts.

Pause.

And begin again.
Needles through the eye.
Bodies cracked open like nuts.
Must have a place.
Dog has a place.

Pause.

And begin again.
Tents in the sultry weather.
Rifles hate holds.
Who is right?
Was Christ?
Is it wrong to love all men?

Pause.

And begin again.
Contagion of murder.
But the small whip hits back.
This is my life, Caesar.
I think it is good to live.

Pause.

And begin again.
Perhaps the shapes will open.
Will flying fly?
Will singing have a song?
Will the shapes of evil fall?
Will the lives of men grow clean?
Will the power be for good?
Will the power of man find its sun?
Will the power of man flame as a sun?
Will the power of man turn against death?
Who is right?
Is war?

Pause.

And begin again.
A narrow line.
Walking on the beautiful ground.
A ledge of fire.
It would take little to be free.
That no man hate another man,
Because he is black;
Because he is yellow;
Because he is white;
Or because he is English;
Or German;
Or rich;
Or poor;
Because we are everyman.

Pause.

And begin again.
It would take little to be free.
That no man live at the expense of another.
Because no man can own what belongs to all.
Because no man can kill what all must use.
Because no man can lie when all are betrayed.
Because no man can hate when all are hated.

And begin again.
I know that the shapes will open.
Flying will fly, and singing will sing.
Because the only power of man is in good.
And all evil shall fail.
Because evil does not work,
Because the white man and the black man,
The Englishman and the German,
Are not real things.
They are only pictures of things.
Their shapes like the shapes of the tree
And the flower, have no lives in names or signs;
They are their lives, and the real is in them.
And what is real shall have life always.

Pause.

I believe in the truth.
I believe that every good thought I have,
All men shall have.
I believe that what is best in me,
Shall be found in every man.
I believe that only the beautiful
Shall survive on the earth.
I believe that the perfect shape of everything
Has been prepared;

And, that we do not fit our own
Is of little consequence.
Man beckons to man on this terrible road.
I believe that we are going into the darkness now;
Hundreds of years will pass before the light
Shines over the world of all men . . .
And I am blinded by its splendor.

Pause.

And begin again

* DYLAN THOMAS *

ESPECIALLY WHEN THE OCTOBER WIND

ESPECIALLY when the October wind
With frosty fingers punishes my hair,
Caught by the crabbing sun I walk on fire
And cast a shadow crab upon the land,
By sea's side, hearing the noise of birds,
Hearing the raven cough in winter sticks,
My busy heart who shudders as she talks
Sheds the syllabic blood and drains her words.

Shut, too, in a tower of words, I mark
On the horizon walking like the trees
The wordy shapes of women, and the rows
Of the star-gestured children in the park.
Some let me make you of the vowelled beeches,
Some of the oaken voices, from the roots
Of many a thorny shire tell you notes,
Some let me make you of the water's speeches.

Behind a pot of ferns the wagging clock
Tells me the hour's word, the neural meaning
Flies on the shafted disc, declaims the morning
And tells the windy weather in the cock.
Some let me make you of the meadow's signs;
The signal grass that tells me all I know
Breaks with the wormy winter through the eye.
Some let me tell you of the raven's sins.

Especially when the October wind
(Some let me make you of autumnal spells,
The spider-tongued, and the loud hill of Wales)
With fist of turnips punishes the land,
Some let me make you of the heartless words.
The heart is drained that, spelling in the scurry
Of chemic blood, warned of the coming fury.
By the sea's side hear the dark-vowelled birds.

EARS IN THE TURRETS HEAR

Ears in the turrets hear
Hands grumble on the door,
Eyes in the gables see
The fingers at the locks.
Shall I unbolt or stay
Alone till the day I die
Unseen by stranger-eyes
In this white house?
Hands, hold you poison or grapes?

Beyond this island bound
By a thin sea of flesh
And a bone coast,
The land lies out of sound
And the hills out of mind.
No bird or flying fish
Disturbs this island's rest.

Ears in this island hear
The wind pass like a fire,
Eyes in this island see
Ships anchor off the bay.
Shall I run to the ships
With the wind in my hair,
Or stay till the day I die
And welcome no sailor?
Ships, hold you poison or grapes?

Hands grumble on the door,
Ships anchor off the bay,

Rain beats the sand and slates.
Shall I let in the stranger,
Shall I welcome the sailor,
Or stay till the day I die?

Hands of the stranger and holds of the ships,
Hold you poison or grapes?

THE HAND THAT SIGNED THE PAPER FELLED A CITY

THE hand that signed the paper felled a city;
Five sovereign fingers taxed the breath,
Doubled the globe of dead and halved a country;
These five kings did a king to death.

The mighty hand leads to a sloping shoulder,
The finger joints are cramped with chalk;
A goose's quill has put an end to murder
That put an end to talk.

The hand that signed the treaty bred a fever,
And famine grew, and locusts came;
Great is the hand that holds dominion over
Man by a scribbled name.

The five kings count the dead but do not soften
The crusted wound nor pat the brow;
A hand rules pity as a hand rules heaven;
Hands have no tears to flow.

AND DEATH SHALL HAVE NO DOMINION

A ND death shall have no dominion.
  Dead men naked they shall be one
With the man in the wind and the west moon;
When their bones are picked clean and the clean bones gone,
They shall have stars at elbow and foot;
Though they go mad they shall be sane,
Though they sink through the sea they shall rise again;
Though lovers be lost love shall not;
And death shall have no dominion.

And death shall have no dominion.
Under the windings of the sea
They lying long shall not die windily;
Twisting on racks when sinews give way,
Strapped to a wheel, yet they shall not break;
Faith in their hands shall snap in two,
And the unicorn evils run them through;
Split all ends up they shan't crack;
And death shall have no dominion.

And death shall have no dominion.
No more may gulls cry at their ears
Or waves break loud on the seashores;
Where blew a flower may a flower no more
Lift its head to the blows of the rain;
Though they be mad and dead as nails,
Heads of the characters hammer through daisies;
Break in the sun till the sun breaks down,
And death shall have no dominion.

SONNET

to my mother

Most near, most dear, most loved and most far,
Under the window where I often found her
Sitting as huge as Asia, seismic with laughter,
Gin and chicken helpless in her Irish hand,
Irresistible as Rabelais but most tender for
The lame dogs and hurt birds that surround her,—
She is a procession no one can follow after
But be like a little dog following a brass band.

She will not glance up at the bomber or condescend
To drop her gin and scuttle to a cellar,
But lean on the mahogany table like a mountain
Whom only faith can move, and so I send
O all my faith and all my love to tell her
That she will move from mourning into morning.

MUNICH ELEGY NUMBER 7

NEVERTHELESS when the hands cross at midnight and noon
  O golden oil spills and from the wheels' mesh
Time produces its patterns of fate on the flesh,
And I shall fall out like golden oil from the clash.
Not then, though, the axle cracks or the wheels veer
    To miss my skull—
I feel the jewelled rims riding up my skin
To leave me drawn and quartered in the rear.

  O may I mourn the mathematics of man
Who when alone is lovely as the solitary tree
Evolving existence in an algebra of leaves
Against the thunderstorm and the appalling flash:
    He is a magnificent one.
But the many of man makes darkness and deceives
Each other with shadow, so that none can see
    The human for the flesh.

    Where shall the unicorn rest
    But in this green breast, where
Mystery is moss and charity is care?
Where else shall sleep the innocent hind
    But in this hand,
Or the lizard and snake lonely from danger
    But along this finger?

Also Sheffield and South Shields shall rust and rot,
    Northumberland crumble, and Durham moulder,
Without the forge of his forehead to keep them hot
    And his back to shoulder them.

Europe, the jig-saw puzzle, without his great grip
    Collapses through the map,
And mad America, without his grand insanity,
    Be sane as a cemetery.

But blood's on his head and a gun's in his hand:—
    It's a suicide that he also threatens;
With a shot of war to put a stop to his grief,
    Whose monument is Europe:
Where the broken column and the laurel garland,
The violin that wails as the evening darkens,
The capital cities lying under gas like a wreath,
    Entomb his hope.

Therefore be generous among friends with kisses,
    Hold parties of domestic dance and song—
    O make the doomed roof ring!
Join me in celebrating the occasions of bliss
That turned a condemned home to a ballroom
Ballooned with laughter and ribboned with love.
    The lights will go out soon
And the sound of the mooning bomber drone above.

* D U N S T A N   T H O M P S O N *

MEMORARE

REMEMBER, at this moment, O somewhere
The plane falls through the indifferent air,
No longer flying the about to be dying
Pilot to any over-the-border disaster, but lying
Like the boyhood toy, by bad luck destroyed.
      The lost lads are gone
      God grace them

Remember how, even now, when the ship sinks,
The sailor, paler than a pearl, only thinks,
Diving through destiny to be invested with coral,
Of himself—saved from the sea caves where no laurel
Lives—and so gives up a gay ghost at land's end.
      The lost lads are gone
      God grace them

Remember, also, as the soldier in amber fires
Too late, his nerves, swerving on exploded tires,
Plunge through the past to exhaust their history
In the silent, never again to be violent mystery,
Which the womb worshiped more than the hero's tomb.
      The lost lads are gone
      God grace them

Remember—do not forget—the numbered, anonymous spy's
Suddenly surprised, not quite clever enough disguise,

And see him, neither gallant nor grim, obeying
The code, sans cipher, of the classroom saying:
O happy and hallowed to die for a flag.
> *The lost lads are gone*
> *God grace them*

Remember the enemy, always remembering you,
Whose heartbreaks heartbeat defeats, who too,
Shedding tears during prayers for the dead, discovers
Himself forever alone, the last of his lovers
Laid low for love, and O at your mercy, murdered.
> *The lost lads are gone*
> *God grace them*

* RALPH GUSTAFSON *

TWO SONNETS

1. ON THE STRUMA MASSACRE

Now as these slaughtered seven hundreds hear
   The vulgar sennet of thine angel sound,
Grant, in thy love, that they may see that ground
Whose promised acres holy footsteps bear.
For they of only this made credulous prayer—
Even for whom thy Son the tempest bound
And waters walked O not those same where, drowned,
Driven by plausible tongues and mute despair,
These faithful roll! No not as they, with board
And spike, who took Thy sweetness then, do we—
Studied in ignorance, and knowing Thee,
For Thine archaic crown of thorns and cord,
Statistics are become Thine agony,
The ocean designate, Gabbatha, Lord.

2. "S.S.R., LOST AT SEA."—*The Times*

What heave of grapnels will resurrect the fabric
Of him, oceans drag, whereof he died,
Drowning sheer fathoms down, liquid to grab on—
Sucked by the liner, violence in her side?
Of no more sorrow than a mottled Grief
In marble. These fantastic in the murk,
Where saltwhite solitary forests leaf,

He swings: the dark anonymously works.
For who shall count the countless hands and limbs
In ditch and wall and wave, dead, dead
In Europe: touch with anguished name and claim
And actual tear, what must be generally said?
O let the heart's tough riggings salvage him,
Only whose lengths can grapple with these dead.

* L A W R E N C E   D U R R E L L *

IN ARCADIA

B Y DIVINATION came the Dorians,
Under a punishment composed an arch.
They invented this valley, they taught
The rock to flow with odourless water.

Fire and a brute art came among them.

Rain fell, tasting of the sky.
Trees grew, composing a grammar.
The river, the river you see was brought down
By force of prayer upon this fertile floor.

Now small skills: the fingers laid upon
The nostrils of flutes, the speech of women
Whose tutors were the birds; who singing
Now civilised their children with the kiss.

Lastly, the tripod sentenced them.

Ash closed on the surviving sons.
The brown bee memorised here, rehearsed
Migration from an inherited habit.
All travellers recorded an empty zone.

Between rocks 'O death,' the survivors.
O world of bushes eaten like a moon,
Kissed by the awkward patience of the ant.
Within a concave blue and void of space.

Something died out by this river: but it seems
Less than a nightingale ago.

* R O Y   F U L L E R *

JANUARY 1940

SWIFT had pains in his head.
Johnson dying in bed
Tapped the dropsy himself.
Blake saw a flea and an elf.
Tennyson could hear the shriek
Of a bat. Pope was a freak.
Emily Dickinson stayed
Indoors for a decade.
Water inflated the belly
Of Hart Crane, and of Shelley.
Coleridge was a dope.
Southwell died on a rope.
Byron had a round white foot.
Smart and Cowper were put
Away. Lawrence was a fidget.
Keats was almost a midget.
Donne, alive in his shroud,
Shakespeare, in the coil of a cloud,
Saw death very well as he
Came crab-wise, dark and massy.
I envy not only their talents
And fertile lack of balance
But the appearance of choice
In their sad and fatal voice.

A WRY SMILE

THE mess is all asleep, my candle burns.
I hear the rain sharp on the iron roof
And dully on the broad leaves by the window.
Already someone moans, another turns
And, clear and startling, cries "Tell me the truth."

The candle throws my shadow on the wall
And gilds my books: tonight I'd like to bring
The poets from their safe and paper beds,
Show them my comrades and the silver pall
Over the airfield, ask them what they'd sing.

Not one of them has had to bear such shame,
Been tortured so constantly by government,
Has had to draw his life out when the age
Made happiness a revolution, fame
Exile, and death the whimsy of a sergeant.

But without envy I remember them,
And without pity look at my condition:
I give myself a wry smile in the mirror
—The poets get a quizzical ahem.
They reflect time, I am the very ticking:

No longer divided—the unhappy echo
Of a great fault in civilization; inadequate,
Perhaps, and sad, but strictly conscious no one
Anywhere can move, nothing occur,
Outside my perfect knowledge or my fate.

THE STATUE

THE noises of the harbour die, the smoke is petrified
Against the thick but vacant, fading light, and shadows slide
From under stone and iron, darkest now. The last birds glide.

Upon this black-boned, white-splashed, far receding vista of grey
Is an equestrian statue, by the ocean, trampling the day,
Its green bronze flaked like petals, catching night before the bay.

Distilled from some sad, endless, sordid period of time,
As from the language of disease might come a consummate rhyme,
It tries to impose its values on the port and on the lime—

The droppings that by chance and from an uncontrollable
And savage life have formed a patina upon the skull;
Abandoned, have blurred a bodied vision once thought spare but
full—

On me, as authority recites to boys the names of queens.
Shall I be dazzled by the dynasties, the gules and greens,
The unbelievable art, and not recall their piteous means?

Last night I sailed upon that sea whose starting place is here,
Evaded the contraptions of the enemy, the mere
Dangers of water, saw the statue and the plinth appear.

Last night between the crowded, stifling decks I saw a man,
Smoking a big curved pipe, who contemplated his great wan
And dirty feet while minute after tedious minute ran—

This in the city now, whose floor is permanent and still,
Among the news of history and sense of an obscure will,
Is all the image I can summon up, my thought's rank kill;

As though there dominated this sea's threshold and this night
Not the raised hooves, the thick snake neck, the profile, and the
    might,
The wrought, eternal bronze, the dead protagonist, the fight,

But that unmoving, pale but living shape that drops no tears
Ridiculous and haunting, which each epoch reappears,
And is what history is not. O love, O human fears!

✳ R U T H   H E R S C H B E R G E R ✳

HYMN TO TEXTURE

DELIVER us into the hands of quartz,
    Of stalks, of surfaces, give us to color,
To sea-green and to grass, to blue,
When trapped in our human life, touch fur.

Place hovering palm on the wet of lilies,
The nails of our claws on rimless silk,
Give us up, we will give ourselves, to rapture,
Swaying like drunkards in sight of milk.

Texture of ozone, and lift of meadows,
Tactual wonder of clay toned dust,
Give us the lesson: inanimate nature
Resolves the animate lust.

Meanwhile our ears on a baffled skull
Receive the blistering shot: give touch
To the oval cheek of a deadly shell,
Caress the unknown future.

IN PANELLED ROOMS

THE love-grip, first excited by the eye,
  Fastens its pleasing mortar; then the thigh
Moves like a tractor rocketing to fate.
The head reclines, the mind will gladly wait;
But pearly blood and sockets made of gum,
Less than immobile, seek the pleasing hum
Of fall and exaltation. Eyebrows made
Of ships and shaped like islands cannot shade
The walnut hull of eyes, the husk of brown
Under whose cover lies the kernel-down,
The certainty of love. Each jointed knee
Strolls in the wake of new fraternity,
And wishes elbows well; itself does grace
To flesh and bone, extracting from its place
All that made Solomon declare of myrrh,
Frankincense, flowers, upon touching her.

THE LUMBERYARD

WE WATCHED our love burn with the lumberyard,
Bats in their wheeling showed our crazéd sense,
We stood in fields where weeds with chiggers scrambled,
And stood the heat flush in our face, immense.

Softly the crowd acclaimed the devastation,
And we, we smiled to see the embers twist,
Tottering towers and poles with flashing wires.
We shifted feet when shifting structures kissed.

Up in the sky the sparks were red stars shuttling,
Planes with a scouter's appetite hung by.
And at our backs the Negro huts were lit
With yellow mist, a ghostly gayety.

Sound above all: the cracking and the crocked,
As bones that, whetted by the warmer flames,
Edged into death, until the crimson glow
Vanquished the knotted amber boards, the names.

All banished, all decided, all cast in;
Far back beyond, the trees made silver white
By steaming flames, rose as cold piles of cloud
To cool this mirror of the blazing night.

And we beheld, we watched, as drunk as all,
And gladdened when the bursting peaked and sprung,
Rejoiced to see the threat of fire win,
And sang to see the worthy timbers wrung.

We watched our love burn with the lumberyard,
Magnificent the sight, the sin, the shame,
The vice profusely lavished; wheeled the bats
Silent as we, but crazed, crazed as the flame.

* WILLIAM ABRAHAMS *

THE MUSEUM

1. CLASSIC

WHO rose up like a goddess from the sea,
A vision of beauty to haunt so many houses,
Dies in a marble stasis, gallery goddess.
And only the prurient children will discern
How wet flanks gleamed in the sunlight, the very waves
Shone admiration through the racing foam.

It comes to this: the bleak memorial halls,
The guide in sour serge, the tired feet,
And faint through the mausoleum walls the sound
Of streetcars. These patterns have their meanings far
From the grove of olive trees, the passionate dancers
Hot in the frenzy of Etruscan summer.
It comes to this: the middle-aged on camp chairs
Sketching those marble limbs that once were love's.

2. RENAISSANCE

Princeling in velvet and furs, the fairhaired boy
With a sly smile and a goblet of gold wine.
Also the costumed dwarf, the chained falcon,
The spotted hound arrogant by the throne.
Such profusion of wealth, such suffocating beauty!
And all set down with a genius for the rich
Self-confident detail. But time is traitorous.

Easily the baize walls confer their apathy.
Time closes in: an anonymity
Of dust and varnish. The sly smile will induce
No further rubies. No emeralds will mingle
With the stuffed bird, the manuscripts swearing
Perpetual devotion. No more gold collars
To please the almost life-like hunting bitch.

3. 19TH CENTURY

A grace like swans, and swanlike gleaming at
The stage's centre, turn and turn again
Those beautiful dancers. O simple to understand
The fashionable painter disowning his faubourg
Of expensive portraits. Simple to understand
How in an age of dying gods this grace
Is godlike. Fairer than swans they float in the blue light,
Over the blue lake hover in a white radiance,
Glide and fall, rise up, circle, like swans,
While legato the music calls each swanlike gesture.

O at the instant the complex is simple,
Time poses no problems, Art is volition,
But already, poised in the future: the apotheosis
Of the meatpacker, the thwarted anguish of the slums.

4. THE PRESENT

Nothing to paint but what the eye can see.
The eye sees the broken faces, the cities
In convulsive disorder, how the bones puncture the flesh,
How the teeth break from the gums, how the tears fall.

Nothing to paint but what the mind discerns.
The mind discerns the implacable insects burrowing,
The fatal complacency of the skyscraper,

The insects honeycombing final triumph.
Nothing to paint but what the heart tells.
The heart tells of love. O still repeats
Strong in its need and confident, of the young
Still turning to one another in the dangerous darkness,
Where the many are hooded and carry knives, where still
There is one who waits, unarmed, and will be kind and gentle.

5. CONCLUSION

The doors are closed. The lights turned down. The dog
Trots through the galleries sniffing the air
For some possible intruder. The streetcars creak
In the night, and the camp chairs are stacked in a storeroom.

O now, surely, the haunting spirit of beauty
Rises from its long sleep, now surely,
In the empty silence, delivers its messages.
The archaic lips open, and reaffirm;
The fairhaired boy reads in the dim light
The perpetual parchment and is glad and proud;
The dancers tremble in a reawakened music;
And even the wrecked towers have an affirmative meaning:
Where love whispers softly, heard at last,
Whispering, consoling, promising: I am Love.

* SAGITTARIUS *

Three Rhymes From QUIVER'S CHOICE

1. ALTERNATIVES

For the Duce's inflated ideas
We can offer but two panaceas—
Either give him Gibraltar,
Suez, Cyprus, and Malta,
Or a kick in the Pantellarias.

2. THE REASON

A rather extreme vegetarian,
Looked down from his summit Bavarian,
He said: 'It's not odd
I'm superior to God,
For the Latter's not even an Aryan.'

3. FRITTO MISTO

> 'The Italian race has remained pure
> for the last 2000 years.'
> —La Difesa della Razza, Rome.

When Alaric mopped up in Rome
With his totalitarians,
Italian dames were not at home
To visiting barbarians,
Disdaining to supply the Goth
With Teuton offspring hardy,

As later they withheld their troth
From lovesick Langobardi.

Their way was equally abrupt
With overlords Byzantine,
Lest Roman blood they might corrupt
With influence levantine.
These steadfast virgins spurned like dirt
The decadent Hellenic,
And never would so much as flirt
With Emirs Saracenic.

Invaders of two thousand years,
Not always of the purest,
Left fewer racial souvenirs
Than any summer tourist.
The mothers of the Coming Race
Abhorred miscegenation
And substituted in its place
Parthenogeneration.

* L A U R I E   L E E *

RIVER

THE morning is white
  with the hot frost of elder,
blizzards of scent
blind the shuddering walls.

The red flames of lizards
wriggle out of the ditches
to suck the black tar
from the smoking road.

There is thirst on my tongue
like the powder of fungus,
my throat is a sandstorm
of thistle and moth.

O where is the river
and where are the willows,
your kisses of hazel
to sweeten my mouth?

You are that stream
where the glass fish dazzle
the flash of their scales
on the star-blue stones.

The heart of cool amber
in baking granite,
the motionless lily
in pools of clay.

Dewdrop of honey,
moisture of bloom
in the sweating rose
and the branded poppy.

O bring me your river,
your moss-green bridges,
the bank of your breasts
with their hill-cold springs;

the voice of the moorhen
diving under your eyelids
and your ankles like swans
in a nest of reeds. . . .

NOTES FOR AN ELEGY

THE alternative to flying is cowardice,
And what is said against it excuses, excuses;
Its want was always heavy in those men's bodies
Who foresaw it in some detail; and failing that,
The rest were shown through its skyey heats and eases
In sleep, awoke uncertain whether their waking cry
Had been falling fear only, or love and falling fear.
When the sudden way was shown, its possibility
In terms of the familiar at last shown,
(How absurdly simple the principle after all!)
Any tyrant should have sensed it was controversial:
Instrument of freedom; rights, not Wrights;
Danger should never be given out publicly.
The men could easily have been disposed of,
They and their fragile vehicle. Then the sky
Would perhaps have darkened, earth shaken, nothing more.
But in practice the martyrdom has been quiet, statistical,
A fair price. This is what airmen believe.

The transition to battle was smooth from here.
Who resents one bond resents another,
And who has unshouldered earth-restraining hand
Is not likely to hear out more reasonable tyrannies.

The woods where he died were dark even at sun-up,
Oak and long-needle pine that had come together
Earlier, and waited for the event at the field's edge.
At sunset when the sky behind was gay
One had seen the lugubrious shapes of the trees,
Bronze and terrible, but had never known the reason,
Never thought they were waiting for someone in particular.
They took him at night, when they were at their darkest.
How they at last convinced him is not known:
The crafty engine would not fall for their softness,
(Oh, where were you then, six hundred cunning horses?)
In the end it had torn hungrily through the brush
To lie alone in the desired clearing. Nor the wings;
(And you, with your wide silver margin of safety?)
They were for the field, surely, where they so often
Had eased their load to ground. No, the invitation
Must have been sent to the aviator in person:
Perhaps a sly suggestion of carelessness,
A whispered invitation perhaps to death,
Death.

      He was not badly disfigured compared to some,
But even a little stream of blood where death is
Will whimper across a forest floor,
Run through the whole forest shouting, shouting.

Him now unpersoned, warm, and quite informal,
Dead as alive, raise softly sober interns;
Lift gently, God, this wholly airborne one
Leads out all his life to this violent wood.

Note that he had not fought one public battle,
Met any fascist with his skill, but died
As it were in bed, the waste conspicuous;

This is a costly wreck and costly to happen on:
Praise and humility sound through its siren shrieks,
And dedication follows in car.

The morning came up foolish with pink clouds
To say that God counts ours a cunning time.
Our losses part of an old secret, somehow no loss.

A KODIAK POEM

PRECIPITOUS is the shape and stance of the spruce
   Pressed against the mountains in gestures of height,
Pleasing to Poussin the white and repetitious peaks.

Fonder mountains surely curl around your homeland,
Fondle the home farms with a warmer green;
Follow these hills for cold only, or for fool's gold.

Easy winds sweep lengthwise along the known places,
Essay brittle windows and are turned away;
Eskimo houses had seal-gut windows that the east-wind drummed.

A fish people now, once fur hunters and fierce,
Fire-needing, they buried their dead with faggots,
And when a man went to their hell, he froze.

Remembering the lands before but much more real,
Look where aloft, you cannot say how except rarely,
The raven, rich in allusion, rides alone.

THE SOLDIER WALKS UNDER THE TREES
OF THE UNIVERSITY

THE walls have been shaded for so many years
   By the green magnificence of these great lives
Their bricks are darkened till the end of time.
(Small touching whites in the perpetual
Darkness that saturates the unwalled world;
Saved from the sky by leaves, and from the earth by stone)
The pupils trust like flowers to the shades
And interminable twilight of these latitudes.

In our zone innocence is born in banks
And cultured in colonies the rich have sown:
The one is spared here what the many share
To write the histories that others are.
The oak escapes the storm that broke the reeds,
They read here; they read, too, of reeds,
Of storms; and are, almost, sublime
In their read ignorance of everything.

The poor are always—somewhere, but not here;
We learn of them where they and Guilt subsist
With Death and Evil: in books, in books, in books.
Ah, sweet to contemplate the causes, not the things!
The soul learns fortitude in libraries,
Enduring patience in another's pain,

And pity for the lives we do not change:
All that the world would be, if it were real.

When will the boughs break blazing from these trees,
The darkened walls float heavenward like soot?
The days when men say: "Where we look is fire—
The iron branches flower in my veins"?
In that night even to be rich is difficult,
The world is something even books believe,
The bombs fall all year long among the states,
And the blood is black upon the unturned leaves.

* HUBERT CREEKMORE *

IT'S ME, OH LORD, STANDING WITH A GUN . . .

THEY crouch in the barge and the palms roll close,
Green echo, high over sand, of waves,
Of gray jelly-fish in smoke puffs whose
Invisible sting is swift and leaden.
 They crouch, tongue-dry, in the boat,
And all the world is a puny beach-head:

World of clean-sliced hemispheres,
Of latitudes of love and crime,
Peopled with the mental smears
Of medieval magic, thinning
 To a short horizon
Under war's tremendous engine.

That glittering hierarchy down
Through which the war blood streams, and great
Einsteinian logistics, drown
Upon this coast of conquest. Here is
 All of war, compact.
It is simple. It is death-fear.

Undiscriminating death
Appraises his approaching guests,
Uniform in gear, beneath
Which shiver bodies, black and white skinned,

But uniform in value
As currency of life. Their insight

Penetrates the island's pull,
Magnetic jointure of here-after.
Across the rail, the Negro full
In death's face stares and blinks, beside him
    Son of owners of slaves,
Floating to a mortal hyphen, tongue-tied.

And the hyphen joins the puzzled past:
The tired way down which they came,
Twin exiles of historic trust—
And fades in the jungle's blinding chaos.
    For on that final range
Men sprawled, too patient in the wave lay,

Letting the gently anxious foam
Entomb their scars in sand. No scales
Enamel the minds of two from whom
All memory soon may flee. The Negro
    And the Southern man
Reflect how inner bondage subtly

Links them to oppose what fought
At home between them: tenant house
Of jerried boards, and house it wrought
Of moonbeam pillars; loom of clod-veined
    Overalls that wove
Tradition's silky gown. The drained blood

Mirrors doubly self and war,
Retreating in the glasses to
Extinction. The Negro fighting for

A freedom fraud, the white for freedom
    Mortgaged to mistrust,
Fight to shield the bigot's long breed.

And while the boat rolled on the waves,
Palm surf roaring at their face,
The Negro felt, not as on slaves,
The white hand on his arm, and heard him:
    "We can do it, can't we?"
And some familiar thing was lost words.

The strakes grate on the shore, defy
Horizon turned foreground of slaughter.
Whether I, the Negro, lie
Here or return, by all these tokens,
    Medals are for white men,
Jim Crow life for me and my folk.

Upon the coral shingle they leap
And rush the smoking jungle. Round
Their legs the salt-curls break and seep,
Crumbling soon the mold of foot-prints.
    Streaks of red, shell-studded,
Blot in sand, in waves are washed mute.

* A L U N   L E W I S *

INDIAN DAY

Dawn's cold imperative compels
  Bazaars and gutters to disturb
Famine's casual ugly tableaux.
Lazarus is lifted from the kerb.

The supple sweeper girl goes by
Brushing the dung of camels from the street
The daylight's silver bangles
Glitter on her naked feet.

II

Yellow ramtilla stiffens in the noon,
Jackals skulk among the screes,
In skinny fields the oxen shiver,
The gods have prophesied disease.

Hedges of spike and rubber, hedges of cactus,
Lawns of bougainvillia, jasmine, zinnia,
Terraces of privilege and loathing,
The masterly shadows of a nightmare

Harden and grow lengthy in the drought.
The moneyed antipathetic faces
Converse in courts of pride and fountains
With ermined sleek injustices.
Gods and dacoits haunt the mountains.

III

The sun the thunder and the hunger grow
Extending stupidly the fields of pain
Ploughing the peasant under with his crop
Denying the great mercy of the rain

Denying what each flowering pear and lime
And every child and each embrace imply—
The love that is imprisoned in each heart
By the famines and fortunes of the century.

IV

Night bibles India in her wilderness
The Frontier Mail screams blazing with such terror
The russet tribesman lays aside his flute
Rigid with Time's hypnotic surging error.

The kindness of the heart lies mute
Caught in the impotence of dreams
Yet all night long the boulders sing
The timeless songs of mountain streams.

IN HOSPITAL: POONA

Last night I did not fight for sleep
But lay awake from midnight while the world
Turned its slow features to the moving deep
Of darkness, till I knew that you were furled,

Beloved, in the same dark watch as I.
And sixty degrees of longitude beside
Vanished as though a swan in ecstasy
Had spanned the distance from your sleeping side.

And like to swan or moon the whole of Wales
Glided within the parish of my care:
I saw the green tide leap on Cardigan,
Your red yacht riding like a legend there,

And the great mountains Dafydd and Llewelyn,
Plynlimmon, Cader Idris and Eryri
Threshing the darkness back from head and fin,
And also the small nameless mining valley

Whose slopes are scratched with streets and sprawling
    graves
Dark in the lap of firwoods and great boulders
Where you lay waiting, listening to the waves—
My hot hands touched your white despondent shoulders

—And then ten thousand miles of daylight grew
Between us, and I heard the wild daws crake
In India's starving throat; whereat I knew
That Time upon the heart can break
But love survives the venom of the snake.

THE JUNGLE

IN MOLE-BLUE indolence the sun
   Plays idly on the stagnant pool
In whose grey bed black swollen leaf
Holds Autumn rotting like an unfrocked priest.
The crocodile slides from the ochre sand
And drives the great translucent fish
Under the boughs across the running gravel.
Windfalls of brittle mast crunch as we come
To quench more than our thirst—our selves—
Beneath this bamboo bridge, this mantled pool
Where sleep exudes a sinister content
As though all strength of mind and limb must pass
And all fidelities and doubts dissolve,
The weighted world a bubble in each head,
The warm pacts of the flesh betrayed
By the nonchalance of a laugh,
The green indifference of this sleep.

II

Wandering and fortuitous the paths
We followed to this rendezvous today
Out of the mines and offices and dives,
The sidestreets of anxiety and want,
Huge cities known and distant as the stars,
Wheeling beyond our destiny and hope.
We did not notice how the accent changed
As shadows ride from precipice to plain
Closing the parks and cordoning the roads,
Clouding the humming cultures of the West—

The weekly bribe we paid the man in black,
The day shift sinking from the sun,
The blinding arc of rivets blown through steel,
The patient queues, headlines and slogans flung
Across a frightened continent, the town
Sullen and out of work, the little home
Semi-detached, suburban, transient
As fever or the anger of the old,
The best ones on some specious pretext gone.

But we who dream beside this jungle pool
Prefer the instinctive rightness of the poised
Pied kingfisher deep darting for a fish
To all the banal rectitude of states,
The dew-bright diamonds on a viper's back
To the slow poison of a meaning lost
And the vituperations of the just.

III

The banyan's branching clerestories close
The noon's harsh splendour to a head of light.
The black spot in the focus grows and grows:
The vagueness of the child, the lover's deep
And inarticulate bewilderment,
The willingness to please that made a wound,
The kneeling darkness and the hungry prayer;
Cargoes of anguish in the holds of joy,
The smooth deceitful stranger in the heart,
The tangled wrack of motives drifting down
An oceanic tide of Wrong.
And though the state has enemies we know
The greater enmity within ourselves.

Some things we cleaned like knives in earth,
Kept from the dew and rust of Time
Instinctive truths and elemental love,
Knowing the force that brings the teal and quail
From Turkestan across the Himalayan snows
To Kashmir and the South alone can guide
That winging wildness home again.

Oh you who want us for ourselves,
Whose love can start the snow-rush in the woods
And melt the glacier in the dark coulisse,
Forgive this strange inconstancy of soul,
The face distorted in a jungle pool
That drowns its image in a mort of leaves.

IV

Grey monkeys gibber, ignorant and wise.
We are the ghosts, and they the denizens;
We are like them anonymous, unknown,
Avoiding what is human, near,
Skirting the villages, the paddy fields
Where boys sit timelessly to scare the crows
On bamboo platforms raised above their lives.

A trackless wilderness divides
Joy from its cause, the motive from the act:
The killing arm uncurls, strokes the soft moss;
The distant world is an obituary,
We do not hear the tappings of its dread.

The act sustains; there is no consequence.
Only aloneness, swinging slowly
Down the cold orbit of an older world
Than any they predicted in the schools,

Stirs the cold forest with a starry wind,
And sudden as the flashing of a sword
The dream exalts the bowed and golden head
And time is swept with a great turbulence,
The old temptation to remould the world.

The bamboos creak like an uneasy house;
The night is shrill with crickets, cold with space.
And if the mute pads on the sand should lift
Annihilating paws and strike us down
Then would some unimportant death resound
With the imprisoned music of the soul?
And we become the world we could not change?
Or does the will's long struggle end
With the last kindness of a foe or friend?

FIFE TUNE
(6/8) for 6 Platoon, 308th I.T.C.

ONE morning in Spring
 We marched from Devizes
All shapes and all sizes
Like beads on a string,
But yet with a swing
We trod the bluemetal
And full to high fettle
We started to sing.

She ran down the stair
A twelve-year-old darling
And laughing and calling
She tossed her bright hair;
Then silent to stare
At the men flowing past her—
These were all she could master
Adoring her there.

It's seldom I'll see
A sweeter or prettier;
I doubt we'll forget her
In two years or three,
And lucky he'll be
She takes for a lover
While we are far over
The treacherous sea.

✳ SIDNEY KEYES ✳

THE BUZZARD

THIS town curled round a hilltop
 Flattened and steeply canted at the sun
Sleeps like a brown snake. The poplars point
Tapering shadows, pendula of fate
Across the turf. The golden sun revolves
On the invisible radius of time
And tufts of cloud swim round, dissolving
Or reappearing as the currents of the moment
Vary up there.
     Life swings on its axis
In motion centripetal to this sphere
Or dust under the burning-glass of sky:
This noontide motion spins a kind of peace.
Thoughts nuzzle too the crystalline
Wall of the curving brain and gape their message
Dumbly and flounce away. A caterpillar
Measures with looping back a mulberry leaf;
This is another way of portioning
The endless moment, another demonstration
Of time's deceit and the geometry of living.
A point projected from the hill's brown arc
Draws out its tangent from the central
And unexpected angle of a tower;

Then comes to rest in space at last, suspended
From the sun's further circle as a spider
Hangs from a twig by unseen filaments.

The buzzard's unreflective eye
Quick swivelling on its axis, concentrates
All planes and angles into one great sphere
Of earth its prey. The terra-cotta town
Dropped on the hill, generates circles spreading
To the horizon; rings of green and grey
Granite or yellow of mimosa thickets
Spin round the central pivot of his vision.
Only the quiet eye of water
Stares back and challenges the symmetry.
Behind the buzzard's lens, all secrets
Of beauty or of form unapprehended
Life's many meanings blend their rays to one
Bright spot of cruelty within his brain.
Buzzard drops down the sky and shadows straddle
Longer on grass and rock. Now dust clouds rise
Along the track; a herd of goats stray past;
Their noise shatters the meaning of the moment
And breaks the circle of extended peace.
Why should we wish to hide within the present,
Hanging above infinity and waiting
For pain to move, a rabbit in the grass?
Unfocus rather the too-watchful eye
And wander singing in the golden haze
Behind the flock, and take with them your pleasure
At random from each leaf or twig. So break
The trance of living symmetry, disprove
The buzzard's callous theorem of small pain
And sprawl at last under a myrtle-tree,

Breathing the fleshy odour of its leaves,
So find a better variant of peace,
Another meaning and another science
In nightfall's final clemency of quiet.

TIMOSHENKO

Hour ten he rose, ten-sworded, every finger
A weighted blade, and strapping round his loins
The courage of attack, he threw the window
Open to look on his appointed night.

Where he lay, beneath the winds and creaking flares
Tangled like lovers or alone assuming
The wanton postures of the drunk with sleep,
An army of twisted limbs and hollow faces
Thrown to and fro between the winds and shadows.
O hear the wind, the wind that shakes the dawn.
And there before the night, he was aware
Of the flayed fields of home, and black with ruin
The helpful earth under the tracks of tanks.
His bladed hand, in pity falling, mimicked
The crumpled hand lamenting the broken plow;
And the oracular metal lips in anger
Squared to the shape of the raped girl's yelling mouth.
He heard the wind explaining nature's sorrow
And humming in the wire hair of the dead.

He turned, and his great shadow on the wall
Swayed like a tree. His eyes grew cold as lead.
Then, in a rage of love and grief and pity,
He made the pencilled map alive with war.

September 1942.

FROM THE WILDERNESS

THE red rock wilderness
Shall be my dwelling-place.

Where the wind saws at the bluffs
And the pebble falls like thunder
I shall watch the clawed sun
Tear the rocks asunder.

My seven-branched cactus
Will never sweat wine:
My own bleeding feet
Shall furnish the sign.

The rock says "Endure."
The wind says "Pursue."
The sun says "I will suck your bones
And afterwards bury you."

IN WESTMINSTER ABBEY

L ET me take this other glove off
  As the *vox humana* swells,
And the beauteous fields of Eden
  Bask beneath the Abbey bells.
Here, where England's statesmen lie,
Listen to a lady's cry.

Gracious Lord, oh bomb the Germans.
  Spare their women for Thy Sake,
And if that is not too easy
  We will pardon Thy Mistake.
But, gracious Lord, whate'er shall be,
Don't let anyone bomb me.

Keep our Empire undismembered
  Guide our Forces by Thy Hand,
Gallant blacks from far Jamaica,
  Honduras and Togoland;
Protect them Lord in all their fights,
And, even more, protect the whites.

Think of what our Nation stands for,
  Books from Boots' and country lanes,
Free speech, free passes, class distinction,
  Democracy and proper drains.

Lord, put beneath Thy special care
One-eighty-nine Cadogan Square.

Although dear Lord I am a sinner,
   I have done no major crime;
Now I'll come to Evening Service
   Whensoever I have time.
So, Lord, reserve for me a crown,
And do not let my shares go down.

I will labour for Thy Kingdom,
   Help our lads to win the war,
Send white feathers to the cowards,
   Join the Women's Army Corps,
Then wash the Steps around Thy Throne
In the Eternal Safety Zone.

Now I feel a little better,
   What a treat to hear Thy Word,
Where the bones of leading statesmen,
   Have so often been interr'd.
And now, dear Lord, I cannot wait
Because I have a luncheon date.

1940

* ROBERT LOWELL *

DEA ROMA

Augustus mended you. He hung the tongue
Of Tullius upon your rostrum, lashed
The money-lenders from your Senate House;
Then Brutus bled his forty-six percent
For *Pax Romana*. Quiet as a mouse
Blood licks your Greek cosmetics with its tongue.

Some years, your legions soldiered through this world
Under the eagles of Lord Lucifer;
But human torches lit the soldier home,
And victims dyed your purple crucifix:
All of the roads and sewers wound to Rome;
Satan is pacing up and down the world.

How many butchers and philosophers
Dirtied the Babylonian purple! Blood
Ran in through pipes of public aqueducts;
Vandal patricians squatted on Rome's lid,
Until Maxentius, floundering in the mud,
Wiped out the scandal of philosophers.

Now sixteen centuries, Eternal City,
Are squandered since the inflated pagan flowed
Under the Milvian Bridge; from the dry Dome
Of Michelangelo, your Fisherman
Walks on the waters of a draining Rome
To bank his catch in the Celestial City.

CHILDREN OF LIGHT

OUR Fathers wrung their bread from stocks and stones
  And fenced their gardens with the Redman's bones;
Embarking from the Nether Land of Holland,
Pilgrims unhouseled by Geneva's night,
You planted here the Serpent's seeds of light;
And here the pivoting searchlights probe to shock
The riotous glass houses built on rock,
And candles gutter in a hall of mirrors,
And light is where the ancient blood of Cain
Is burning, burning the unburied grain.

ON THE EVE OF THE FEAST OF THE IMMACULATE CONCEPTION 1942

Mother of God, whose burly love
 Turns swords to plowshares, come, improve
 On the big wars
And make·this holiday with Mars
Your Feast Day, while Bellona's bluff
Courage or call it what you please
 Plays blindman's buff
 Through virtue's knees.

Freedom and Eisenhower have won
Significant laurels where the Hun
 And Roman kneel
To lick the dust from Mars' bootheel
Like foppish bloodhounds; yet you sleep
Out our distemper's evil day
 And hear no sheep
 Or hangdog bay!

Bring me tonight no axe to grind
On wheels of the Utopian mind:
 Six thousand years
Cain's blood has drummed into my ears,
Shall I wring plums from Plato's bush
When Burma's and Bizerte's dead
 Must puff and push
 Blood into bread?

Oh, if soldiers mind you well
They shall find you are their belle

And belly too;
Christ's bread and beauty came by you,
Celestial Hoyden, when our Lord
Gave up the weary Ghost and died,
    You shook a sword
    From his torn side.

Over the seas and far away
They feast the fair and bloody day
    When mankind's Mother,
Jesus' Mother, like another
Nimrod danced on Satan's head.
The old Snake lopes to his shelled hole;
    Man eats the Dead
    From pole to pole.

WHERE THE RAINBOW ENDS

I saw the sky descending, black and white
  Not blue, on Boston where the winters wore
The occidental death's heads from the slates
And Hunger's skin and bone retrievers tore
The chickadee and shrike. The thorntree waits
Its victim and tonight
Arson will eat the deadwood to the foot
Of Ararat: The scythers, Time and Death,
Helmed locusts, move upon the tree of breath;
The wild ingrafted olive and the root

Are withered, and a winter drifts to where
The Pepperpot, ironic rainbow, spans
Charles River and its scales of scorched-earth miles,
The tree-dabbed suburb where construction plans
The wrath of God. About the Chapel, piles
Of dead leaves char the air,
And I am a red arrow on this graph
Of revelations. Every dove is sold,
The Chapel's sharp-skinned eagle shifts its hold
On Serpent-Time, the Rainbow's epitaph.

In Boston serpents whistle at the cold.
The victim climbs the altar-steps and sings:
"Hosannah to the lion, lamb and beast
Who fans the furnace-fire of Is with wings:
I breathe the ether of my marriage-feast."
At the unhouseled table, gold

And a fair cloth. I kneel and the wings beat
My cheek. What can the dove of Jesus give
You now but wisdom, exile? Stand and live,
The dove has brought an olive-branch to eat.

CARON, NON TI CRUCCIARE

"And with Him they crucify two thieves, the one on
His right hand, the other on His left."

I

MY BEAUTY is departed: they will square
My hands and feet, and Omar's coarse-hair tent
Towers above the Kedron's Torrent, Sent,
Ben Himnon and the hide-bound outlands where
The little fox runs shivering to its lair,
Fearful lest the short-sighted Orient
Mistake it for this shambles of dissent
Where the red victims of the gallows stare
And dazzle the trenched highways with their blood.
My brothers, if I call you brothers, see:
The blood of Abel, crying from the dead
Sticks to my shaven skull and eyes. What good
Are *lebensraum* and bread to Israel dead
And rotten on the cross-beams of the Tree?

II

This is the hour of darkness and the clocks
Of Heaven bawl and falter and the Ram
Kicks over his loose traces, earthquake rocks
The stolid temple of Jerusalem,
Whose cornerstone is rocking with a will
To scatter Jew and Roman to the wind;
The wolves steal up on tiptoe for the kill.
Our beauty is departed. All have sinned.
We are a chosen people. Satan, be still;
We huddled against the gallows lest we die.

O why did God climb out on this bald hill,
That Young Man, worse than prodigal, and lie
Upon the gallows of our brotherhood?
The wolves go round in circles in the wood.

III

I wandered footloose in the wastes of Nod
And damned the day and age when I was born.
I weary of this curse, Almighty God,
Which solely falls on my cleft heel and horn;
My shepherd brother led the lepers back
To Jordan. Then I strayed to Babylon
Where gold-dust sands the sidewalks, lost the track
Of Abel through the fallow to thy Son.
Here merchants trim the sheep and goats in mills
Where woolen turns to gold and dollar bills:
The merchants snare us in the golden net
Of Mammon. O Jerusalem, I said,
If I forget thee, may my hand forget
Her cunning. Let the stranger eat my bread.

IV

"There is a woman, if you find her, Son,"
My worldly father whispered, "Where each street
Bubbles and bursts with houses of concrete,
There you shall know the whore of Babylon."
In this way Cain's instruction was begun,
Mother of God, before I could repeat
An *Ave* or know the fabulous clay feet
Of Babylon are dynamite and gun;
Mother of God, I lie here without bail.
Instruct a lasher of the sheep and goat
In Jonah, who three nights of midnights lay

Buried inside the belly of the whale,
Then, grappling Nineveh by its mule's throat,
Hauled a great city to the Scapegoat's hay.

V

Behind his sliding window, Dives sits
To turn out Lazarus, if he should knock;
Wealth is a weighty sorrow. But my wits
Are addled by the sepulchre, the rock,
By splinters of the Godhead in a head
That knows the devils Saul and Joshua smote
From Salem repossess their old homestead
And keep up open-house to feast the Goat;
O tame and uniform conceits of man
And human reason, you should light the night
By burning! Goat-foot Satan, I have lain,
Clutching my nothing close as death, tonight
And heard you hooting, when our women ran;
Your goat horns rattle on the whited pane.

VI

We saw Mount Sinai and the Holy Land
In Egypt, compound of black earth and green
Between a powdered mountain and red sand
Scoured by the silver air-lines: we have seen
The sworded Seraphim, the serpent-tree,
The apple, once more distant than light-years,
Falling like burning brands about our ears.
The hydra-headed delta choked with sea;
On that sarcophagus of the Nile's mud
And mummies, the Destroyer clamped a lid,
Weightier than King Cheops' pyramid,—
Coffin within a coffin. In whose blood,

Or Jordan, will our spiked and burdened hands
Cup water for a mummy and his lands?

VII

But peace, in Israel bearded elders keep
The peace as they have always kept it. No
Wolves break into these pastures where the sheep
Wait for the hireling hind to shear them. O
People, let us sleep out this night in peace.
Jehovah nods, the doors of Janus slam,
Cocks on the weathervanes will never cease
Crowing for our defilement of the Lamb.
Lamb in the manger, come into our house:
Here you may find and buy all you can eat,
Dirt cheap. On high, till cockcrow, Lord of Hosts,
The gallows' bird is singing to his spouse,
And mad-cap Lamb is gambolling in the street
And splatters blood on the polluted posts.

VIII

Virgil, who heralded this golden age,
Unctuous with olives of perpetual peace,
Had heard the cackle of the Capitol Geese,
And Caesar toss the sponge and patronage
Of Empire to his prostituted page.
The gold is tarnished and the geese are grease,
Jason has stripped the sheep for golden fleece,
The last brass hat has banged about the stage.
But who will pipe a new song? In our land
Caesar has given his scarlet coat away.
But who will pipe a new song? In our land
Caesar has given his crown of thorns away.
But who will pipe the young sheep back to fold?
Caesar has cut his throat to kill the cold.

IX

God is my shepherd and looks after me.
See how I hang. My bones eat through the skin
And flesh they carried here upon the chin
And lipping clutch of their cupidity;
Now here, now there, the sparrow and the sea
Gull splinter the groined eyeballs of my sin,
Caesar, more beaks of birds than needles in
The fathoms of the Bayeux Tapestry;
Our beauty is departed. Who'll discuss
Our scandal, for we are terror and speak:
"Remember how the Dove came down to us,
Broke through your armor of imperial bronze
And beat with olive-branch and bleeding beak
And picked the Lord's Annointed to the bones."

X

I made this Babel. Pushed against the wall,
With splintered hands and knees and sky-sick blood,
I pieced together scaffolding, O God,
To swing my cloven heels into the tall
Third heaven of heavens, where the Prophet Paul
Fathoms that Jacob's Ladder is the wood
Of Christ the Goat, whose hanging is too good
For my unnourished horns, gone wooden, all
Splintered. God even of the goats, that was:
The fearful night is over and the mist
Is clearing from the undemolished shore
Of Paradise, where homing angels pass
With the dunged sheep into the manger. Christ
Swings from this Tower of Babel to the floor.

✱ DEMETRIOS CAPETANAKIS ✱

ABEL

MY BROTHER Cain, the wounded, liked to sit
    Brushing my shoulder by the staring water
Of life, or death, in cinemas half-lit
By scenes of peace that always turned to slaughter.

He liked to talk to me. His eager voice
Whispered the puzzle of his bleeding thirst,
Or prayed me not to make my final choice
Unless we had a chat about it first.

And then he chose the final pain for me.
I do not blame his nature: he's my brother;
Nor what you call the times: our love was free,
Would be the same at any time; but rather

The ageless ambiguity of things,
Which makes our life mean death, our love be hate.
My blood that streams across the bedroom sings
"I am my brother opening the gate."

LAZARUS

THIS knock means death. I heard it once before
As I was struggling to remember one,
Just one thing, crying in my fever for
Help, help. Then the door opened, yet no Son

Came in to whisper what I had to know.
Only my sisters wetted me with tears,
But tears are barren symbols. Love is slow,
And when she comes she neither speaks nor hears;

She only kisses and revives the dead
Perhaps in vain. Because what is the use
Of miracles unheard-of, since instead
Of trying to remember the great News

Revealed to me alone by Death and Love,
I struggled to forget them and become
Like everybody else? I longed to move
As if I never had been overcome

By mysteries which made my sisters shiver
As they prepared the supper for our Friend.
He came and we received Him as the Giver,
But did not ask Him when our joy would end.

And now I hear the knock I heard before,
And strive to make up for the holy time,
But I cannot remember, and the door
Creaks letting in my unambiguous crime.

* THOMAS MERTON *

THE TRAPPIST ABBEY: MATINS
Our Lady of Gethsemani, Kentucky

WHEN the full fields begin to smell of sunrise
  And the valleys sing in their sleep,
The pilgrim moon pours over the solemn darkness
Her waterfalls of silence,
And then departs, up the long avenue of trees.

The stars hide, in the glade, their light, like tears,
And tremble where some train runs, lost,
Baying in eastward mysteries of distance,
Where fire flares, somewhere, over a sink of cities.

Now kindle in the windows of this ladyhouse, my soul,
Your childish, clear awakeness:
Burn in the country night
Your wise and sleepless lamp.
For, from the frowning tower, the windy belfry,
Sudden the bells come, bridegrooms,
And fill the echoing dark with love and fear.

Wake in the windows of Gethsemani, my soul, my sister,
For the past years, with smokey torches, come,
Bringing betrayal from the burning world
And bloodying the glade with pitch flame.

Wake in the cloisters of the lonely night, my soul, my sister,
Where the apostles gather, who were, one time, scattered,
And mourn God's blood in the place of His betrayal,
And weep with Peter at the triple cock-crow.

FOR MY BROTHER
Reported Missing in Action, 1943

SWEET brother, if I do not sleep
My eyes are flowers for your tomb;
And if I cannot eat my bread,
My fasts shall live like willows where you died.
If in the heat I find no water for my thirst,
My thirst shall turn to springs for you, poor traveller.

Where, in what desolate and smokey country,
Lies your poor body, lost and dead?
And in what landscape of disaster
Has your unhappy spirit lost its road?

Come, in my labor find a resting place
And in my sorrows lay your head,
Or rather take my life and blood
And buy yourself a better bed—
Or take my breath and take my death
And buy yourself a better rest.

When all the men of war are shot
And flags have fallen into dust,
Your cross and mine shall tell men still
Christ died on each, for both of us.

For in the wreckage of your April Christ lies slain,
And Christ weeps in the ruins of my spring:
The money of Whose tears shall fall
Into your weak and friendless hand,

And buy you back to your own land:
The silence of Whose tears shall fall
Like bells upon your alien tomb.
Hear them and come: they call you home.

* K A R L   S H A P I R O *

AUTO WRECK

Its quick soft silver bell beating, beating,
And down the dark one ruby flare
Pulsing out red light like an artery,
The ambulence at top speed floating down
Past beacons and illuminated clocks
Wings in a heavy curve, dips down,
And brakes speed, entering the crowd.
The doors leap open, emptying light;
Stretchers are laid out, the mangled lifted
And stowed into the little hospital.
Then the bell, breaking the hush, tolls once,
And the ambulance with its terrible cargo
Rocking, slightly rocking, moves away,
As the doors, an afterthought, are closed.

We are deranged, walking among the cops
Who sweep glass and are large and composed.
One is still making notes unde the light.
One with a bucket douches ponds of blood
Into the street and gutter.
One hangs lanterns on the wrecks that cling,
Empty husks of locusts, to iron poles.

Our throats were tight as tourniquets,
Our feet were bound with splints, but now,

Like convalescents intimate and gauche,
We speak through sickly smiles and warn
With the stubborn saw of common sense,
The grim joke and the banal resolution.
The traffic moves around with care,
But we remain, touching a wound
That opens to our richest horror.
Already old, the question Who shall die?
Becomes unspoken Who is innocent?
For death in war is done by hands;
Suicide has cause and stillbirth, logic;
And cancer, simple as a flower, blooms.
But this invites the occult mind,
Cancels our physics with a sneer,
And spatters all we know of dénouement
Across the expedient and wicked stones.

THE FLY

O HIDEOUS little bat, the size of snot,
  With polyhedral eye and shabby clothes,
To populate the stinking cat you walk
The promontory of the dead man's nose,
Climb with the fine leg of a Duncan-Phyfe
     The smoking mountains of my food
         And in a comic mood
     In mid-air take to bed a wife.

Riding and riding with your filth of hair
On gluey foot or wing, forever coy,
Hot from the compost and green sweet decay,
Sounding your buzzer like an urchin toy—
You dot all whiteness with diminutive stool,
     In the tight belly of the dead
         Burrow with hungry head
     And inlay maggots like a jewel.

At your approach the great horse stomps and paws
Bringing the hurricane of his heavy tail;
Shod in disease you dare to kiss my hand
Which sweeps against you like an angry flail;
Still you return, return, trusting your wing
     To draw you from the hunter's reach
         That learns to kill to teach
     Disorder to the tinier thing.

My peace is your disaster. For your death
Children like spiders cup their pretty hands
And wives resort to chemistry of war.

In fens of sticky paper and quicksands
You glue yourself to death. Where you are stuck
    You struggle hideously and beg
        You amputate your leg
      Imbedded in the amber muck.

But I, a man, must swat you with my hate,
Slap you across the air and crush your flight,
Must mangle with my shoe and smear your blood,
Expose your little guts pasty and white,
Knock your head sidewise like a drunkard's hat,
    Pin your wings under like a crow's,
      Tear off your flimsy clothes
    And beat you as one beats a rat.

Then like Gargantua I stride among
The corpses strewn like raisins in the dust,
The broken bodies of the narrow dead
That catch the throat with fingers of disgust.
I sweep. One gyrates like a top and falls
    And stunned, stone blind, and deaf
      Buzzes its frightful F
    And dies between three cannibals.

NIGGER

A ND did ever a man go black with sun in a Belgian swamp,
On a feathery African plain where the sunburnt lioness lies,
And a cocoanut monkey grove where the cockatoos scratch the
skies,
And the zebras striped with moonlight grasses gaze and stomp?

With a swatch of the baboon's crimson bottom cut for a lip,
And a brace of elephant ivories hung for a tusky smile,
With the muscles as level and lazy and long as the lifting Nile,
And a penis as loaded and supple and limp as the slaver's whip?

Are you beautiful still when you walk downtown in a knife-cut
coat
And your yellow shoes dance at the corner curb like a brand new
car,
And the buck with the arching pick looks over the new-laid tar
As you cock your eye like a cuckoo bird on a two-o'clock note?

When you got so little in steel-rim specs, when you caught that
French,
When you wrote that book and you made that speech in the bot-
tom south,
When you beat that fiddle and sang that role or Othello's mouth,
When you blew that horn for the shirt-sleeve mob and the snaky
wench?

When you boxed that hun, when you raped that trash that you
didn't rape,
When you caught that slug with a belly of fire and a face of gray,

When you felt that loop and you took that boot from a KKK,
And your hands hung down and your face went out in a blast of
    grape?

Did the Lord say yes, did the Lord say no, did you ask the Lord
When the jaw came down, when the cotton blossomed out of your
    bones?
Are you coming to peace, O Booker T. Lincoln Roosevelt Jones,
And is Jesus riding to raise your wage and to cut that cord?

THE LEG

A MONG the iodoform, in twilight-sleep,
    What have I lost? he first inquires,
Peers in the middle distance where a pain,
Ghost of a nurse, hastily moves, and day,
Her blinding presence pressing in his eyes
And now his ears. They are handling him
With rubber gloves. He wants to get up.

One day beside some flowers near his nose
He will be thinking, *When will I look at it?*
And pain, still in the middle distance, will reply,
At what? and he will know it's gone,
O where! and begin to tremble and cry,
He will begin to cry as a child cries
Whose puppy is mangled under a screaming wheel.

Later, as if deliberately, his fingers
Begin to explore the stump. He learns a shape
That is comfortable and tucked in like a sock.
This has a sense of humor, this can despise
The finest surgical limb, the dignity of limping,
The nonsense of wheel-chairs. Now he smiles to the wall.
The amputation becomes an acquisition.

For the leg is wondering where he is (all is not lost)
And surely he has a duty to the leg;
He is its injury, the leg is his orphan,
He must cultivate the mind of the leg,
Pray for the part that is missing, pray for peace

In the image of man, pray, pray for its safety,
And after a little it will die quietly.

The body, what is it, Father, but a sign
To love the force that grows us, to give back
What in Thy palm is senselessness and mud?
Knead, knead the substance of our understanding
Which must be beautiful in flesh to walk,
That if Thou take me angrily in hand
And hurl me to the shark, I shall not die!

FROM ESSAY ON RIME

1. FORM

FORM is the build of any organism
    Living or dead, of a whole tree or a leaf,
A whole poem or a word. In prosody,
Where all is motion, form is the interaction
O all the parts of rhythm that produce
The sensory effect of single rhythm. In past
Eras of art the chief preoccupation
Was not with craft, not with mechanics, but
With the end-product, its effect and use.
Some t me in our grandfather's generation
Rime took to looking at itse'f as form,
X-rayed its own anatomy, discussed
The trend of art toward science, until by dint
Of hypnotism a means became an end.

2. SPEECH AND POETRY

In one of the most widely circulated
Anthologies of current rime, a speech,
The actual peroration of a man
Fated to die, is set within the text
Beside the most exemplary and abstruse
Of modern poems. Vanzetti's broken English
Seen in the context of self-conscious art
In company with the works of gifted minds
At perfect ease, argues a new confusion.
By what philosophy the editor
Attempts to hold this tragic martyred thing
A hostage to the literary cause

Is, in a sense, our present argument.
For much of modern rime denotes this bent
To cancel out the distance and the line
Between the language of spontaneous nature
And that of formal artifice. So basic
A solecism cries out for explanation.

Compare the plea for innocence in a play,
Bassanio's for instance with the words
Vanzetti used before the New England court.
One lives and dies in the imagination;
Its reference to existence is oblique
And only by suggestion can impinge
Upon the behavior of the audience
The other is what the audien·e knows as *real,*
A fact of the statistical world, as like
An actor's agonizing as true blood
To a splash of crimson paint upon a dress.
Our editor pursues the rule of thumb
Allowed by poets themselves in his collection.

3. THE RATIO OF RIME TO LANGUAGE

I do not here attempt the definition
Of rime, which is the province of esthetics,
But to point out its ratio to language.
In the mathematical sense, rime is a power,
Prose raised to the numerical exponent
Of three or six or even n, depending
Upon the propensity of the literature
At a particular time and on the bent
Of the particular poet. It is therefore
A heightening and a measure of intensity.

In the physical sense, rime is the nuclear
And vital element of speech and prose,
The very protoplasm of the tongue,
Or that organic substance which survives
The structures it creates. Words are as lives,
Deaths and mutations, and the poet learns
Through search for life, the biology of rime.
In the theological sense, rime is
    the ghost
And prose the flesh of language. Poets may boast
That they have known the mystic rose of good,
The blessed face of truth, the host of beauty;
They press the oil and elevate the wine,
For poetry like philosophy is divine
And wells up from the uncreated will.

4. BELIEF AND POETRY

Belief, it may be, is fortuitous
In rime; there are perhaps as many poets
Who shrug heir shoulders at the word as there
Are those who clutch it like a talisman.
Shakespeare, we think, believed in God and country
And the nobility of man. What else?
The greatest poet has left us no account
Of his theology or his metaphysics;
This in our day is almost tantamount
To calling him a fool or a barbarian.
Certain it is that we regard belief
As the tap-root of art. So various
And multifoliate are our breeds of faith
That we could furnish a herbarium
With the American specimens alone.

5. THE POETRY OF IDEAS

One need but ask Where is the literature
Of nature, where the love poem and the plain
Statement of feel'ng? How and when and why
Did we conceive our horror for emotion,
Our fear of beauty? Whence the isolation
And proud withdrawal of the intellectual
Into the cool control-room of the brain?
At what point in the history of art
Has such a cleavage between audience
And poet existed? When before has rime
Relied so heavily on the interpreter,
The analyst and the critic? Finally how
Has poetry as the vision of the soul
Descended to the poetry of sensation,
And that translated to the perceptive kind,
Evolved into the poetry of ideas?

* APPENDIX *

WILLIAM ABRAHAMS was born in Boston in 1919. At Harvard, from which he was graduated in 1941, he edited the *Advocate*, studied under Robert Hillyer, was twice awarded the Lloyd McKim Garrison poetry prize. He was associated with Dunstan Thompson and Harry Brown on the editorial staff of *Vice Versa* when inducted into the Army in 1942. There he wrote his first novel, *Interval in Carolina* (1945) and began his second, *By the Beautiful Sea*. His few published poems appear to affirm the future through a Rilkean recreation and rejection of the past.

JAMES AGEE was born in Knoxville, Tennessee, in 1909. His first book, with a foreword by Archibald MacLeish was published in 1934 by the Yale University Press. Its title, *Permit Me Voyage*, is taken from the last line of one of Hart Crane's "Voyages." After graduation from Harvard in 1932 Agee came to New York, joining that remarkable coterie of poets and free-thinkers, the editorial staff of *Fortune*. His verse, ornate as any Elizabethan's, is nevertheless pungent with an imagery struck from contemporary flint. His prose (*Let us now Praise Famous Men*, 1941) is unique for its orchestration of fury and humility, its self-consciousness of guilt and its splendor of observation. In recent years Agee has contributed a column, "Films," to *The Nation*.

CONRAD AIKEN, equally distinguished as poet, critic and anthologist, was born in Georgia in 1889. After graduation from Harvard, he lived in Massachusetts until 1921; thereafter, until very recently, in Sussex, England. His novels, like his poems, are concerned with psychological problems. The mood, generally, is nostalgic. His *Selected Poems,* 1929, was awarded the Pulitzer Prize. During the war Aiken returned to Massachusetts and wrote a civilian's tribute to G.I. tribulations entitled *The Soldier.*

W. H. AUDEN is the strongest and most versatile member of that generation of English poets, including Spender and Day Lewis, which first made its voice heard at Oxford in the thirties. He was born in 1907; has taught school; was first a Marxist, then a seeker after religious certainty; did journalistic service for the Spanish Loyalist and Chinese causes; received the King's Prize for poetry in 1937 from George VI; in 1939 came to the United States, becoming a citizen in 1946. Auden's style, the equipment of a major poet, is a highly personal blend of Byronic wit and Freudian symbolism; yet when he wishes to (witness the poem "Prologue") he can employ rhetoric in the grand manner. In addition to his poems, and his plays (with Christopher Isherwood), Auden is the co-author of the entertaining travel-diary, *Letters from Iceland* (with Louis MacNeice), and has edited several anthologies. His *Collected Poems* were published in 1945.

GEORGE BARKER'S first book, *Poems,* was published in 1933 in London. After the incumbency of William Empson, he went to Japan as a teacher in the Imperial University at Tokyo, returning to England during the war by way of the United States as Empson had done, and spending some time in New York with Oscar Williams. The poems in his later books, *Calamiterror, Munich Elegies* and *Lament and Triumph* reveal a preoccupation with Freud and a virtuosity in expressing the world's crises in terms of sex symbolism that does not always avoid vulgarity. Barker's metrical skill is capable of containing his lurid vocabulary in strict patterns, but the idea is often lost in the ambiguities of rhetoric.

STEPHEN VINCENT BENÉT, born in Bethlehem, Pennsylvania, in 1898, published a vigorous collection of poetic monologues, *Five Men and Pompey,* before he entered Yale in 1916. Producing in quick succession novels, ballads and short stories, he made a great name for himself in 1928 with the appearance of the novel-length narrative poem *John Brown's Body*. Although perhaps the most popular poem of our time (it has sold 169,000 copies and is still selling), *John Brown's Body* does not contain its author's best work—that combination of metrical experiment, elfish humor and social indignation which made *Burning City*, 1936, memorable Benét's *Western Star* appeared in 1943, the year of his death.

WILLIAM ROSE BENÉT, the elder brother of Stephen Vincent, was born in 1886 and graduated from Yale in 1907. He served in the First World War, and in 1924 helped to found the *Saturday Review of Literature* of which he is still the poetry editor. In addition to his poetry (the most characteristic experiments and ballads are to be found in the collection *Man Possessed*, 1927), Benét edited the posthumous *Collected Poems* of his second wife, Elinor Wylie.

JOHN BETJEMAN, poet-satirist and architectural draftsman, was born in England in 1906. Author of *Ghastly Good Taste*, *Continual Dew* and *Old For New Chancels*, the poem in this collection first appeared in *The New Statesman & Nation*, where it was immediately attacked by a Church journal as characteristic of the liberal weekly's "anti-Christian attitude." The author replied that "Of course the poem is written from a Christian standpoint and is a satire on the sort of person who turns God into a wishing-well for preserving the *status quo*." Betjeman's verses have been highly praised by Evelyn Waugh and W. H. Auden, among others.

JOHN PEALE BISHOP was born in 1892 and died in 1944. His first book, *The Undertaker's Garland*, was written in collaboration with his friend Edmund Wilson. His poems appeared in *Now with his Love* (1933) and *Minute Particulars* (1935). His *Selected Poems* were published in 1941. His poetry, from the earlier imagist exercises to the later more sensual and ambitious pieces, is delicate, aristocratic and classical.

LOUISE BOGAN says she has looked for privacy and anonymity in her life, and her poetry reflects this search. The intricacy of feeling in her lyrics is polished by a brilliant craftsmanship to an almost frozen but classic impersonalness. Of Irish descent, she was born in Maine, studied for a year at Boston University, married in 1916 and again in 1925, has written the poetry reviews in the *New Yorker* and is presently Curator of Poetry at the Library of Congress. Her poems appeared in *Body of This Death* (1923), *Dark Summer* (1929), *The Sleeping Fury* (1937) and *Poems and New Poems* (1941).

KAY BOYLE's poetry, on which she herself sets an inadequate value, is less intellectualized than her novels and stories, equally experimental; it is also, for one who has spent much of her life as an expatriate in France, strongly American. The best of it appeared in *A Glad Day* (1938) and in a long poem on flight which Miss Boyle has never completed. Its author acknowledges the influence of Lola Ridge with whom she worked on *Broom*, and the encouragement of Eugene Jolas, who published some of it in *transition*. Miss Boyle's prose works for which she is better known include *Wedding Day and Other Stories* (1929); *Plagued by the Nightingale* (1930); the *Crazy Hunter* (1940) and *Armistice Diary* (1942). Born in Minnesota in 1903, she is presently living with her six children in New York City.

R. P. BLACKMUR was born in Massachusetts in 1904, of Scotch descent. He was one of the group at Harvard who with Lincoln Kirstein and Varian Fry founded and edited *The Hound and Horn* in 1929. He worked on the *Kenyon Review* for a while and then came to the Creative English department at Princeton at the call of Allen Tate, where he still teaches. Blackmur's criticism, which goes in strong for "line-by-line" analysis and an almost microscopic weighing of "sensibility" is not at all like his poetry, which has a rough vigor and a healthy emphasis on primary emotions. The criticism is collected in *The Double Agent* (1935) and *The Expense of Greatness* (1940), the poetry in *From Jordan's Delight* (1938) and *The Second World* (1942).

ROBERT BRIDGES, born in England in 1844 and educated at Oxford, was Poet Laureate from 1913 until his death in 1930. His lyrics, as well as his ambitious long poem, *The Testament of Beauty*, are distinguished by their conventional, pietistic subject-matter, and by a style, which, though subtle, is so deliberately patterned after classical models as to approach pedantry. He discovered Gerard Manley Hopkins in the eighties without fully understanding his genius, and edited the first collection of that poet's work.

ROY CAMPBELL was born in Natal, South Africa, in 1902. A latter-day Byron with the vitality of a major poet, the violence of *The Flaming Terrapin*, the satire of *The Georgiad* and the symbolism of *Adamastor* led Edith Sitwell to hail him as "a poetic tornado" and his many admirers in England to hope that a stricter discipline and a larger, more democratic vision would fulfill his promise. Instead Campbell, who had already won a reputation as a professional bullfighter and as the steer-throwing champion of Provence (1932–3), became the slave of his egotism, his worship of action and his passion for authority. In 1935 he joined the Catholic Church. Throughout the Spanish Civil War he fought with Franco's forces and is now living in Toledo. His last volume of poems, published in 1939, was appropriately entitled *Flowering Rifle*.

DEMETRIOS CAPETANAKIS died in England in 1944, aged 32. He had left his native Greece in 1939, learning, as by a miracle, to write English poetry of the first order, and had become a legendary figure even before his death. Once a disciple of Stefan George, the reading of Thomas Gray convinced him that the German poet's mind "was too much of one piece to understand the dialectic mystery of existence, whose reality is born of nothingness, whose light comes from darkness, whose greatest hope is brought about by utmost despair." "Nothingness," he had written in his essay on Rimbaud, "might save or destroy those who face it, but those who ignore it are condemned to unreality," and it was the genius of English poetry, he came to realize, that it questioned everything to the point where "the truth of something in man's existence, revealed by suffering and the awareness of nothingness," became unquestionable. When Capetanakis' half-dozen essays and a like number of poems are brought together in book form by his friend John Lehmann it will be revealed how overpowering and fruitful this doctrine was both in his criticism and his poetry. He wanted his poetry above all to be *disturbing*, and this is exactly the quality of "Abel" with its terrifying depth of pity for Cain whose "eager voice/ Whispered the puzzle of his bleeding thirst," and of "Emily Dickinson" with its opening stanzas:

> I stand like a deserted church
> That would much rather be
> A garden with a hopping bird,
> Or with a humming bee.
>
> I did not want eternity,
> I only begged for time:
> In the trim head of chastity
> The bells of madness chime . . .

LEWIS CARROLL, the pen-name of the mathematician, C. L. Dodgson, is as well known to the world as his masterpiece, *Alice in Wonderland*. He was born in Cheshire, England, in 1832 and died in 1898. The immortal nonsense rhyme included in this volume has contributed at least four new words of common usage to the language—and it is still a treasury.

EUNICE CLARK (Mrs. John Knox Jessup) was born in New York City in 1911 and spent her childhood in Roxbury, Connecticut. The granddaughter of John Bates Clark, classic American economist and teacher of Veblen, and the sister of the novelist Eleanor Clark, she graduated from Vassar College in 1933 where she edited the *Vassar Miscellany News*. In 1936 she was a member of the editorial staff of *Fortune*. Her poems appeared in *Poetry*, *Common Sense*, the *Nation* and the *New Republic*.

SARAH N. CLEGHORN was born in 1876 at Norfolk, Virginia. She lives near Manchester, Vermont. She spent a year at Radcliffe, has taught at Manumit School and Vassar College, and her poems have appeared during the last thirty years everywhere from the old *Masses* and the *American* to the *Atlantic Monthly* and *Century*. Robert Frost, in his introduction to her autobiography, *Threescore*, contends that there is more "high explosive for righteousness" in a single line of Sarah Cleghorn's famous poem about the golf links than in the prose that labors under "several atmospheres of revolution." It originally appeared in 1915 in Franklin P. Adams' column in the *Tribune*.

MALCOLM COWLEY was born in the mining country of Pennsylvania in 1898. After his years at Harvard he went abroad with the earlier "exiles," edited *Secession*, contributed to *Broom* and *transition*. Better known as a critic and as literary editor of the *New Republic*, Cowley's poems (*Blue Juniata*, 1929, *The Dry Season*, 1941) record the moods and attitudes of the Lost Generation far more profoundly than the autobiographical *Exile's Return*.

HART CRANE was born in Ohio in 1899. His integrity as an artist contrasted always with—was perhaps the function of—his inability to reconcile himself with his family and with society. His poetry, from the "imagism" of "Sunday Morning Apples" to the only partially successful myth-making of *The Bridge*, is difficult in proportion to its prodigious ambition and to its author's failure to find any resolution for his personal conflicts. But the grandeur of lines like

For joy rides in stupendous coverings

has not been rivalled in our time. Crane leapt into the Atlantic from the stern of the S.S. *Orizaba* in 1932. He was returning from the terrible sojourn in Mexico he describes so poignantly in "Purgatorio." His poetry, as well as his life, are analyzed in that paragon of what a poet's biography should be, *Hart Crane* by Philip Horton.

HUBERT CREEKMORE's third collection of poems is to be called *The Long Reprieve* and records the experiences of his third year in the U. S. Navy, as an officer stationed in the French island of New Caledonia. Cacophony, reverse rhyme, anti-climax and broken rhythms are used with striking effect to portray the anarchy of war and the cynicism of its backwash. Creekmore, who is now working for New Directions and completing a novel, was born in Mississippi in 1907, attended the University of Mississippi and took his Master's degree at Columbia with an essay on Ezra Pound. His earlier poems were collected in *Personal Sun* (1940) and *The Stone Ants* (1943).

E. E. CUMMINGS, born in 1894, educated but not tamed at Harvard, first achieved celebrity among the discriminating with his powerful war novel, *The Enormous Room*. After years abroad, Cummings returned to live in New York and Vermont. His poetry, recently collected in a single volume, is well described by Louis Untermeyer as "a jumble of imaginative exuberance, cool precision and archaic affectations. His is a mind which is in quick succession, lyrical, fantastic, grotesque, pathetic, savage." It should be said in addition that Cummings is a first-rate humorist, and despite his unabating eccentricity, one of the most original lyrical talents at work today. His description of Soviet Russia, *Eimi*, 1933, was a shock to those who hoped his literary iconoclasm would feel at home in Moscow. His *Collected Poems* were published in 1938. *50 Poems* and *1 × 1* appeared in 1940 and 1944.

WALTER DE LA MARE, born in 1873 in Kent, England, must spend a good part of his life in dread of the next anthologist who will neglect a hundred almost equally worthy poems to reprint "The Listeners." What irony, that the poem the Romantics and masters of neo-Gothic mystery never quite wrote, should have been finally achieved by a man who spent eighteen years of his life working for the Standard Oil Company! Equally renowned for his children's books (*Peacock Pie*, etc.) and the novel *Memoirs of a Midget*, De La Mare's poetry is notable for the subtlety with which its archaic diction and floating rhythms convey a spectral beauty.

REUEL DENNEY was born in New York City in 1913, attended Dartmouth, taught school in Buffalo, farmed in Vermont and is now one of the editors of *Fortune*. Although he has written several experimental plays ("The Calculators," "The Headless Horseman") his only published work so far has been *The Connecticut River*, a group of poems in an earthy and delightfully personal style which was published in 1939.

BABETTE DEUTSCH'S latest collection of poems, *Take Them, Stranger* went beyond the quality that stamped most strikingly her earlier work— poignant reflection of the world's wrong; there was a control and a quiet assurance that was new. With her husband, Avrahm Yarmolinsky, Miss Deutsch had already made a major contribution through her translations to the appreciation of Russian poetry; and in her critical work (*This Modern Poetry*, 1935) to the appreciation of poetry generally. Born in New York City, she graduated from Barnard College and was for a while secretary to the late Thorstein Veblen.

LAWRENCE DURRELL's poetic descent is from Auden and Dylan Thomas. In his first book of poems, *A Private Country* (1943), the Audenesque is most pronounced in the Byronic "Ballad of the Good Lord Nelson":

> 'England Expects' was the motto he gave
> When he thought of little Emma out on Biscay's wave,
> And remembered working on her like a galley-slave . . .
> If they'd treat their women in the Nelson way
> There'd be fewer frigid husbands every day
> And many more heroes on the Bay of Biscay
> Aboard the Victory, Victory O.'

Thomas's influence is apparent in the remarkable sequence "The Sonnet of Hamlet" and in the poem in this collection, but Durrell's individuality emerges both in the sureness of his technique and in the Eastern Mediterranean setting which he has made his own, following extended duty in the British government service abroad.

RICHARD EBERHART was born in Austin, Minnesota, in 1904, a fact which will be less obvious to the reader of his poetry than that he was educated at Cambridge and published by Oxford, taught English at St. Mark's School, tutored the son of the King of Siam and compounded an elegant poetic idiom from close study of the styles of Donne, Blake and Hopkins. Nevertheless it is important. For the *energy* ("Spirit won't keep/But like the laughter in the throat/It shocks out over the teeth/In a stony springing brook") and the *images* ("Opportunity, tired cup of tin") are as American as Mauldin and Mark Twain. The famous and overanthologized "Groundhog," for all its closing invocation of China, Greece, Alexander, Montaigne and Saint Theresa, is strictly a confession of the New England conscience, closer in spirit to Emerson and Dickinson than to the English metaphysicals. The matchless lyrics, "If I could only live . . ." and "I walked out to the graveyard . . ." actually derive their strength from the "moral answer" which they seem to spurn. The unique war poems like "Dam Neck, Virginia" and "The Fury of Aerial Bombardment" are less unique for the atmosphere of mysticism in which they seem to float than for the mechanical curiosity and administrative competence which they fail to conceal. This dualism of Eberhart the exquisite and Eberhart the executive accounts both for the great unevenness of *Reading the Spirit* and *Song and Idea* and for exciting fireworks when in the best poems the two Eberharts stubbornly join hands.

T. S. ELIOT was born in 1888 in St. Louis and educated at Harvard and Oxford. The radical symbolist experimentor of "Prufrock," "Gerontion" and *The Waste Land*, after living in England two decades described himself as "classicist in literature, royalist in politics, Anglo-Catholic in religion."

But if Eliot has become thrice subdued in keeping with the pedantic perfection of his later verse and the schoolmasterly dogmatism of his essays, his championship of younger talent in *The Criterion*, the power of his popular verse-dramas, *Murder in the Cathedral* and *Family Reunion*, are answer enough to those who have prematurely written his obituary. Prophet of frustration, later of sophisticated piety, the artist remains master throughout. The philosophies, even the ornate style studded with literary allusion and quotation, may date quickly. The word-magic of poems like "The Hollow Men" and "Ash Wednesday" is deathless. Eliot's 'war poem,' *Four Quartets*, appeared in 1943.

WILLIAM EMPSON's first book, *Seven Types of Ambiguity*, was published shortly after he left Cambridge in 1929. His early *Poems* appeared in 1935 and the later *The Gathering Storm* in 1940 after teaching and travelling in the Orient and in the United States. "Many people," he writes in a note to the later collection, "like myself prefer to read poetry mixed with prose; it gives you more to go by; the conventions of poetry have been getting far off from normal life, so that to have a prose bridge makes reading poetry seem more natural. . . . The fashion for obscure poetry, as a recent development, came in at about the same time as the fashion for crossword puzzles; and it seems to me that this revival of puzzle interest in poetry, an old and natural thing, has got a bad name merely by failing to know itself and refusing to publish the answer."

PAUL ENGLE was born in Cedar Rapids, Iowa, in 1910; studied at the University of Iowa, Columbia and Oxford. His first book, *American Song*, was highly praised; his second and third, *Break the Heart's Anger* and *Corn*, roundly thumped. So far, Engle has been the slave of his own exuberance. He has attempted the difficult task of carrying the Whitman-Sandburg tradition into a generation socially rebellious but nurtured on symbolism.

KENNETH FEARING, born in Chicago in 1902, worked as a millhand and journalist until the publication of his first book of poems, *Angel Arms*, in 1929. Already original for his kaleidoscopic realism, the development of *Poems*, 1935, may be appreciated by comparing the introductory poem of Part IV in this anthology with the later "Dirge." Whether the virtuosity of Fearing's bludgeoning manner would mature to a broader idiom was one of the important questions of "post-depression" poetry. It was not answered by the appearance of *Collected Poems* in 1940.

ROBERT FITZGERALD'S poetry is distinguished by two qualities, its elegance and its capacity to evoke the past. In his early *Poems* (1935) imagism and the early Eliot intrude, but in *A Wreath for the Sea* (1943) moment and mood are fixed with sheer magic, figures recreated out of the past with a poignancy that is breathtaking. Fitzgerald was born in Geneva, New York, in 1910. He studied classical languages at Trinity College, Cambridge, in 1931–2, and attended Harvard the following year. From 1933 to 1935 he worked on the city staff of the *New York Herald-Tribune* and from 1936 to 1942 (intermittently) on *Time*. From 1943 to 1945 he served with the Navy in the Pacific. His translations of Euripides' *Alcestis* and of Sophocles' *Antigone* and *Oedipus at Colonus* (the first two in collaboration with Dudley Fitts) are unrivalled.

ROBERT FROST, the poet *par excellence* of New England and already a classic in his own country, continues to create with unflagging distinction though his philosophy and style seem static. He was born in San Francisco in 1875 and was, off and on, a shoemaker, textile worker, student (Dartmouth and Harvard), teacher, editor, farmer—and unappreciated poet. His fame, when it came, was great, and has remained so. It began in England, where he lived from 1912 to 1915. Frost's poetry is precise, sly, meditative, sympathetic; always bucolic and generally didactic in a transcendental but conversational sort of way. He has described himself as one of two kinds of realist: not the kind "who offers a good deal of dirt with his potato to show that it is a real one," but rather "the one who is satisfied with the potato brushed clean."

ROY FULLER's poetry, like that of his contemporaries Alun Lewis, Terrence Tiller, John Heath-Stubbs and Sidney Keyes, is exciting for its embodiment of a sense of great change in the world. In Fuller that sense is expressed with such overwhelming honesty that the writing tends often to be devoid of ornament, knotted with the concentration of thought, oblivious to metrical experiment or contemporary "new directions." Conversely, this self-contained dedication is the writing's strength. Published in 1942 when the poet was thirty and had just been transferred from the British Navy to the Fleet Air Arm, *The Middle of a War* expressed an agony of spirit that had not been heard in English poetry since Owen and which constituted the first real literary expression of World War II. If Fuller never achieved in his next book *A Lost Season* quite the intensity of such poems as "Spring: 1942" and "Troopship," he did in poems like "The Giraffes" and "In Africa" broaden his focus by suggesting a mystery from which civilization might expect rejuvenation.

JEAN GARRIGUE, whose *Thirty-Six Poems and a Few Songs* appeared in New Directions' *Five Young American Poets 1944*, was there described as a contemplative lyricist, but she might also be called a metaphysical imagist. Without resembling any of them her much more flowing style sometimes recalls in its precise "memoranda" Marianne Moore, in its temporal fixity Turner, a less violent Eberhart, a more color-conscious Marguerite Young. She herself describes poetry as an art of "many-jointed" relationship, something that "illuminates in a cold, perpetual heat. The forestation of symbol around all of the events that have the integrity which obliges the poet to use them . . ." Born in Indiana and a graduate of the University of Chicago, Jean Garrigue now lives in New York City.

ROBERT GRAVES was born in 1895 and during World War I served in France in the same regiment as Siegfried Sassoon, achieving fame first as a war poet, as the biographer of T. E. Lawrence and as the author of *Good-bye to All That*, and then twenty years later still greater fame as the historical novelist of *I, Claudius* and *Hercules, My Shipmate* and the pitiless biographer of John Milton. How good the poet was who had been writing quietly all this time was revealed to American readers with the publication of *Collected Poems* in 1938. The rather humorless and priggish Foreword to this book, beyond acknowledging a debt to his wife the poet Laura Riding, throws one spark of light on Graves' unquestionable vitality as a poet. "To manifest poetic faith," he says, "by a close and energetic study of the disgusting, the contemptible and the evil is not very far in the direction of poetic serenity, but it has been the behaviour most natural to a man of my physical and literary inheritances."

HORACE GREGORY was born in Wisconsin in 1898, attended the University there, and lives in New York. A man of letters in the full creative sense—urban, Irish, full of a restless, generous energy—his poetry found stiff competition in the occupations of criticism and teaching, and in the championship of younger talent. His lyrical gift, tempered by a strong sense of social injustice and disorder, reached maturity in *No Retreat*, 1933. But his elliptical philosophic verse (*Chorus for Survival*, 1935), his translations from Catullus, his critique of D. H. Lawrence's symbolism (*Pilgrim of the Apocalypse*) are equally vigorous. His wife, Marya Zaturenska, is a lyric poet celebrated in her own right. (Randolph Bourne, whose courageous career is celebrated in Gregory's second poem of this collection, was the crippled editor of the *New Republic* who fought a single-handed intellectual battle against America's entrance into the First World War.)

RALPH GUSTAFSON, a graduate of Bishop's University and Oxford, and at present with the British Information Service in New York, was born in Quebec province, Canada, in 1909. The most original if not the most considerable poet to come out of Canada, he has edited three discriminating anthologies of Canadian writing. His verse play, *Alfred The Great*, was published in London in 1937, and his collected lyrics appeared in New York in 1944 under the title *Flight into Darkness*. Gustafson is a religious poet in the sense that his poetry reasserts the dignity of man as a reflection of man's idea of God; in his best poems ecstasy provides its own meaning, but frequently the effect of a private language is conveyed and the destination is lost in a labyrinth of short-cuts.

THOMAS HARDY was born near Dorchester, England, in 1840. He died in 1928. Renowned as a novelist, the author of *The Return of the Native* and *Tess of the D'Urbervilles*, his first and last love was poetry, and to poetry went the essence of his homely genius. His verse has been criticized as harsh, its philosophy as fatalistic. It is the harshness of a giant's uncompromising strength, the fatalism of one who loved humanity too well to tell it pretty fables.

ALFRED HAYES was born in London, England, in 1911, but has lived in New York City 31 of his 36 years. He has worked as a reporter on a tabloid, for the WPA Federal Theatre's "Living Newspapers," and has contributed verse to the *New Masses*, *Trial Balances*, and the *New Republic*. In 1943 he entered the Army. The influence of Browning, and possibly Masters, may be felt in the powerful "Death of the Craneman," but these were healthy influences in 1934 and Hayes made the resultant style his own.

RUTH HERSCHBERGER studied at the University of Chicago and at Black Mountain College and is now living in New York City. Like her friends and equally talented contemporaries, Jean Garrigue and Marguerite Young, Miss Herschberger came from the Middle West (she was born in Chicago in 1917, the daughter of a celebrated football player) and like them she received her first encouragement from Ransom's *Kenyon Review*, but her poetry is less metaphysical, less mannered and more sensuous. Her work has appeared also in *Accent, Common Sense, Partisan Review* and *Portfolio*.

GERARD MANLEY HOPKINS may be fated, through the sheer intensity of his vision, to remain a poet's poet, though it is difficult to see how such a translucent poem as "Pied Beauty" will escape the anthologies of the future. He was born in 1844, spent most of his life as a Jesuit priest and teacher of Greek metrics. He died in 1889. His poems, first published by Bridges in 1918, only achieved influence with the second edition of 1930. If Hopkins' style still appears difficult it is because, as one of his editors has said, his is "a passionate emotion which seems to try to utter all its words in one," and an equally passionate intellect "striving at once to recognize and explain both the singleness and division of the accepted universe. . . . Others have sung *about* their intellectual exaltations; in none has the intellect itself been more the song." In addition to Hopkins' collected poems, the reader should not miss his superb letters, and the recently published *Note-Books and Papers* with reproductions of his exquisite Leonardo-like pen drawings.

A. E. HOUSMAN has compared poetry to a secretion—"whether a natural secretion, like turpentine in the fir, or a morbid secretion, like the pearl in the oyster." It is to the latter that one must turn for explanation of the pessimistic spell of *The Shropshire Lad*. Housman was born in 1859, and with the exception of the echo of *Last Poems* 30 years later, this slender sheaf was his only contribution to poetry in the 78 years of his life. It was a great contribution, and immediately popular, but the scholarly editor of Manilius' forgotten works made a fetish of his shattered inspiration, preferring to comment acidly in Latin upon the foibles of another day than to trust himself again to the buffetings of an uncloistered world. It was the world's misfortune, perhaps, that this perfectionist in a minor key who had succeeded in stripping poetry to the bone merely in linking the moods of adolescent melancholy and good cheer, should have been assured immortality before he was 40.

RANDALL JARRELL's criticism is on the prowl for ultimate complexities and his poetry is packed hard with them. If, in his reviews, he sometimes slaps a poet down too readily for leaning on the past or using a well-worn rhyme, so in his poetry the idea seems always to dictate the form—and the rhythm, in extremities, to be sacrificed to the odd word or the violent image. This was more true of Jarrell's first book, *Blood for a Stranger* (1942), written angrily out of the guilt and frustration of life as a University of Texas teacher, than of his second, *Little Friend, Little Friend* (1945) in which, as a sergeant training B-29 crews, the poet is confronted with the greater anonymity and suffering of war and manages to give his verse a more human referent and a freer pace.

ROBINSON JEFFERS was born in Pittsburgh in 1887. He spent some of his youth abroad, but has lived most of his life in the tower he built for himself on the cliff above Carmel, California. He has been aptly described by William Harlan Hale as a latter-day Whitman, looking outward from the Pacific coast, rather than inward from the Atlantic, toward death rather than toward life. The sweep of Whitman is in his majestic verse, but the love has turned to hate, at best to pity and disgust. "Roan Stallion" was one of the first, and remains the best of that succession of long poems in which Jeffers celebrated the introversion of the race, usually through the symbol of incestuous, self-destructive love. His *Selected Poetry* was published in 1937.

JOSEPHINE W. JOHNSON, author of the Pulitzer-Prize-winning *Now in November* and several other novels, was born in 1910 in Missouri and attended Washington University where she studied painting. She lives on a farm in St. Louis County and has been active in union organizing work. Her poetry, while conventional in style, is remarkable for its emotional honesty and the sinew with which it handles social issues.

JAMES JOYCE, like another major novelist, the author of *Wuthering Heights*, is a minor poet but a fine one. He was born in Dublin in 1882 and lived in Zurich and Trieste and Paris in the years between the Wars. With the publication of *Ulysses* by Sylvia Beach in 1922, worshippers and imitators, charlatans and censors, perched on his doorstep and he became a legend. The great novelist died in 1941 in France, two years after the publication of his last work, *Finnegans Wake*. In Joyce's poetry, the lyricism of his prose is attenuated to a flute-like key, not often stirring and tragic as in "I hear An Army," but full of sentiment, subdued and like the title of his first book, *Chamber Music*.

SIDNEY KEYES, born at Dartford, Kent, in 1922, and killed in Tunisia twenty years later, lived a life as dedicated to art and as full of dramatic spiritual developments as though he had foreseen its exact duration. At 5 he was poring over legend and history, and rejecting *The Children's Encyclopaedia* as inaccurate. At 16 he was writing poems of a reserved duality but already in his own precisely quiet style. At 17 he was visiting France and beginning to see in the natural world that had always pre-occupied him a meaningful symbolism. At 18 he entered Oxford, shared his creative life with the gifted poet John Heath-Stubbs. At 19 he entered the Army and in the words of his friend and the editor of his *Collected Poems*, Michael Meyer, "came into immediate contact with the material world. Love and Death, inextricably entwined, became vital problems instead of subjects for laboratory analysis. . . . He lost his duality. He found his imaginary fears shared by thousands, and became the spokesman of a generation." In his own words Keyes conceived the function of poetry to be "to express the eternal meaning which resides in the physical world, and show the relationship between the eternal and its physical counterpart."

D. H. LAWRENCE was born in 1885 in the mining country of England and died in Nice, France, in 1930 after a tortured life spent wandering through Europe and Australia, Arizona and Mexico. What he sought— the 'noble savage,' masculine civilization, sex unperverted by guilt of mind or war of wills—he never found. His works, marred by a self-conscious sense of liberation and the zeal to convert or castigate, but burning with the intensity of his quest, are the result. The poems suffer more than the novels from the hysteria of the propagandist who will stop for no formal discipline; but poet and novelist are equal parts of the man, and at their best equally great. "The Ship of Death," found in a number of versions in his papers after his death, was Lawrence's last poem.

LAURIE LEE is a young English poet whose first book, *The Sun My Monument*, appeared in 1944.

ALUN LEWIS was born in 1915. He was teaching school in one of the mining valleys of his native Wales when the war began. His first book, *Raider's Dawn*, reflected this background and his reactions to a year of soldiering in England. *The Last Inspection* complemented these observations in prose. His last book, *Ha! Ha! Among the Trumpets*, from which the poems in this anthology are chosen, was published posthumously after the poet's death at Arakan, Burma, in 1944. "For myself," wrote Lewis modestly to Robert Graves in one of his last letters, "I can't claim as much hold on the universal as some poets and consider my poems as expressions of personal experience." But he added: "When I wrote a poem about the jungle I found it had become a criticism of the Western world . . . I wanted to fuse the finite and the infinite in action." And in another letter (to his wife): "They (the poems) are universal statements if they're anything." His last poems, with their unforgettable fusion of place and time, are more than that; they express triumphantly what Lewis thought they had failed to express: "At once the passion of Love, the coldness of Death . . . and the fire that beats against resignation."

C. DAY LEWIS was born in Ireland in 1904 and educated at Oxford with Auden, Spender, Rex Warner and others of that younger group for whom he was to become a John the Baptist. His verse is more studied and programmatic than theirs, but his versatility (he is the author of several novels and is a first-rate critic) have won him equal respect.

VACHEL LINDSAY was born in Springfield, Illinois, in 1879. One of the most characteristic yet individual of American poets, he tramped the country, "bringing beauty to the people," inventing a popular music for its raucous blend of megalomania and idealism, selling his poems for bread, chanting from platforms like any other revivalist, exhausting himself and his art in one grand, generous splurge of emotion. There is Lindsay the prophet; there is Lindsay the crank; Lindsay the weaver of delicate phantasies for children; Lindsay the indignant Socialist. He may not have realized his goal of a "communal art," but he came closer to celebrating his country in terms that its people could appreciate than any other contemporary. He died in 1931.

PARE LORENTZ, born in West Virginia in 1905, attended West Virginia Wesleyan and served for a time as motion picture critic on such magazines as *Judge*, *Vanity Fair* and *McCalls*. He wrote and directed two great documentary films, *The Plow That Broke The Plains* and *The River*. It was the second of these, produced by the Farm Security Administration, that was hailed as a new literary form when the book, combining soundtrack and pictures, appeared. Archibald MacLeish (in *Land of the Free*) and Erskine Caldwell and Margaret Bourke-White (*You Have Seen Their Faces*) had anticipated this development; but Lorentz's open-space cadences were a sturdy contribution to the Whitman tradition.

AMY LOWELL, of the Boston Lowells, but who smoked cigars and shocked her contemporaries even more with her free verse, was born in 1874 in Brookline, Mass. Renowned for her promotion of the Imagist movement, she was an able craftswoman and a healthy influence in the 1912–20 renaissance, but her poetry, with little but its glittering finish to recommend it, seems dated today. Her two-volume life of Keats is still the standard biography. She died in 1925.

ROBERT LOWELL, whose first book, *Land of Unlikeness* (1944), left no doubt of his stature as a poet, had already been publicly marked as a Catholic, a conscientious objector and a violator of family tradition. Son of a retired naval commander, great-grandson of a martial poet and anti-papist, and heir to a Boston family tradition that boasted members in every war since the Revolution, he tried to enlist twice, then became convinced that total war with its thought-control and pattern-bombings was unprincipled and anti-Christian. In October, 1943, Lowell was sentenced to a year and day in Federal prison. Since his release he has been living with his wife Jean Stafford, the novelist, first at Westport, Connecticut, more recently at Damariscotta Mills, Maine, and working on a second book, *Lord Weary's Castle*, which will include the sonnet sequence in this anthology. Lowell's early writing was encouraged by Eberhart at St. Mark's School, and by John Crowe Ransom at Kenyon College, but owes little to either. The weight of the imagery and the familiarity with which God is invoked recall Crashaw, Vaughan and Donne, but the landscape is New England and the outrageous skill with which all centuries are forced to march through the present is Lowell's alone.

HUGH MACDIARMID is the pen-name of Christopher M. Grieve, a Scotsman born in 1892 and educated at Edinburgh University. As a student he joined the Fabian Society. Through World War I he served in the Medical Corps, refusing to accept rank. As a Socialist, after the war, he helped to found the National Party of Scotland, from which he was subsequently expelled as a Communist. In 1936 he was expelled from the Communist Party for demanding Scottish autonomy, but was reinstated the same year. His "recreation" was once given in the English *Who's Who* as "Anglo-phobia" and he then lived in one of the northernmost of the Shetland Islands. Much of MacDiarmid's poetry is in the Scots vernacular, and he has been compared to Robert Burns for the national-proletarian bite of his scurrilous lyrics. He is at his worst when he gets literary about "the eternal lightning of Lenin's bones"; at his best when he writes straight, letting the indignation generate the poetry.

ARCHIBALD MACLEISH was born in 1892. He graduated from Yale, where he excelled as scholar and athlete, and began the practice of law in Boston after attending the Harvard Law School. He had already seen war service in France and published one book of verse. Abandoning law, MacLeish travelled in France and Persia during the 20's, finally joining the editorial staff of *Fortune* where he was considered their ablest chronicler of the nation's industrial and political affairs. During World War II

MacLeish denounced *The Irresponsibles*, headed the Office of Facts and Figures and the Library of Congress, served briefly as Assistant Secretary of State. From *The Hamlet of A. MacLeish* to the lyrics of *New Found Land* and the nostalgic *Conquistador* in narrative terza-rima, through the social satire of *Frescoes* and the trail-blazing radio play, *The Fall of the City*, MacLeish had developed as a poet. After *Air Raid* (1940) he wrote few poems, and those few of an "official" character.

ARCHIBALD FLEMING MACLIESH was born in 1911. At Princeton in 1931 he collaborated on the undergraduate prize play. After the publication of *The Island Called Pharos* in 1934, MacLiesh lived in New City, N. Y. and devoted his talents to the writing of drama in verse. *The Destroyers* was published in 1940; *Cone of Silence*, a novel, in 1942. The long poem "Exploration by Air" was featured in *The Poetry of Flight* by the present editor. It recorded MacLiesh's first (and unsurpassed) observations of the meaning of flight, an experience that was subsequently broadened by a year training fighter pilots at Shaw Field and two years ferrying planes for the Air Transport Command.

LOUIS MACNEICE was born in Ireland in 1907 and attended Oxford. A close friend of Auden, and the Oxford poets generally, he went his own way from the beginning, eschewing politics and beating out a somewhat crabbed but powerful style of his own. Satire is the prevailing weather in his landscapes. Spare solidity characterizes his authentic translation of Aeschylus' *Agamemnon*. Following the war, in which MacNeice served as a fire-watcher and writer for the BBC his war poems were published in *Springboard*.

JOHN MANIFOLD was born in Melbourne, Australia, in 1915 and educated at Cambridge. Escaping from Germany, where he was working as translator for a publishing firm in 1939, he joined the British Army, became a Captain in the Intelligence Corps, and served in West Africa, France, and Germany. His poems, which are to be published in the United

States in 1946, have the brashness as well as the freshness of a new conti-nent about them: the lyrics have much of the lilt and vigor of Burns; the satires are crude, belligerent and naively Marxist.

EDWIN MARKHAM was born in Oregon in 1852 and lived until his recent death in Staten Island, New York. No poem ever published in America has had the instant and lasting popularity of "The Man with the Hoe" which appeared in 1899. Conventional in form, inspired by the still more conventional Millet painting, its indignation and rugged strength are still challenging.

JOHN MASEFIELD, the present Poet Laureate of England, was born in 1878 and won an early fame with *Salt-Water Ballads* and the narratives, *Dauber* and *The Widow in the Bye Street*. The rude sincerity of his early work and the quotable lilt of such "anthology pieces" as "Cargoes" and "Sea Fever" are still prized above the magnificent narrative sweep and technical virtuosity of *Reynard the Fox*

EDGAR LEE MASTERS was born in Kansas in 1869. As a realistic, psychological "novelist," if not as a poet, he takes his place beside Dreiser, Anderson and Dos Passos. For *Spoon River Anthology*, contributing little to the musical and architectural in poetry, remains a masterpiece of col-lective characterization. Neither ingratiating nor epigrammatic, Masters' weapon is blunt, effective.

WILLIAM MEREDITH was born in New York City in 1919 and gradu-ated from Princeton in 1940, serving the following year as a reporter on the *New York Times* until his induction into the Army. From 1941 to 1942 he did public relations work as an enlisted man in the Air Corps. In 1942 he was transferred to the Navy, won his wings and served as a naval aviator in the Aleutian Campaign (1942–1943) and in the Central Pacific (1944–1945). He is presently stationed at the Army and Navy Staff College in Washington, D. C. Meredith's *Love Letter from an Impossible Land* was published in 1944 with a preface by Archibald MacLeish who remarked that "because the experience of this war, fought with new weapons in remote and unimaginable places, is an experience strange to most of us . . . the communication itself is oblique—seen from the corner of the eye like the movement of danger at night."

THOMAS MERTON, a Cistercian monk of the Strict Observance who became a Trappist at Our Lady of Gethsemani, Kentucky, in 1941, has this to say about religious poetry: "It won't get better until Christians are more serious about the ascetic element essential to their faith. Asceticism is necessary to smelt down the truths of dogma into concrete religious experience, because without it there can be no love of God. However, many Catholics who truly love God and might otherwise have something to say about it, are paralyzed by the lack of a corresponding literary asceticism: *i.e.* they passively accept the cheapest and most trashy literary standards that a materialistic culture has to offer." Merton was born at Prades, France, in 1915. His father was an artist who had come to France from New Zealand. The poet was educated at the Lycee of Montauban and at Clare College, Cambridge, taking his M.A. at Columbia and teaching thereafter for several years at the Franciscan college of St. Bonaventure in upstate New York. His *Thirty Poems* was published by New Directions in 1944.

EDNA ST. VINCENT MILLAY was born in Maine in 1892 and had written the famous "Renascence" before she attended Vassar College in 1913. Her intense feminism and hunger for beauty struck a responsive chord and she became the idol of more than one generation of rebellious young women. To modern poetry she brought a new freedom of mood and movement and an attractive bitter-sweetness. Critics who looked for major poetry to follow the flowering of Miss Millay's talent were disappointed by the somewhat archaic rhetoric of *Fatal Interview* and the studied slow-motion of *Conversation at Midnight.* During the War, Miss Millay succumbed to the temptation to be topical, producing in *The Ballad of Lidice* a poem that honored neither its author nor the subject.

MARIANNE MOORE was editor of that focus of revolutionary writing, *The Dial*, from 1925 to 1929. She was born in 1887 and now lives in Brooklyn. Her impressive *Selected Poems* was published in 1935 with a preface by T. S. Eliot who said: "Miss Moore is one of those few who have done the language some service in my lifetime . . . carrying on that struggle for the maintenance of a living speech, for the maintenance of its strength, its subtlety, for the preservation of quality of feeling, which must be kept up in every generation." "In Distrust of Merits," a poem of civilian guilt and humility, which appeared in *Nevertheless* (1944) was hailed by W. H. Auden as the outstanding war poem of World War II.

OGDEN NASH was born in 1902 and has worked in various advertising and editorial capacities, including a term on the staff of the *New Yorker*, where most of the horrific rhymes of *Hard Lines* and subsequent volumes first appeared. Lines like "The Bronx?/No, thonx!" may not be immortal, but they will live until the things they hold up to ridicule become something new and less strange.

WILFRED OWEN was killed at the age of 25 in the battle for the Sambre Canal, November 4, 1918. He was, to quote the words of his friend, editor and fellow Englishman, Edmund Blunden, "one of those destined beings who, without pride of self, 'see, as from a tower, the end of all.' Outwardly he was quiet, unobtrusive, full of good sense; inwardly he could not help regarding the world with the dignity of a seer." A woman who knew him as a young officer, already tending toward a profound pacifism, describes his sensitive, acutely sympathetic nature: "Direct personal experience and individual development can hardly be said to have existed for him. He could only suffer, or rejoice, vicariously." Like Keats, he knew that he would be among the English poets after his death, but he never lived to see his single small volume in print. "He was a man of absolute integrity of mind," wrote Siegfried Sassoon, another poet-friend. "He never wrote his poems (as so many war poets did) to make the effect of a personal gesture."

DOROTHY PARKER, who was born in New Jersey in 1893, is even more famous as a wit than as the author of the most acidulous *vers de societé* of her time. She claims to have learnt nothing at school "except that if you spit on a pencil eraser, it will erase ink." Superstitious, pessimistic, gregarious and something of a radical, she writes movie scenarios and short stories, as well as the verse collected in *Not So Deep as a Well.*

KENNETH PATCHEN was born in 1911 in Ohio of a miner's family and worked in the steel mills before attending the Experimental College of the University of Wisconsin. He settled in New York about the time his first book of poems, *Before the Brave*, was published in 1936. From 1939 to 1945 the variety and volume of his work has been astounding, *First Will and Testament* and *Cloth of the Tempest* containing his richest poetry, *The Journal of Albion Moonlight* and *Memoirs of a Shy Pornographer* his most ambitious fantasies in prose. Patchen never tires of baiting the bourgeois, the professor, the war monger, the businessman, the politician and the pundit. He does not stop to explain any of these phenomena; he is too busy denouncing them. Nor does he stop to integrate or perfect his own formal arrangements. Yet Patchen has undeniable gifts. Unlike other poets he never caters to the popular style. War has not softened his pacifism, nor anti-Stalinism his revolutionary ardor, nor recognition his delight in experiment—the deliberate derangement of words and ideas. The *Memoirs* reveals, moreover, an American humorist more daring than Perelman and as original as Thurber. If one wishes occasionally that Patchen would grow up and take his tongue out of his cheek, one is more frequently delighted that in his world magic and mystification persist.

RUTH PITTER was born in Essex in 1897. To make a living during World War I she studied woodwork and painting and now operates a hand-painted-gift business in Chelsea. Scorning the dependency of the Bohemian, she prides herself on being "frugal, industrious and provident."

Of her poetry (she began writing it at the age of 5) she says: "It occurs in the form of a mood out of which phrases gradually crystallize and a rhythm emerges. . . . You can make poetry out of yourself; prose takes experience and drudgery." Miss Pitter's poetry certainly is the kind that is spun out of the self, but the craftsmanship is of a high order. The poem in this collection is taken from *The Spirit Watches* (1939).

EZRA POUND, the *enfant terrible* of modern poetry, was born in Idaho in 1885 and lived abroad (in London, Paris and Rapallo, Italy) from 1908 to 1945. Instigator of movements—Imagism, Vorticism, Objectivism, Social Credit—the classic and oriental erudition, the conversational formalism of his art have exerted an acknowledged and profound influence on such widely different talents as Eliot, MacLeish, Hemingway, Ford Madox Ford, Joyce and Yeats. His early lyrics are fresh, but always faintly literary. His interminable *Cantos* are a badly assimilated potpourri of history, economics, science, and especially literature. At their best they rise to symphonic impressionism. In 1945, Pound, who had been broadcasting throughout World War II for Mussolini's Italy, was seized and brought to trial for treason by the invading Allied forces.

FREDERIC PROKOSCH was born in Wisconsin in 1909. He was educated at Harvard, Yale and Cambridge. Making something of a reputation at home and abroad as a scholar and champion squash-racquets player, his novels (*The Asiatics, The Seven Who Fled, Night of the Poor, Age of Thunder*) have been notable for an almost sickly response to the beauty of things past. The same feeling, intensified, inspires his verse. Prokosch's *Chosen Poems* were published in 1944.

JOHN CROWE RANSOM was born in Tennessee in 1888 and studied at Vanderbilt and Oxford Universities. He taught at the former and edited several publications (notably *The Fugitive*) devoted to the cultivation of letters in the South. With *Chills and Fever*, 1924, he set the pace for the elegant intellectualism that has stamped most Southern poetry since.

The matter of his poems is trivial; the philosophy, ironic; the style, superbly deft. Recently Ransom has edited the *Kenyon Review*. His *Selected Poems* were published in 1945.

KENNETH REXROTH, poet, abstract painter and mountaineer, was born in Indiana in 1905. His political evolution took him from the IWW (as a youngster) through Stalinism (League of American Writers) to Christian Anarchism (influenced by Kropotkin, Berkman, Vanzetti, Lawrence and especially Albert Schweitzer, and by the English personalist revolt against the modern war-making state). His evolution as a poet took him from neo-imagism (he edited the *Objectivists' Anthology* in Paris in 1932) to the intimate classicism of *The Phoenix and the Tortoise* (1944) from which the poems in the present anthology are selected. Rexroth, who now lives in San Francisco and is working on a series of verse plays, believes that "poetry is best when it is personal, speech from one to another; purposive, written out of some definable subjective need and objective motivation; 'simple, sensuous and passionate' or at least made up of such elements or articulated around them. I find hallucination and rhetoric dull, pernicious and silly. Cataclysms are all alike and it is not a human function to create them. Being human is being responsible, totally."

LOLA RIDGE's radical, "class-conscious" poetry antedates by a generation most of the work commonly described in those terms. She was born in Ireland, coming to New York in 1907 and publishing *The Ghetto and Other Poems* in 1918. Her later long poems, tenuous and mystical, intense and unpopular, tended to obscure the historical importance of her early inventions.

EDWIN ARLINGTON ROBINSON was born in Maine in 1869. He spent several years at Harvard and from 1893 to 1910 worked at a succession of clerical jobs in New York City, one of which he secured through President Theodore Roosevelt who had read *Captain Craig*. With *The Man Against the Sky*, Robinson's reputation as the master philosophic poet of his time was made. He began to present character, specifically the "little man" of the American lower middle class and farm, with a realism and economy new to American poetry. From then on, as Untermeyer remarks, "Frustration and defeat are like an organ-point heard below the varying music of his verse; failure is almost glorified." In later years, as Robinson turned out Tennysonian tragedies with a New England background to meet the cost of living-for-letters, his work became more bleakly moral, his blank verse more uncompromisingly spare. He died in 1935, a lonely man but praised and honored for his single-minded devotion to poetry.

SELDEN RODMAN was born in New York City in 1909 and graduated from Yale in 1931 where he founded and edited the polemical *Harkness Hoot* with William Harlan Hale. He is the author of *Mortal Triumph and Other Poems; Lawrence: The Last Crusade; The Airmen; The Poetry of Flight; The Revolutionists* and (with Richard Eberhart) *War and the Poet*. With Alfred M. Bingham he edited the political monthly *Common Sense* from 1932 to 1943. From 1943 to 1945 he served in the Army with the Office of Strategic Services.

MURIEL RUKEYSER's first book, *Theory of Flight*, was hailed in 1935 as "One of those rare first volumes which impress by their achievement more than by their promise." She was twenty-one at the time, born in New York, had attended Vassar and had already begun those travels to stormcenters of revolt from which the material for her best work has been invariably drawn. "Her poems," said Philip Blair Rice, "not only present and celebrate experience, but evaluate it." And, added Stephen Vincent Benét, "When Miss Rukeyser speaks her politics—and she speaks with sincerity and fire—she does so like a poet, not like a slightly worn phonograph record." *U. S. 1* (1938) was followed by *A Turning Wind* (1939). In 1942 Miss Rukeyser's remarkable study of the mathematician Willard Gibbs appeared. Her war poem, *Wake Island,* was a disappointment to her admirers.

SAGITTARIUS is the pen-name of Olga Katzin, who was in a real sense (and comparable to the cartoonist Lowe) the conscience of England during the dark days before and after Munich. Her weekly barb appeared in *The New Statesman and Nation*, and continues to appear— 'alas,' one is tempted to add—for the poet who was obliged to say in 1937:

> Franco trusts to Britain
> Not to let him down . . .

had to take up the theme again in 1944 with the question:

> Shall Greek Resistance be put down
> To prop the quislings of the Crown?

and in 1945, surveying post-war oratory:

> Habituated to disguise,
> The spokesmen of united nations
> Their aims omit to advertise,
> And only tell their aspirations.

Whatever else 1945 failed to accomplish, it saw the publication for the first time in one volume, *Quiver's Choice*, of all Miss Katzin's lethal arrows. The satirist was born in London in 1896.

CARL SANDBURG was born in Illinois in 1878. He received his apprenticeship to the mantle of Walt Whitman in such varied occupations as reporter, scene-shifter, athlete, dish-washer, harvest hand, copywriter, salesman, Socialist organizer, itinerant guitar-player and soldier in the Spanish-American War. Not until 1914, with the appearance of the famous "Chicago" in Harriet Monroe's *Poetry*, did he establish his reputation as a poet. Like Whitman, Sandburg employed the common speech of the people, including slang—but less self-consciously. Like Whitman also, his work was fired with a democratic zeal and an identification with the traditions of a growing country, especially the folklore of its receding frontier. His most recent collection, *The People, Yes*, had all of the salt and more sense of form than his earlier work. He is the author of a monumental biography of Abraham Lincoln, and edited *The American Songbag*. He lived until recently at Hobart, Michigan.

SIEGFRIED SASSOON, wounded and invalided home in 1917 after three years in the trenches, threw his Military Cross in the Channel and announced publicly that he would serve no more. Hoping for a courts martial, he was declared "temporarily insane" and shipped to Palestine where he fought two years more. In 1920 he toured the United States, delivering anti-war talks and reading his poems. Sassoon's war poems of protest were surpassed in their time only by Owen's; his later poetry has been thin but never meretricious and sometimes intense; *Memoirs of a Fox-Hunting Man* (1928) and *Memoirs of an Infantry Officer* (1930) contain his finest prose. He was born in 1886.

DELMORE SCHWARTZ was born in 1914 in Brooklyn and was educated at New York University and Harvard. He taught for a number of years at the latter, and wrote while there his verse play *Shenandoah*. The earlier *In Dreams Begin Responsibilities* contains his best work. Precocious, versatile and productive, he had published verse, criticism, drama, short stories, written a novel, before this book of poems appeared in the autumn of 1938. In each of these media, Schwartz was predominantly concerned with "the values by which people live, as distinct from their beliefs and explicit avowals of choice."

KARL SHAPIRO was born in Baltimore in 1913 and his first book, *Poems*, was privately printed there in 1935. His first characteristic verse appeared in New Directions' *Five Young American Poets 1941*, in which he stated that poetry "has no sense of time, no idea of growth or progress, and no ambition . . . I write about myself, my house, my street, and my city, and not about 'America,' the word that is the chief enemy of modern poetry." *Person, Place and Thing* appeared the following year when its author had already reached Australia with an advance unit of the Medical Corps, and immediately established his reputation as the most accomplished technician in the post-Auden school and the spokesman of a new poetic generation. *The Place of Love* (privately printed in Australia) and *V-Letter* (1944) bore witness to his technical resourcefulness and his increasing ability to probe the human situation without rhetorical tricks, but *Essay on Rime* (published after Shapiro's return to the United States in 1945) though arousing popular admiration for the extraordinary ease with which it analyzed the confusions of modern poetics was at the same time severely criticized for the glibness with which it disposed of all but the accepted masters, for a tone of anti-intellectualism carried over from certain poems in *V-Letter*, and for its failure to fill the vacuum it created. Shapiro is now living with his wife and child on a farm in Connecticut.

EDITH SITWELL was writing surrealist poetry long before André Breton invented the word or Pavel Tchelitchew painted her portrait. "The Bat," like the better-known "Sir Beelzebub" and "The King of China's Daughter" typifies that brittle style with which, as Louis Untermeyer remarked, the general reader associates her—"the artificer of a papier-maché universe, a juggler amusing herself in a world where grass is shrill, fire furry, where rains hang like wooden stalactites, where the creaking air, combed seas, and spangled emotions are equally automatic." The other Sitwell, the Sitwell of "Still Falls the Rain," achieved her maturity in *Street Song* (1942) and *Green Song and Other Poems* (1944), taking her place with the great mystical poets of an earlier religious generation. Edith Sitwell was born in 1887 of a titled family. Her two brothers, Osbert and Sacheverell, are distinguished men of letters in their own right. She lives in London.

STEPHEN SPENDER is one of the few poets whose first reviewers have not had cause to regret that they compared him to Shelley. Not